D0140272

Photojournalism
and Foreign Policy

Recent Titles in the
Praeger Series in Political Communication
Robert E. Denton, Jr., *General Editor*

Campaign Craft: The Strategies, Tactics, and Art of Political Campaign Management
Daniel M. Shea

Inside Political Campaigns: Theory and Practice
Karen S. Johnson-Cartee and Gary A. Copeland

Rhetorical Studies of National Political Debates—1996
Robert V. Friedenberg, editor

Communication Consultants in Political Campaigns: Ballot Box Warriors
Robert V. Friedenberg

Manipulation of the American Voter: Political Campaign Commercials
Karen S. Johnson-Cartee and Gary A. Copeland

Presidential Crisis Rhetoric and the Press in the Post–Cold War World
Jim A. Kuypers

The 1996 Presidential Campaign: A Communication Perspective
Robert E. Denton, Jr., editor

Reconciling Free Trade, Fair Trade, and Interdependence: The Rhetoric of Presidential
Economic Leadership
Delia B. Conti

Politics and Politicians in American Film
Phillip L. Gianos

Electronic Whistle-Stops: The Impact of the Internet on American Politics
Gary W. Selnow

Newspapers of Record in a Digital Age: From Hot Type to Hot Link
Shannon E. Martin and Kathleen A. Hansen

Campaign '96: A Functional Analysis of Acclaiming, Attacking, and Defending
William L. Benoit, Joseph R. Blaney, and P. M. Pier

Photojournalism and Foreign Policy

Icons of Outrage in International Crises

David D. Perlmutter

Praeger Series in Political Communication

PRAEGER

Westport, Connecticut
London

TR 820
.P44
1998

Library of Congress Cataloging-in-Publication Data

Perlmutter, David D., 1962–
    Photojournalism and foreign policy : icons of outrage in
international crises / David D. Perlmutter.
        p.   cm.—(Praeger series in political communication, ISSN
1062–5623)
    Includes bibliographical references and index.
    ISBN 0–275–95812–4 (alk. paper).—ISBN 0–275–96362–4 (pbk. :
alk. paper)
    1. Photojournalism.   2. International relations.   I. Title.
II. Series.
TR820.P44   1998
070.4′9—dc21   98–16908

British Library Cataloguing in Publication Data is available.

Copyright © 1998 by David D. Perlmutter

All rights reserved. No portion of this book may be
reproduced, by any process or technique, without the
express written consent of the publisher.

Library of Congress Catalog Card Number: 98–16908
ISBN: 0–275–95812–4
        0–275–96362–4 (pbk.)
ISSN: 1062–5623

First published in 1998

Praeger Publishers, 88 Post Road West, Westport, CT 06881
An imprint of Greenwood Publishing Group, Inc.

Printed in the United States of America

The paper used in this book complies with the
Permanent Paper Standard issued by the National
Information Standards Organization (Z39.48–1984).

10 9 8 7 6 5 4 3 2 1

To my parents.

AUH 3065   C2 5870

MAR 3 1 1999

Contents

Series Foreword

Those of us from the discipline of communication studies have long believed that communication is prior to all other fields of inquiry. In several other forums I have argued that the essence of politics is "talk" or human interaction.[1] Such interaction may be formal or informal, verbal or nonverbal, public or private, but it is always persuasive, forcing us consciously or subconsciously to interpret, to evaluate, and to act. Communication is the vehicle for human action.

From this perspective, it is not surprising that Aristotle recognized the natural kinship of politics and communication in his writings *Politics* and *Rhetoric*. In the former, he established that humans are "political beings [who] alone of the animals [are] furnished with the faculty of language."[2] In the latter, he began his systematic analysis of discourse by proclaiming that "rhetorical study, in its strict sense, is concerned with the modes of persuasion."[3] Thus, it was recognized over twenty-three hundred years ago that politics and communication go hand in hand because they are essential parts of human nature.

In 1981, Dan Nimmo and Keith Sanders proclaimed that political communication was an emerging field.[4] Although its origin, as noted, dates back centuries, a "self-consciously cross-disciplinary" focus began in the late 1950s. Thousands of books and articles later, colleges and universities offer a variety of graduate and undergraduate coursework in the area in such diverse departments as communication, mass communication, journalism, political science, and sociology.[5] In Nimmo and Sanders's early assessment, the "key areas of inquiry" included rhetorical analysis, propaganda analysis, attitude change studies, voting studies, government and the news media, functional and systems analyses, technological changes, media technologies, campaign techniques, and research techniques.[6] In a survey of the state of the field in 1983, the same authors and Lynda Kaid found additional, more specific areas of concerns such as the presidency, political polls, public opinion, debates, and advertising.[7] Since the first study, they have also noted a shift away from the rather strict behavioral approach.

A decade later, Dan Nimmo and David Swanson argued that "political communication has developed some identity as a more or less distinct domain of scholarly work."[8] The scope and concerns of the area have further expanded to include critical theories and cultural studies. Although there is no precise definition, method, or disciplinary home of the area of inquiry, its primary domain comprises the role, processes, and effects of communication within the context of politics broadly defined.

In 1985, the editors of *Political Communication Yearbook: 1984* noted that "more things are happening in the study, teaching, and practice of political communication than can be captured within the space limitations of the relatively few publications available."[9] In addition, they argued that the backgrounds of "those involved in the field [are] so varied and pluralist in outlook and approach, . . . it [is] a mistake to adhere slavishly to any set format in shaping the content."[10] More recently, Swanson and Nimmo have called for "ways of over-coming the unhappy consequences of fragmentation within a framework that respects, encourages, and benefits from diverse scholarly commitments, agendas, and approaches."[11]

In agreement with these assessments of the area and with gentle encouragement, in 1988 Praeger established the series entitled "Praeger Series in Political Communication." The series is open to all qualitative and quantitative methodologies as well as contemporary and historical studies. The key to characterizing the studies in the series is the focus on communication variables or activities within a political context or dimension. As of this writing, over seventy volumes have been published and numerous impressive works are forthcoming. Scholars from the disciplines of communication, history, journalism, political science, and sociology have participated in the series.

I am, without shame or modesty, a fan of the series. The joy of serving as its editor is in participating in the dialogue of the field of political communication and in reading the contributors' works. I invite you to join me.

Robert E. Denton, Jr.

NOTES

1. See Robert E. Denton, Jr., *The Symbolic Dimensions of the American Presidency* (Prospect Heights, IL: Waveland Press, 1982); Robert E. Denton, Jr., and Gary Woodward, *Political Communication in America* (New York: Praeger, 1985; 2d ed., 1990); Robert E. Denton, Jr., and Dan Hahn, *Presidential Communication* (New York: Praeger, 1986); and Robert E. Denton, Jr., *The Primetime Presidency of Ronald Reagan* (New York: Praeger, 1988).

2. Aristotle, *The Politics of Aristotle*, trans. Ernest Barker (New York: Oxford University Press, 1970), p. 5.

3. Aristotle, *Rhetoric*, trans. Rhys Roberts (New York: The Modern Library, 1954), p. 22.

4. Dan Nimmo and Keith Sanders, "Introduction: The Emergence of Political Communication as a Field," in *Handbook of Political Communication*, eds. Dan Nimmo and Keith Sanders (Beverly Hills, CA: Sage, 1981), pp. 11–36.

5. Ibid., p. 15.

6. Ibid., pp. 17–27.

7. Keith Sanders, Lynda Kaid, and Dan Nimmo, eds. *Political Communication Yearbook: 1984* (Carbondale, IL: Southern Illinois University, 1985), pp. 283–308.

8. Dan Nimmo and David Swanson, "The Field of Political Communication: Beyond the Voter Persuasion Paradigm," in *New Directions in Political Communication*, eds. David Swanson and Dan Nimmo (Beverly Hills, CA: Sage, 1990), p. 8.

9. Sanders, Kaid, and Nimmo, *Political Communication Yearbook: 1984*, p. xiv.

10. Ibid.

11. Nimmo and Swanson, "The Field of Political Communication," p. 11.

Preface

Every photographer dreams of capturing that one great shot, that
magical moment of passage from life into death.[1]

—David Hume Kennerly
Pulitzer Prize-Winning Combat Photographer

In this book I explore the interplay of news images and public, press,
and political reaction. I do so not by attempting to look at *all* pictures in
the press, but rather by examining what prominent people in politics,
media, and the academy—the "discourse elites"—proclaim to themselves, to the public, and to posterity to be the crucial, key, important
images. Such pictures are the icons of legend and romantic description,
the Pulitzer Prize winners that herald page one and lead the newscast but
also stir controversy and reaction often subsumed under the word
"outrage." The icon of outrage, then, is used here as a mirror to the
cultural, political, and historical argumentation that surrounds pictures in
the press. Such pictures are also worthy of attention because the last
three decades are replete with anecdotes, often stemming from the
testimony of powerful leaders and influential commentators, that icons
of outrage can drive policy. Indeed, it has become almost assumed
wisdom that a picture—an executed Viet Cong[2] prisoner on the streets
of Saigon, a lone protester facing tanks at Tiananmen, the battered face
of a captured American pilot in Somalia—can trigger the emotional
reaction of world opinion and force the hand of policy makers. I suggest
a phenomenon that might be dubbed the *first person effect* where
discourse elites feel that a picture has an effect on them (or should have
one) and then, often falsely, project this effect on the general viewing
public. The purpose of this book is to assess such assumptions, and, I
hope, encourage greater prudence before automatically attributing to a
news photograph, icon or not, the power to change the world, scar the

nation, outrage the people or make or break policy. Even while expressing skepticism about the power of images, however, I recognize that widespread perception of the magnitude of that power may itself influence foreign policy discourse and action.

In the first chapter of the book, the lay theory of *visual determinism* is broken down into its correlated, if not always explicitly coiterated, hypotheses. Among these is that both the public and political leaders draw their views and understanding of world events from news media, especially television. News pictures have a special ability to focus attention on one time, place, event and issue, to the point where any item not pictured in the press is generally ignored by everyone. The speed with which pictures from foreign events arrive has bypassed the "normal" channels of foreign policy decision making. Furthermore, the ability of images to evoke an emotional response—anger, agitation, sympathy—obscures the reasoned and rational bases for policy-making. Finally, it is also taken for granted that pictures have discrete meanings, cross-culturally and cross-temporally transportable messages. The only ways to control the genie of press imagery, therefore, are to censor it, to manipulate it, or to create new persuasive images. These hypotheses suggest widespread belief in a "hypodermic needle" model of visual effects on policy and opinion where pictures have a special power to drive people to change attitude, and that, crucially, the direction of that changed attitude or galvanization is preordained.

Continuing, I argue that certain pictures are the center of public and elite discourse. I introduce the term "icon of outrage" to identify a picture that seems to demand our attention. It is allegedly stored in our collective memories, though in practice the memories of those who study or work with images are more resolute than those of the general public. In any case, one thing or many things about a given image have made it famous. It is a picture to which most of us who grew up in a given time or generation or culture have some vague or definite connection. For the generation of World War II, the Joe Rosenthal photograph of the flag-raising at Iwo Jima may be one example; for the Vietnam generation, the screaming woman at Kent State may come to mind; for the post–baby boom generation, perhaps it is the young man facing the tanks at Tiananmen, or the bomb's-eye view of a building in Baghdad.

Cross-generational memory and recognition of such images, on the other hand, may be weak. In this light, I try to delineate common characteristics of icons of outrage. These range from their prominence in the press to their resonance with certain "primordial" themes in human life. They may also have aesthetic appeal as "great shots" (drawn from our conventions of visual imagery). Yet, I question if this necessarily makes them politically powerful. More important, the visual journalists of the world produce many striking images each day to plug into the news stream: few are made icons. Icons of outrage, then, are rarely born great; rather, journalists, academics and politicians, and only to a very small extent the public, thrust greatness upon them. Furthermore, their significance, their meanings, and their relevance to historical events are not transcendent but are the subjects of often bitter political argumentation.

These criteria are illustrated in the analysis of a recent icon of outrage: the picture of a Sudanese child and a vulture (Figure 1).

The next three chapters are devoted to case studies of notorious crises in American foreign policy and the allegedly famous images—the icons of outrage—chosen to represent them. The cases address respectively issues surrounding American participation in a war; political protest in a nation of major interest to the United States; and the view of human disasters (such as famine) abroad and the subsequent "humanitarian intervention" by U.S. military forces. These cases, I believe, cover the range of issues and challenges facing policy makers, the press, and the public in the realm of foreign affairs.

Chapter Two examines the brief, violent but critical events of 1968, when Viet Cong and North Vietnamese forces launched surprise attacks all over South Vietnam, and in particular captured the ancient capital of Hue and parts of the U.S. embassy complex in Saigon. The uprising was eventually turned back; the American military considered it a terrific defeat for the Communist forces. In contradistinction, most observers agreed that Tet was a public relations catastrophe for American policy in Vietnam. At the time, and still today, supporters of the war effort accuse the press of eroding public support by portraying Tet as a U.S. setback through graphic images of material destruction, atrocities, and U.S. casualties. A single important image (taken on both still and motion picture film) will be focused on: a South Vietnamese police chief executing a Viet Cong suspect at close range (Figure 2). The picture did seem to occasion outrage, or at least concern, among many discourse elites. Evidence of wider public reaction, however, is missing; furthermore, the frames of discourse and social contexts through which the image was presented and absorbed may actually have discouraged sympathy for the "victim" of the shooting. The abdication of decisive leadership during Tet by the number one agenda-setter and shaper, President Lyndon Johnson, may also have affected interpretation of the icon and of the event itself.

In Chapter Three, I discuss the events at Tiananmen Square in 1989. For a few months, one of the most visualized foreign conflicts in the history of global media splashed out on the televisions and front pages of the world. Protests by Chinese students about living conditions in university dormitories ballooned until by June millions of students, intellectuals, and ordinary workers were marching in the streets of China's major cities, demanding a host of political reforms. The American press eagerly dubbed it a "Democracy" movement. Yet, despite the fact that the whole world's media were witnessing the events, the protests were crushed. How did the flood of pictures of protesting students and rampaging government troopers affect American opinion and policy? Several icons of outrage emerged from the cameras of western media; the man facing the tanks (Figure 3) was the most notorious.

The Tiananmen incident reveals many of the hidden rules of the global visual news system: for example, the need for photojournalists to create visually identifiable villains and heroes. The events also illustrate how pictures can affect opinion but not policy; essential trade and diplomatic ties with the People's Republic of China remained firm despite any real or feigned outrage. The rhetoric of solidarity with the man who stood against the tanks seemed widespread, but the effects of his bravery were fleeting. Expressions of outrage by the Bush administration proved an effective tool—in the long term—for displacing any radical challenges to the president's moderate China policy. Finally, Tiananmen is also a useful case to explore why certain pictures do *not* become celebrated and how such absences reveal the constructed and imposed nature of the icon of outrage.

Chapter Four explores what nearly the entire cohort of discourse elites, from presidents to anchor people, described as the "mission of mercy": the U.S. military intervention in Somalia. Later, this action was cited as a "humiliating failure." American soldiers were sent to supervise and protect the distribution of food in Somalia, a country whose government, infrastructure, and society were shattered by civil war and whose people were starving. The bookends of the story were summed up by two opposing types of images. When the intervention began, newspapers, newsmagazines, and newscasts featured generic icons of one subject: starvation. When the intervention collapsed, its failure was exemplified by pictures of the naked bodies of American servicemen desecrated by Somali mobs, and the battered face of a captured American helicopter pilot.

The Somalia case is examined as indicative of two crucial genres of pictures in global visual news flow: the starving African child and the American casualty. Analysis is made of how such pictures operate in the public mind, and how they may battle to affect opinion. The allegation that the former images "got us in" to Somalia and the latter "drove us out" is critiqued. Special focus is directed toward the elements missing from the framing of such pictures, including American culpability in the initial starvation and our provocation of the disastrous battle that created the final set of pictures. The colliding icons of Somalia illustrate that what a picture shows is often only camouflage for other images not seen, frames of discourse unchallenged, and contexts unrevealed.

The final chapter extrapolates from the observations made in the case studies of Tet, Tiananmen, and Somalia, and to a lesser degree the Sudan, examined in the book. An image can have aesthetic power but no lasting political influence; the two qualities may coincide but should not be conflated. In general, the content, context, and framing of an icon of outrage seem to be more influential than the picture itself. In some cases, the icon of outrage may have had no impact on general opinion; in others, such as the brutalities visited on American soldiers in Somalia, a strong impact seems to have been directed by the combination of the image and its subject content. Yet, whatever the effects of images are, there is clearly a perception among the public, the press, and our leaders that images *are* powerful; this perception can be more influential than its less sensational reality.

Icons of outrage, then, may change the world because we believe they can, and perhaps because we want them to. Ironically, for all its supposed power, we know very little about the icon and how it is created. Press, public, and even the political structure would be better served if icons were more thoroughly engaged. Yet, the evidence is that icons of outrage are not independent actors, unguided missiles that carry pristine messages and impart monodirectional stimuli. Icons can be managed as tools of foreign policy argumentation, enactment, and destabilization. Because their essential meanings are subject to debate, they also have the potential, like any weapon, no matter how costly or well designed, for backfiring on their creators, employers, and champions. Understanding them, however, is predicated on asserting they are the products of a commercial system. Icons are sought, bought, and marketed and, as with any media product, audiences may grow jaded and fatigued at their repetition.

NOTES

1. D. H. Kennerly, "Foreword," in *Battle Eye: A History of American Combat Photography*, ed. by N. B. Moyes (New York: Metrobooks, 1996), p. 7.

2. As discussed briefly in Chapter 4 on the Somalia crisis, it is always an act of framing to characterize by name an individual, group, or institution, especially those who have contested missions and legacies; was General Aidid a Somali "warlord" or "clan leader"? The term "Viet Cong," which was originally employed by the South Vietnamese government as an anti-communist pejorative against all dissidents, including but not exclusively communist guerrilla fighters, is an example. I have tried to use "National Liberation Front" occasionally for balance, but of course 99 percent of American readers would not only not recognize but would be confused by the term, and disagree with the group's self-definition.

Acknowledgments

Many people advised and assisted in the creation of this book. Some of them are not aware of their contribution because it was to earlier work that eventually led to the present volume. These include Hannah Gourgey, Larry Gross, Carolyn Marvin, Paul Messaris, and particularly Joseph Turow. Special thanks is also extended to Mike Griffin and Dona Schwartz.

I wish to thank Tsan-Kuo Chang for advice on mass media and foreign policy; Jane Perrone, my research assistant, for grinding labor above and beyond the call of assistantship; Anne Jett, who read and commented on an earlier draft of this work; and Cpt. Scott Belgarde, U.S. Army Reserve, for his careful reading of the manuscript for military and political terminology and content.

Gratitude is extended to Greenwood's editor Jim Sabin for supporting the manuscript and making suggestions that improved it. Terry Park and his team's guidance in proofing and designing the copy was also invaluable. I am grateful to Robert E. Denton, Jr. for allowing me to make my contribution to the Political Communication Series.

Most important, I want to thank my wife, Christie, who has been an astute critic of my writing and this work's steadiest advocate.

Figure 1
Sudan, 1993
Kevin Carter/SYGMA

Figure 2
Saigon, 1968
Eddie Adams/ASSOCIATED PRESS

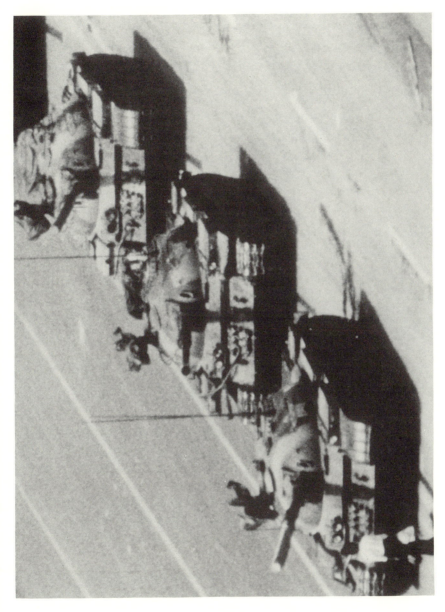

Figure 3
Beijing, 1989
Charles Cole/SIPA

Chapter One

In Search of Icons of Outrage

THE "PROBLEM" OF VISUAL IMAGES
AND FOREIGN POLICY

The idea that a picture can drive political policy and public opinion—the concept of visual determinism—is not novel.[1] In the world's first major treatise on governance, Plato's *Republic*, the philosopher expressed concern about the nefarious effects on public opinion and political decision-making by vivid visual images.[2] Today, many people believe that the "problem" of pictures influencing policy and opinion has hypertrophied in the late twentieth century. The allegation that news images have an especially resonant ability to drive, alter, or overturn foreign policy has received currency and generated controversy since the Vietnam War. Among those who espouse such a belief are presidents, members of the foreign policy establishment, and reputable and influential reporters and pundits. In contrast, most mass communication researchers and some journalists and politicians are quite skeptical about any theory of news that posits strong or powerful effects on viewers regardless of informational context, cultural prejudice, or interpersonal influence. Claims of the powerful effects of pictures in the press, however, are so persistent, and made by such influential and powerful voices in media and the political structure, that they cannot be dismissed merely as hyperbole. Claims made about the links between pictures in the press and foreign policy and public opinion form a common web of implicit and explicit assumptions, each flowing from the other in supportive logic. My purpose here is to list them, and to partially critique them; further assessment will be conducted in the case study chapters to come.

Policy Makers Survey the Foreign Affairs Environment
Through Mass Media[3]

The basic, and least controversial, premise of the lay theory of visual determinism is that politicians, like many of us, watch TV (and read newspapers and magazines) to monitor the world environment. As Jarol Manheim has concluded, "In foreign affairs, even public officials can have a hard time gathering information, so even they may be dependent on the media for some portion of their understanding of events." He continues, "They [in some cases] know little more than we know."[4] This information gap may be widened in those situations where the flow of news pictures seems the most enticing: fastbreaking stories from foreign lands. Anecdotal revelations of the attention that policy elites pay to mass media abound. It is said that President Clinton—the first president who grew up with TV—"prefers CNN to daily [CIA] intelligence briefings."[5] Yet the utility of media knows no generational bounds. George Bush apparently faithfully watched the Larry King show on CNN as a "barometer" to gauge "how the public was responding" to his actions and policies.[6] During the Persian Gulf conflict, the *Washington Post* noted that the "White House . . . is preoccupied with the war."[7] The solution in a previous era would have been more frequent or intensified intelligence briefings; this time, however, the situation was addressed by installing televisions in each staff person's office. The diplomatic sophism "we are monitoring the situation" increasingly means watching it on TV. Even foreign government representatives have admitted: "We get a lot of our information like you do . . . from CNN."[8] In sum, TV news might be seen as the modern "great equalizer" where mighty and low all have, at least in the first minutes or hours of a major story, access to the same information. As one CNN executive noted, during the Gulf war, "Everyone with access to CNN, including the president, was receiving the news of the beginning of the war, from the very target, at the very same instant."[9]

News is Visual

If politicians are learning about the world through television images, then television and other news media must satisfy the demand for vivid, kinetic visuals to draw their attention.[10] As journalist Edward Girardet suggests, "When such bang-bang footage is not available, the story does not appear quickly and powerfully for viewers. . . . Journalists, particularly television cameramen, are under pressure to bring back spectacular images to satisfy network appetites."[11] NBC's Jim Lederman similarly states that, "Television news is enslaved to images. If an idea cannot be recorded in the form of an image, it will rarely, if ever, be given extensive time on a nightly network newscast."[12] In the language of the powerful image model, the news values that define a good story are identical to those that spur reaction from the public: "Clear, dramatic pictures are the key to both 'good television' and to the impact a given story will have on viewers."[13] Similarly, a *Newsweek* editorial stated: "Everyone knows there are three key ingredients to a good magazine piece: reporting that informs, writing that enlightens and photos that capture the drama that words can't always convey."[14]

The Instantaneousness of Media Imagery Bypasses the Normal Channels of Political Decision-Making

During the Vietnam War, news film took about 24 hours to be processed from the battle front to the TV screen.[15] By the time of the 1973 Arab-Israeli War, improved satellite technology had reduced transit time to several hours.[16] During the Persian Gulf War, visual news could be seen by viewers live.[17] Many believe that this compression of the traditional news cycle bypasses the normal channels of journalistic filtration and government deliberation. This instantaneousness is seen as a threat to the traditional mechanisms and timetables of foreign affairs decision-making. As researchers Steven Livingston and Todd Eachus have argued, the CNN phenomenon—the relentless flood of news images into the national consciousness—creates a tension with the measured and deliberative folkways of national decision makers. "On one hand is the perceived need of various foreign policy actors to manage policy in an atmosphere of relative isolation, sheltered from the vicissitudes of public pressure. On the other are various news media creating those very pressures."[18] Such perceptions are evident in the complaints made by those within the diplomatic hierarchy and those who report on it. For example, Secretary of State Warren Christopher complained that "television images cannot be the North Star of America's foreign policy."[19]

Pictures Cannot Lie and Their "Meanings" Are Fixed

Another aspect of the claim that pictures in the press have power is that the veridicality and verisimilitude of those images are rarely doubted. No one looks at a news photograph and thinks "that's just his opinion," although they may claim a photo was posed or staged. As Richard C. Leone, president of the Twentieth Century Fund, has observed, "The pervasiveness of the belief that CNN is where you go to find out 'what's really happening' is startling."[20] For example, former President Jimmy Carter recalled the following incident:

When the coup attempt was made against Gorbachev, the leaders of the coup called the president of Kazakhstan and said "we have taken control of the Russian government, and Gorbachev has agreed that we are in control." And the president of Kazakhstan said "that is a lie because I'm watching it on CNN and I know that what CNN says is true and what you've told me is not true."[21]

Yet, even when the verity of a picture is questioned, it is typically done so on a limited, nonstructural basis: is it true? During one of Boris Yeltsin's long bouts of illness, a video tape was released by the Russian government showing him convalescing and looking reasonably animated. The video, it turned out, was heavily edited. Hours of tape of a torpid Yeltsin were scanned for a few seconds of vitality; the doctor and worried attendants were cropped out. "Our job was to show he looked better than in reality," recalled one of the editors.[22] The "reality" they spoke of was distorted by editing. Yet, photojournalism has its codes of production as much as any other component of the news industry.[23] It always distorts reality on some levels; it is always selective about what reality it represents. Moreover, the "truth" of an image, whether or not it shows something that really happened, is less important than the struggle to define what the image means for national policy. Paradoxically, the assumed natural objectivity of visual news undermines its adherence to journalistic ideals of neutrality; no newspaper is expected to show both *visual* sides of a story.

Pictures Strike an Emotional Response in Viewers That Overrides Reason

Descending straight from Plato, a fifth corollary of the visual determinism hypothesis is the emotional impact of the images; pictures, it is alleged, hit the heart and cloud the mind. *Time* magazine writer Lance Morrow argues, in line with many other journalists, that still and video images "are mainlined directly into the democracy's emotional bloodstream without the mediation of conscious thought."[24] George F. Will speculated that "heart-rending pictures of agony will soften hearts and prompt [unwarranted and foolish] humanitarian interventions."[25] Media critic Tom Shales concluded that "shocking and heartbreaking" TV pictures of starving children in Somalia helped motivate the American response.[26] Veteran diplomat and statesman George F. Kennan agreed that visual images of Somalia in the press created a compassion that drove the United States to unwarranted intervention.[27] Such emotions can direct policy, or affect it. In response to President Clinton's decision to use force in Bosnia in support of the Muslim-led government, Senator Bob Dole asked the president to "tell the American people as much as we abhor the pictures [of the victimization of the Muslims] why it is in our national interest to intervene."[28] Another conservative critic of American interventionism argued that "by exacerbating fears and stoking passions, the news media create public predispositions for action (or inaction) that take precedence over any calculus of long-range policy considerations, thereby making it impossible for elites to play their accustomed role."[29] Pictures, therefore, can lay the groundwork for policy by setting up public expectations.

Second, the feelings that such images are said to incite are taken as distinct, uniform, transcendental. We are all assumed to abhor and be moved by the same pictures and to arrive at the same emotional response. The only variation, like the truth value of the image, is taken as being binary: we can, as veteran diplomats say they do, keep our eyes dry and be sensible, not get overwrought. If we did get emotional, however, the attitude and kind of emotional response is assumed to be the same regardless of the observer. Having another response, an emotion of a different kind, is seen as deviance. This view might reflect a *first person effect*, where people react to a mediated stimulus in a certain way, and then assume that others must be reacting in the same way. Typically, such first person assumptions are expressed by political and journalistic elites—discourse elites—and then imposed on the public.[30] This gives rise to the standard incantation that "all America" was "shocked" by a given picture. Yet, outrage is in the eye of the beholder; it is quite possible, for example, to see pictures of burned children and be unmoved because those children are categorized as the enemy. Here again, images seem to stimulate politicians' rhetoric rather than their actions, and elicit poetics, not policy. Admitting emotional impact from a news video may be, for the modern diplomat and office-holder, a form of ritual response ("I was shocked") that requires no commensurate action.

Pictures Drive Policy

In addition to the other influences of pictures in the press, we are told that "pictures drive foreign policy." Again the anecdotal evidence and admission of this phenomenon are widespread and made by key opinion-makers and shapers. Sometimes a general "CNN effect" subsuming the flood of imagery and its instantaneousness and vividness is ascribed as being able to influence, affect, or drive foreign policy. Diplomat Rozanne Ridgway, for example, claimed that the Somalia misadventure demonstrated that "pictures of starving children would rightly encourage Americans to press their government to intervene, then equally dramatic pictures of American casualties would force a premature withdrawal before the job was done."[31] Conversely, Madeleine Albright, in seeking support for U.S. policy in Bosnia while she was U.N. Ambassador, noted that it was through television imagery that the American people "will understand how important this is to the United States for moral reasons."[32] Rep. Luis V. Gutierrez (D-Florida) reported that he was turned against the intervention in Somalia when he saw pictures of the bodies of American servicemen dragged through the streets of Mogadishu. "I saw the picture of the mutilation and I saw the picture of the American hostage. . . . They caused me great pain and consternation as I'm sure they did to every American."[33] The White House assured the public that President Clinton "finds those pictures reprehensible, and he wants to make sure something is done about that."[34] During a debate to impose severe restrictions on China's trade with the United States in the wake of the Tiananmen events, Rep. Nancy Pelosi (D-California) brandished the photograph of the man facing the tanks and proclaimed, "We have an opportunity today in this chamber to stand with that man for democracy."[35] In this manner, policy is explained by pointing at specific images in the press.

FRAMING IMAGES

The visual determinism hypothesis contradicts much traditional research in mass communication and political science. As Tsan-Kuo Chang points out, there is a middle ground between purely mechanical interpretations of the press being "a legitimate and powerful contender" and the view of its being "a docile and submissive official agent."[36] This middle ground includes the work of scholars from a variety of disciplines who are attempting to build a theoretical framework for the interaction between the American press and policy-making in foreign affairs.[37] According to this research, press power is limited at best. For example, in a comprehensive survey of prestige press coverage (in written reports) of China from 1950 to 1984, Chang found that:

In the process of China policy making, the direction of influence among foreign policy makers, the press, and public opinion can therefore be reasonably described as moving from the central players to those in the outer circle, with the press serving as magnifier of official actions and decisions in the public sphere.[38]

Such a conception parallels that of political scientist Graham T. Allison, who proposed that there are many "actors" or "players" in the foreign policy game who bargain and maneuver with each other, sometimes in accordance, sometimes in conflict.[39] These include constitutional actors like the executive branch, represented in the person of the president, and the legislative branch, represented by Congress. Other players range from ethnic lobbies, corporations, and other nations to major and minor individuals and institutions of the government bureaucracy. Many minor players may have greater power in areas of their expertise, fiat, or lobbying interest.

Foreign policy making can also be both unified and fractionalized, depending on the issue, the event, and the context. Perhaps the only unifying element of all policy debates and decisions is the perception of the need to explain and sell policies to the people. As one writer has characterized this relationship, no other nation is as resolute as the United States in acting upon "ritualistic deference to [the worth of] public opinion."[40]

The opinions of the different publics within the citizenry can only be effectively addressed through mass media. The press serve as a conduit for political leaders to address their constituencies and to influence other opinion leaders. While discourse elites comprise most of the voices, by-lines, and sources in news, they also believe that the public is listening and watching. Crucially, the assumptions also work in the reverse; political elites not only monitor mass media to find out what is going on but also to assess what is of interest to the public.[41]

Of all actors, the president traditionally has the greatest power to influence, direct or perpetuate American foreign policy. His constitutional powers make him the "ultimate decision-maker."[42] His every action is a "visbyte"; his every statement has built-in news value; his every whim is a potential policy; and to many inside and outside the country, he physically embodies the nation. It is the president who can set the agenda of interest and action in foreign affairs.[43] Chang's study found that editorials in the *New York Times* and *Washington Post* regarding China from 1950 to 1984 basically reflected the agenda, attitudes and utterances of the executive branch.[44] Likewise, in my own analysis of pictorial coverage of China in the *New York Times, Newsweek* and *Time* from 1949 to 1989, I found that the political stance of the U.S. government (as directed by the president) was the consistent determinant of the connotative intent of the images.[45]

In addition, one of the extra-constitutional powers is a leader's popularity; public approval of the man seems to positively influence approval of his policies.[46] In one study, as many as 40 percent of respondents indicated that a mere statement of preference by the president would lead them to alter their opinion on a foreign policy question.[47] Political scientists have also categorized a "rally 'round the flag" syndrome in which the president can, albeit temporarily, mobilize public opinion in his favor through decisive actions during foreign crises.[48] These powers of action and persuasion are not pervasive; a thousand minor issues of foreign policy are enacted every day without presidential utterance and imposition. The president, however, can set broad guidelines and pick and choose issues that, simply by his selection, become the foci of others' attention, if not action.

One crucial power, primarily available to the president but potentially accessible to other players in the foreign policy system, is the power to frame an issue. Framing's main contribution as a research paradigm is that it is equally applicable to the production, transmission, and reception of messages.[49] As Robert Entman defines it, "To frame is to select some aspects of a perceived reality and make them more salient in a communicating text in such a way as to promote a particular problem definition, causal interpretation, moral evaluation, and/or treatment recommendation."[50] Words or pictures to describe an event impose a frame; the selection of a particular event as being newsworthy is in itself a framing choice. Much of public discourse involves disputes or consensus over such frames. The implication is that the way that media frame issues, events, and texts influence how the public interprets mediated reality.

The media frame a person, an issue, or an event by selecting it for coverage; limiting or expanding the amount of coverage; suggesting its status and relative associations; and appointing spokespeople to present "sides" of the issue. They also supply a complex array of tones, nuances, contexts, and boundaries of controversy to the framed story. More important for our purposes, media also supply (or serve as conduits for) pictures associated with a story. Ascribing metonymy to a news photograph—for example, "This was the scene that summed up Africa's problems"—is the most potentially powerful visual framing device. Gaye Tuchman portrays the frame as reducing the range of possible meanings of any event into industrially acceptable categories: "The news frame organizes everyday reality and the news frame is part and parcel of everyday reality."[51] Frames, thus, are tools for attempting to impose meaning "as well as psychological stimuli for audiences to process."[52] Which visual images do and do not appear in the press, what is and is not said about them, the context which they are said to represent and the context in which they appear, constitute media frames.

Framing and the popularity of political leaders are intimately linked.

Enacting foreign affairs decision-making has much to do with the perception of who holds power: how the framer of an issue is her or himself framed by the audience. William Clinton's first term as president was a case study in how such powers may wane and wax. Several factors conspired to undermine his authority in foreign policy early on. First, he had no foreign affairs background or tenure to call upon as a source of credibility. In the election he had styled himself as the "man from Hope" and criticized President Bush for being overly concerned with foreign affairs. Second, in 1994, a Republican victory in Congressional elections was seen as a referendum on Clinton's performance. This gave the oversight responsibility to his political enemies. Third, until 1996, low poll ratings served as a signal of the public's perception that Clinton was weak and unlikely to win reelection. In 1994, as Robert Denton and Rachel Holloway point out, the face of Bill Clinton was "the most negative political image available."[53] Finally, Clinton was portrayed in many press accounts—and in other sources such as the *Doonesbury* comic strip—as a waffler, an indecision-maker.

These perceptions of weakness and vulnerability affected his policy-making powers. His own party comrades in congressional committees thought it prudent not to be seen as close allies of their president.[54] Foreign leaders learned that the "White House is no longer the only stop required of a visiting dignitary here in Washington."[55] Such political realities and the perceptions (real or false) of weakness or failure in turn affect the reaction of the press to the president's foreign policy initiatives and actions. A "blood in the water" phenomenon may allow mass media to challenge, or to serve as the conduit for other elites challenging presidential hegemony in foreign affairs. In short, the president's power to frame an image of foreign policy is partly determined by how political and journalistic elites and, by extension, the public, frame him.

Frames also govern which events are allowed to constitute news from foreign lands. The sociologist Herbert Gans has described the seven most prevalent foreign news stories in print and television.[56] They include:

1. American actions abroad, ranging from wars to visits by the president.
2. Foreign activity that affects America, such as a war that threatens oil supplies.
3. Relations with totalitarian countries, especially when these are seen as dysfunctional and thus are contrary to American ideals.
4. Foreign elections and transfers of power (including coverage of European royalty).
5. Major wars.
6. Disasters (natural or otherwise) that cause great loss of life.
7. The antics and oppressions of foreign dictators, especially if they have unfriendly relations with the United States.

These subjects have two elements in common. They are potential sources of good visuals. They also generally relate to American issues and concerns. Defining those concerns, are, of course, an enterprise of the government as well as the press.

In sum, the mass media may serve as a player (sometimes acquiescent, sometimes antagonistic) in the process of making foreign policy. The press may also be the platform through which many of the other groups declaim their views and enact persuasion strategies, especially those aimed at the general public. Whatever the degree of their independence or subservience to the political power structure in foreign affairs, the news media serve as "a continuous and articulate link between foreign policy officials in the government and those people on the outside who follow events."[57] Once information (both verbal and visual) actually appears in media, however, it may act to confirm its own importance to the discourse elites *even if they are the sole and original source of the information.* Yet, as I think will become clear in the case studies to follow, most discourse elites (including many academics) tend to overestimate the numbers of people who really follow foreign affairs news. The public interest and mood that elites think they are sensing may be fictive, or, by extension, may be created by their own agenda and proclamations.

WHOSE ICONS ARE THEY, ANYWAY?

In the spring of 1996, I distributed a questionnaire in an introductory mass communication class. I gave 146 students a series of prompts, including brief descriptions of historical events, their dates, and locations. I provided one entry as follows:

February 1968, America's war in Vietnam. Communist, Viet Cong and North Vietnamese units launch attacks throughout South Vietnam on American and South Vietnamese targets. The attacks occur on the Vietnamese lunar new year, Tet. The event is known as the Tet offensive, and some people believe it was the turning point of America's effort in Vietnam. Several famous photographs emerged from the fighting. Can you name or describe any of them?

I allowed space on the paper for students to either write an answer or to draw a picture from memory. My intention in this survey was simply to find out how famous, for these mostly 17- to 20-year-olds, were "famous" pictures.[58] Overwhelmingly, the verdict was that pictures with which I, as a student of American photographic history, was intimately familiar, were largely unknown to my students. For the Tet question, for example, over 90 percent of the class gave vague answers, such as "pictures of fighting." Revealingly, fully 20 percent of the class provided answers that seemed drawn from Hollywood movies, such as *Platoon*, or the *China Beach* TV series, or even *M*A*S*H*. Individual students did recall or draw approximations of certain images. Several drew or described a young girl fleeing a napalm attack. A dozen students remembered a picture of a helicopter taking off from the U.S. embassy in Saigon. Both of these pictures, of course, were from Vietnam, but from different times, 1972 and 1975 respectively. In the general survey, almost across the board, my students performed dismally in associating famous images, that is, images that professors of visual communication, photojournalists or historians might readily call to mind, with the conflicts from which they originated. Only ten students gave the answer that I would have provided. They drew or described a picture of one Vietnamese man, his arm outstretched, holding a pistol to the head of another who cringed, ready to receive a bullet.

In another class, I tried reversing the experiment, showing the famous images without captioning and gauging whether the subjects could cite their source event. These images were august members of the pantheon of photojournalism: Robert Capa's *Dying Spanish Militiaman* (1936); Eddie Adams's *Saigon Street Execution* (1968), described above; Dorothea Lange's *Migrant Mother* (1936); Joe Rosenthal's *Old Glory Goes up on Mt. Suribachi* (1945); the photo by an unknown Nazi photographer of a small boy emerging from the rubble of the Warsaw ghetto (1943); Alberto Korda's portrait of Che Guevara (1960); Charles Moore's police dogs attacking black civil rights marchers in Birmingham, Alabama (1963); Bob Jackson's *Jack Ruby Shooting Lee Harvey Oswald* (1963); John Paul Filo's *Girl Screaming over a Dead Body at Kent State* (1970); Huynh Cong Ut's *Naked Little Girl and Other Children Fleeing Napalm Strike* (1972); Charles Cole's picture of a man confronting a column of tanks at Tiananmen (1989); and a still shot from a Pentagon Gulf War video of a missile's eye view of an Iraqi building (1991). In this test, many students were able to correctly associate an image with an event, most often for the Gulf War. Yet, very few could give me any detail about the exact context and circumstance of the picture's creation and provenance. Many vaguely recalled that they had "seen it somewhere before," though such an answer could have been more an artifact of the subjects trying to please their professor than a true measure of their familiarity with the icons.

I admit that at the time I viewed these results dejectedly, probably in the same way that a traditional professor of English might feel a twinge of sadness at discovering that his freshman class had only casually heard of Shakespeare, Hemingway, and Orwell, and certainly not read them. For those of us who study visual communication, these images are familiar companions. I thought I was studying visual texts that were at the center of American culture; I was reminded by my students that historical images may have only a slight chance of surviving the event and the generation from which they sprang. What my cohort considers to be the powerful, the important, the widely known, may very well have faded from the immediate cultural landscape as completely as the poems of Callimachus or the essays of Montaigne. Moreover, such findings coincide with recent work on collective memory which suggests that recollections of news events "tend to be a function of having experienced an event during adolescence or early adulthood."[59] In my students' case, images from the Gulf War—"experienced" through mass media, of course—stirred the connecting neurons; icons of Vietnam and previous eras fell flat.[60] The icons of one generation or one audience are the enigmas, or at best, the shadows of another generation or audience.

Are we justified, then, in using the word "icon" for a picture of dubious renown? The term has several roots and implications of interest. First, icon is derived from the Greek word *eikon* meaning image or reflection.[61] Pictures may be iconic, but not all pictures are icons in that few in the news stream achieve fame and attention. There are two types of icons of outrage that will be examined in this book. The *discrete* icon is a single image with a definite set of elements—the famous photo or footage. Many frames were taken of the Marines raising the flag at Mount Suribachi; only one shot is the icon that is so familiar to the wartime generation. This does not mean that the icon must be wholly unique, as in the case of a work of art where only one original exists, though innumerable copies may be produced. When Joe Rosenthal took the picture of the second flag raising at Iwo Jima, to his right was U.S. Marine photographer Sgt. William H. Genaust with a motion picture camera, who filmed the flag raising from an almost identical angle. Often icon-producing events, such as the lone man facing the tanks in Beijing, may be photographed or filmed by more than a single journalist.

The second type of icon is the *generic*, in which certain elements are repeated over and over, from image to image, so that despite varying subjects, times, and locations, the basic scene becomes a familiar staple, a visual cliché.[62] An example, elaborated on below and in the chapter on Somalia, is the "hungry child in Africa." These words may not attune one's memory or focus to a single sharp image taken at one moment by one photographer. Rather they probably elicit a vague mental picture of a black-skinned, naked, crying baby with a bloated belly. There is no doubt that the hungry child image is strongly triggered by the prime words "Africa" and "hunger." Of course, the subjects are interchangeable; the child may be Ethiopian, Sudanese, Somali, or Liberian. The generic scene then is infamous; the cast and the backdrop may differ from picture to picture.

DEFINING THE ICON

Who is in charge of electing pictures to "greatness" and maintaining their fame when they are so easily lost to each new generation? There is no definitive production cycle describing how a picture becomes an icon. As well, some pictures can be iconic without engendering outrage, or at least the kind of strong, evocative reaction that the pictures studied in this book are said by many to provoke. Nevertheless, common formal, thematic, contextual, and discursive elements are attributed to icons. Several more distinguish the icon that is said to engender strong negative reaction: outrage.

Celebrity

The first major criterion for justifiably calling a picture an icon is its fame. A famous image is one which people can identify when prompted, or are vaguely familiar with even if little is known about the context of events. As my class experiment suggested, this aspect of celebrity is quite fleeting. Nevertheless, in terms of generational icons, certain pictures are better known to the public than others. The celebrity status of a picture is often signaled by the fact people assume others must know of it. Congressman Neil Abercrombie (D-Hawaii), in memorial demonstrations outside the Chinese embassy on June 4, 1991, two years after the Tiananmen events, referred to the man facing the tanks picture as one that he kept "outside my office to remind myself that democracy isn't free, that there is always a price to be paid."[63] Abercrombie did not show the picture, but told reporters and others present, "I'm sure all of you have seen it."

Accordingly, an image has achieved celebrity status if it is surrounded by discourse that pre-interprets the meaning, significance and relevance of the picture. Because so many words are devoted to a single image, and these words are articulated by important, influential people in society from presidents to anchor people, the mere quantity and focus of this discourse implies that the picture is important. The effort magnifies the celebrity. Often the denotation that an image is important is explicit; discourse elites tell us it is important, that it is a key image. I argue, however, that celebrity—or common fame—is not something on which the people, the viewing public, vote. Susan Moeller, whose *Shooting War* is a perceptive study of the culture and values of war photographers, argues that "the public sifts out the ordinary or banal images and remembers the extraordinary or the picturesque."[64] While she is correct that the public plays some role as a larger audience—who read the newspaper and watch TV news programs—her own role, and the role of others who collect and comment on news photography is more important in this selection process. There is, after all, no people's "photograph of the year" award.

Certainly, once a picture is in the marketplace—the images of the captured and desecrated Americans in Somalia are one example—the public may react. Yet, fame arises largely through publicity and by the approval of cognoscenti. Certain people have the power, through written publication or oral commentary, to bestow labels of importance on images or events. These are the photos that win Pulitzer Prizes and that reappear in books devoted to describing famous photographs. They become items of political importance and are reverentially treated *objets d'art*.

Prominence

Another distinction of an icon is how prominent is its appearance in print or transmission. Is it the front page or cover shot, or does it lead a newscast?[65] As a famous person is more likely to be in the "front of the line" of the flow of news, so is the picture that is considered to be well known and important. Prominence is one of the least ambiguous qualities of the icon. The video images of Michael Durant, the American helicopter copilot captured by Somalis, were on the front cover of *Time*, *Newsweek*, almost every newspaper in North America, and many international publications, as well as leading or figuring prominently in most newscasts. In this sense, an icon is a picture that is much more visible than any other. Its greater likelihood to achieve a higher rank in our collective memory is influenced by its place order in the agenda of media. Prominence can be historically imposed as well; pictures may stay famous because they are featured as famous in textbooks and histories from which they arose. They are also more likely to be chosen by writers, editors, and publishers to make the covers of books. The same qualities that discourse elites saw or imposed on the image to make it prominent in the press may also attract bookstand sales; or, as discussed below, they may seem the natural choice to adorn a historical study because they are thought to sum up a great event or era.

Frequency

Related to the prominence of a picture is its quantitative representation in media sources. An icon is much more likely to be not only the front page image, but to appear in many publications, newscasts, and books on history, photojournalism, and visual cultural analysis. Traditional forms of content analysis sampling are best at uncovering this element. Frequency as well contributes to assumed "power." A flood of repetitious, similar images may have more of an influence than a single, non-recurring one. The importance of frequency is underscored in that tens of thousands of news pictures appear somewhere in the world's media outlets every day, but most are swept into forgotten archives, never to arise again. Many of these pictures are technically interesting and competent executions within the codes of visual journalism. A mere handful each year, however, have greatness thrust upon them. As in most qualities cited here, the effect of frequent repetition on our appreciation of the picture is circular. We see it often; it is thus important enough to be often seen.

Profit

Frequency, incorporated with celebrity and prominence, has another implication, one that is often unacknowledged by those outside the business of visual journalism: icons sell. The icon by its nature will appear in many venues for years, even decades. Each appearance earns the copyright holder a fee, especially for the celebrity images repeated in thousands of publications. Such fees are not inconsiderable; the pictures that illustrate this book, for example, cost $200 to $500 each for rights to a simple printing of one quarter page in black-and-white. In short, the icon is a commodity, but also a pearl of great price, a brand name to be licensed in the marketplace of visual news. It is commodified in the sense that thousands of copies are produced for the marketplace, but it is not fully a commodity like a bar of soap because there is an original. Some icons, such as the generic, can be shot to order—for example, a hungry child. The more sensational, specific icons adopt the uniqueness of *objets d'art*; they are commensurably more valuable.

It follows that what appears inside the icon is marketable as well, though usually of no profit to those humans caught in some moment of supreme suffering. The making of the product may inflict pain on the subjects. Rakiya Omaar, a Somali and the former executive director of Africa Watch, noted:

Anyone who has watched a Western film crew in an African famine will know just how much effort it takes to compose the "right" image. Photogenic starving children are hard to find, even in Somalia. Somali doctors and nurses have expressed shock at the conduct of film crews in hospitals. They rush through crowded corridors, leaping over stretchers, dashing to film the agony before it passes. They hold bedside vigils to record the moment of death. When the Italian actress Sophia Loren visited Somalia last month, the paparazzi trampled on children as they scrambled to film her feeding a little girl.[66]

Such behavior may not be pervasive, but the mad competition for the picture of the starlet with the dying baby would not occur if that image was produced simply to document historical events or to reveal human misery in order to arrest it.[67] Yet, journalists are loathe to admit that they are selling or marketing a product. The icon, however, despite being surrounded by discourse that appreciates its aesthetic, emotive, and political qualities, is at its core a thing of cash value.

Instantaneousness

Icons typically achieve fame immediately, then enter the ranks of important images as time passes. Joe Rosenthal's Iwo Jima Marines, Eddie Adams's Saigon execution photo, and a host of other pictures meet this qualification; all were instant stars. Some icons might experience a delay between the moment of their creation and their publication; Dorothea Lange's *Migrant Mother* of the Depression is one example, as is the picture of the Jewish boy rounded up by German soldiers in the Warsaw ghetto. Once appearing in print, however, and in the public eye, their celebrity status is rapidly imposed. In the age of the satellite dish, the quality of instant fame becomes even more operative. Images are captured and then beamed to waiting electronic and print media outlets within minutes. This does not abrogate the fact that discourse elites chose these instant icons to appear, and then chose to frame them as "important" and "powerful."

Transposability

Icons are often replicated across media. The image of the man with the tanks at Tiananmen, for example, is included in the CD-ROM edition of Bartlett's Quotations because, its compiler explained, "the situation is likely to be repeated over and over, though probably not in so visually powerful a way."[68] "Quoting" or transposing an icon across media and in many media sources helps to facilitate retention. The Eddie Adams picture, for example, is a central image in Billy Joel's music video *We Didn't Start the Fire*, as presumably a symbol of the instability of the 1960s. The Iwo Jima flag-raising was replicated in posters, advertising, statuary, and in many editorial cartoons, often stripped of its original context, but at least immortalizing the basic form of the image. In light of experiments such as those described above, however, it is not certain that new audiences will recognize the original icon and its context. However, as Paul Messaris, who earlier conducted similar studies, notes, subjects might not be familiar with the prototype image, but might understand the basic intent of the reference.[69] This is true when the original is reprinted, but it is also quite possible when it is quoted in an editorial cartoon or a parody. For example, Figure 1 [see discussion below] shows a photograph taken in 1993 of a vulture and an African girl. The picture's potential for transposability, however, was identified by an editorial writer in the *Cleveland Plain Dealer*:

If I were an editorial cartoonist I would draw a cartoon modeled on [the] photo. On the vulture's body I would write the words "104th Congress." Over the body of that starving little girl I would write "America's school children." I would follow that the next day with a picture of a school—"the feeding station"— about to be raided and reduced in the name of Gingrich's "Contract with America."[70]

Such a cartoon, if drawn, would not require its audience to be intimately familiar with the icon; an understanding of the habits of vultures and an awareness of contemporary politics is enough. Alternately, one can recognize the allusion without agreeing with the analogy.

Fame of Subjects

Another, perhaps less vital, criterion for an icon is the recognizability or notoriety of its subjects. In "hard" news (visual and verbal) political elites are far more likely to be the focus of attention because they are considered more newsworthy.[71] Icons often draw their fame from the presence of a well-known person: Ronald Reagan grimacing after an assassination attempt; Robert Kennedy dying on a hotel floor. Many pictures are *only* famous because of their human subjects. Korda's Che Guevara picture became an icon, reproduced in different variations in hundreds of settings as a symbol of the heroic revolutionary, because its single object of importance was the face of Che himself.[72] An identically stylized portrait of almost anyone else in the Cuban revolutionary hierarchy probably would not have achieved such notoriety. It was Che whose charisma, youth and good looks assisted the photographer; it is no coincidence that capitalism had earlier recognized these qualities when Che had worked briefly as a model for a motorcycle company's publicity campaign. The photo's climb to immortality was also boosted by the dashing exploits and later martyrdom and beatification (among the political left) of its subject.

Yet, in many icons the subjects are unknown, ordinary people caught up in some important moment or some striking composition that eventually is lifted to iconic status. Interestingly, being a member of the population of an icon does not necessarily mean personal fame outside the narrow discourse of students of visual culture. Sometimes an ordinary icon dweller—such as the Pima Indian Ira Hayes, one of the men raising the flag on Mt. Suribachi—will achieve fame because of his or her presence in an image; in Hayes' case, the notoriety was enhanced by the tragic circumstances of his subsequent life and death. Yet, his situation is atypical. Only a handful of persons alive today could name the young man facing the tanks at Tiananmen, the migrant mother, the woman kneeling at Kent State, or the man shooting the gun during the Tet offensive.

The fame of its subject is also one way for a picture to achieve some degree of retroactive attention. For example, in the *Süddeutscher Verlag* archive in Germany there resides a black-and-white photograph showing a huge, densely packed mass of people. They mill about the Odeonsplatz square in Munich, some more celebratory than others, in the wake of the general mobilization for war by the imperial government. The photo is dated August 1, 1914, a critical moment in world history to be sure, but the image itself achieved no great renown at the time. It had no visual elements or historical actions or persons that would make it a candidate for iconic status. It has some claim to metonymy: the arrival of war was greeted with enthusiasm by many people throughout Europe. No individual in the mass is distinct, except in magnification. Subsequent analysis, however, highlighted one pale, reed-thin, dark haired, heavily mustached figure, his face caught in an expression of orgasmic joy; it is very likely a young Adolf Hitler. At the time, the picture was not a sensation. However, because of the chance inclusion of a subject who later achieved supreme notoriety, it is an object of curiosity and even fascination among historians today.

Importance of Events

Another criterion for iconic status is that the event pictured has significance in itself. Quite often, icons are tied to important social events or historical occurrences. Obviously a certain degree of concomitance is at work; famous events are more likely to draw cameras and thus increase the number of pictures taken of them. In turn, event fame may add to the reasons discourse elites focus on a picture. Often the previous criteria—the importance of the dramatis personae, and the importance of the events—coincide. In such cases, even an aesthetically mundane visual scene is elevated to iconic status. For example, whenever presidents visit leaders in other lands, there is typically news film or still photography of the two leaders meeting and shaking hands. This favorite of diplomatic aides is held in low regard by photojournalists and nicknamed the "grip-and-grin" shot. Such pictures are news staples, but they rarely receive more than fleeting prominence and then only because of the fame of the participants. An exception occurred when, on September 13, 1993, Israeli Prime Minister Itzhak Rabin and Palestinian Liberation Organization Chairman Yassir Arafat shook hands at a White House ceremony to mark the signing of a peace treaty. CBS news anchor Dan Rather, an indisputable member of the discourse elite corps, dubbed it "the picture of the decade so far." ABC's Peter Jennings agreed, "That's the image that will be flashed around the world. That is the picture which will endure."[73] "The photo said it all," according to *USA Today*.[74]

Metonymy

This last ascription, "said it all," suggests another criterion that icons of photojournalism seem to share, though quite unimportant pictures are subject to this condition as well: their employment as metonyms. Pictures of single events are used to exemplify general conditions—*si non è vero è ben' trovato*. As Roland Barthes notes, "Metonymic logic is that of the unconscious."[75] The use of one image to illustrate a news story implies, without need of a caption, that the picture represents the greater event. This "summing up" quality is a special value of the news picture. For example, Carol Moseley-Braun (D-Illinois) stated on the floor of the Senate that she was "moved" by a picture from Bosnia of elderly Muslims being evacuated from the Serb onslaught in wheelbarrows. "This photograph," she proclaimed, "crystallized the ethnic cleansing the Serbs forced on the Muslims."[76]

On an objective level this process is illogical. Visual images are chronologically and spatially limited anecdotes about specific incidents.[77] All photographs are snapshots. Occasionally a photograph, such as the "blue ball" picture of the earth taken by American astronauts from the moon, seems to be comprehensive, to take in a wide range of space—to legitimately "encapsulate" the earth. As we shall see in the case studies to follow, it is more problematic to claim that a portrait of a few individuals summed up a war or an era. For behind every icon's metonymy is more than one story. The seeming naturalness of the imposed metonym masks the variability of its context. This is true when narratives seem compelling, familiar, and are assiduously replicated. For example, an image of police beating a suspect (e.g., Rodney King) suggests that there is a nationwide problem of police brutality. The problem may or may not exist, but the compelling image brings it to the fore especially if it ties into cultural conventions and expectations.[78] The inclination to present a picture as an explicit or implicit metonym is almost overwhelming, for journalists, scholars, and politicians. Yet, in truth, no picture ever says it all.

Primordiality and/or Cultural Resonance

This dual feature of an icon reaches furthest into the uncertain realm of the mystical. When we make allusions to biblical or classical historical scenes related to an icon, we suggest that it taps into some deeper human sensibility. This is not only because such scenes are part of our common cultural history (at least in the mind of the first person observer), but also because certain images may call to mind primordial themes. Jung's archetypes present the most accessible instances: shapes, forms, and ideas that recur across cultures. In a more concrete vein, Tamar Liebes and Elihu Katz, in their study of the reception of the

Dallas TV show in Israel, have suggested that while audiences may differentially interpret meanings and significance of events or attend to different sets of information, at the same time such audiences may also find certain themes to have strong currency, because they are in a sense cross-cultural.[79] Liebes and Katz give the example of conflict between father and son as one such primordial theme in television drama.

Likewise, commentators on icons may connect them with other, previous, icons. The migrant mother, for example, may remind us of the Madonna and Child. The man facing the tanks at Tiananmen recalls—to some observers—David's confrontation with Goliath. In short, the icon of outrage may remain a subject of interest long after the events that have spawned it have collapsed, because of this quasi-religious attachment to past archetypes and themes. This process, however, is not unilinear. Once we make a picture an icon, it too becomes a frame to which newer images will be compared. Every icon, therefore, creates a new standard for new icons.

Striking Composition

Finally, icons may share certain visual qualities. Few details of camera effect or mise-en-scène (the arrangement of objects in the frame) seem to unify the icons. One general criterion is "the decisive moment." This photographic term refers to the one moment in the taking of a picture when all the elements (including lighting, angle, and subject position, action and expression) are "right." Coined by the French photographer Henri Cartier-Bresson, it is a standard quasi-description of superior images in photojournalism where "the subject and the compositional elements form a union."[80] Freelance photographer Henry Grossman has argued that the best pictures are those that contain "revealing juxtapositions."[81] Indeed, many icons seem to capture moments of visual conflict: a man facing a row of tanks, attack dogs mauling citizens, and so on. Other icons—the flag raising at Iwo Jima, for example—seem to present a visual tension. Still others seem to be iconic simply because they capture some insight into human character against the backdrop of historical events. Yet, some icons are technically poor photographs. Many of the shots of the man standing alone against the tanks near Tiananmen Square are out of focus. The picture of the woman screaming over the dead student at Kent State is no stirring example of photo sense: in violation of the rules of photography, a fence post grows out of the woman's head.

One formal element that most icons seem to share, however, is their spareness. As James Barron of the *New York Times* noted, the man with tanks image "was powerful in its simplicity."[82] Almost all icons have very few distinct visual elements, or rather, they are shot, cropped, or printed to exclude all those elements that the photographer and editors, following the values of the trade, deem unessential to the "main point" of the picture. Simplicity and iconicity seem to go hand-in-hand. In many cases, any visual complexity (and thus, much context) is physically removed from the image. In the original negative of the Eddie Adams Saigon photo, other figures exist on both the left and right sides of the main subjects. These are almost always cropped out when the picture is reprinted in books and magazines. This naturally gives more vivid distinction to the action involving the executioner and victim.

Yet, the aesthetic judgment that a picture's composition is striking may not be universal, let alone held by the creator. Stuart Franklin, one of the photographers who pictured the Tiananmen tank encounter from the Beijing Hotel, expressed in an interview three years later that he wasn't that impressed, aesthetically, with the image: "The guy isn't even gesticulating." Franklin felt that some of his other pictures, and those by his colleagues, that showed more dynamic interaction between protesters and soldiers, including facial tension, action, and gesturing, were better images by the standards of photojournalism. He also professed, characteristic of a professional photojournalist, exasperation about the heights of rhetorical fancy that others have attached to the image: "All that stuff about man against the machine. . . . You can go off into desperate vagaries."[83] Of course, those vagaries are part of the discourse about icons.

At the same time, and this is a subtle distinction that can never be expressed in social scientific language: the people who create and interpret icons also live within the system they manage. Journalists, commentators, academics and other students of visual culture, and politicians do not grow up outside of the conventions of photojournalism. Whether or not such conventions are naturalistic—that is, have a basis in hardwired human cognitive processes—the system still influences those who oversee it. The imposition of the status of icon on a news photograph is rarely the result of conspiracy. Many of the pictures cited as summing up great events are both interesting and striking visual compositions. There is something in them that objectively captures our eye, even though the conventions that influence that capturing may be subjective. Because photojournalism permeates modern life, we all share the same standards to some extent.

Thus, a president, as much as a photo editor, might be expected to agree that a photograph of a vulture juxtaposed with a small girl, or a man shooting another man point-blank in the temple, or a young man confronting a column of tanks, or the naked bodies of U.S. soldiers dragged through the streets of a third-world city, are all "great" pictures. However, that such pictures have also changed the world is a shakier assertion. A striking, visually fascinating photograph or video can have an aesthetic power that intrigues everyone, but at the same time has less political impact than we would assume or might attribute to it. And that is one of the main points of this book: the aesthetic appeal of an image must not lead us to imagine, without evidence, that the picture must be commensurably changing hearts and minds. We must keep in mind that many striking compositions of life and death moments fleetingly appear in the news stream every day and then are subsequently buried forever in archives.

DEFINING OUTRAGE

Such are some of the criteria for the notorious photo, the icon; but what of the ascription of outrage attached to so many icons? Several further qualities may contribute to the unity of the term "icon of outrage."

Emotional Reaction

Tragedies, wars, and other disasters of human existence are often the sources of news icons. This does not mean that what is shown within the image is always violence. The migrant mother could be an icon of patient suffering. The flag raising can be seen as a symbol of triumph. However, the events connected with the icon are typically tragic. Certainly, photojournalists feel that extremes of human suffering make good news photography. The photocorrespondent's most basic rule, it is suggested, is that no body equals no story.[84]

What makes an icon into a subject of outrage, then, is more nebulous. Here again, we measure the status of the picture by what people say about it, especially the discourse elites who have the power to confer icon status. I use the term "outrage" flexibly. Many words attached to images will signify that some felt the picture occasioned a strong, emotional reaction. Such words include: horrifying, shocking, haunting, powerful and searing. One example is AP photographer Malcolm Browne's picture of Quang Duc, a Buddhist monk, shortly after immolating himself on a Saigon street (1963).[85] Typically, the picture is annotated as one that occasioned a reaction of "shock and dismay." Such images are taken as having an impact that goes beyond historical identification, aesthetic appreciation, or ascription of political significance. In a word, people have expressed that this image is important; it has affected them or others. Reaction by common folk is harder to judge. Few surveys are done of viewers' attitudes towards news pictures. This does not impede the discourse elites from claiming, for example, that "all Americans are shocked" by a given image.

In addition, photojournalists, though their work has a certain perceived objectivity, are aware of the potential shock value of what falls into their viewfinder. It is not an exaggeration to say that every freelancer in a war zone is looking for the Pulitzer winner that will establish his career. On the other hand, journalists with a cause to support may see outrage as a necessary tool for ideological mobilization. For example, in his recent memoir of experiences in the former Yugoslavia, David Rieff admitted that he and his fellow journalists, very early in the war, "took the side" of the Bosnian government and subsequently consciously chose to maximize the production of evocative images of Serbian atrocities and horrors that they assumed would force the world to intervene.[86] In other words, we have a member of the press claiming that many reports and pictures from Bosnia were (and presumably are) propaganda designed to affect foreign policy in Europe and America. Whether such autonomy of thought and action actually exists, of course, is another question, one that will be explored here. In any case, people can attach the term "outrage," or something like it, to an image of an event. They tell us that it shows something to get angry about, something tragic, something worthy of action, not of dispassion.

That noted, no picture is *naturally* the subject of outrage, in the same way that no image is a natural metonym. Outrage is a quality that stems from human cultural perspective. Many readers may object here, claiming that certain images—a child crying in hunger, or a man being beaten by the police, or civilians being bayoneted—are somehow universals, that all those who witness them will feel empathy and concern. While no action may result from this pity, at the least it will produce upset or outrage. This, however, is not always the case. Too many images that vocal elites in one culture have deemed objects of outrage have been interpreted wholly differently by others. We need look no further for examples than the photographs and films of the destruction of European Jews by the Nazis. These were produced as documents or souvenir shapshots by the perpetrators of the Holocaust. One man's icon of outrage is another man's trophy photo; yet, the picture does not change, only the prejudices of the beholder.

Effects

Another criterion of icons of outrage is that they are often held to have the power to "change the world."[87] Sometimes such changes are directly documentable, at least in limited degrees. There is absolutely no doubt that photographs of pathetic scenes, that stir outrage and evoke strong visceral response, exist in photography. That response can be measured in letters or phone calls to Congressmen, but also in the financial contributions of ordinary citizens. A minor case in point was illustrated in *National Geographic*. William Albert Allard, while traveling in the Andes, took a photograph that appeared in a March, 1982 article titled "The Two Souls of Peru." In the foreground is a small boy in a ragged sweater and a knit cap. The boy is crying, his face creased in anguish. In the background, a dusty field extends to the horizon. An old man walks stooped, and we see the corpses of several plump, woolly sheep. The photograph was taken shortly after "the six sheep that this Peruvian shepherd boy had been tending for his family had just been struck and killed by a taxi." After the photo appeared in the magazine, the editors of *National Geographic* reported that they had been inundated with funds from sympathetic readers who had "spontaneously contributed more than $4,000 to replace the sheep [and that] through CARE in Peru, the boy, Eduardo Condor Ramos, was found, and Assistant Executive Director Ronald Burkard presented him with six new animals. . . . Eduardo, incredulous, broke into tears again and said, 'God will pay you.'"[88]

Another example of influence, this one from the Bosnia war, was that of five-year-old Sarajevan girl Irma Hadzimuratovic.[89] Irma had been wounded in a mortar attack on July 30, 1993, that killed her mother and left the youngster with severe spinal injuries. Like many wounded children of the war she was confined to the overfilled French hospital of the city. Frustrated because he lacked medicine to treat her and other victims, one of the doctors asked a western film crew to do a story on Irma. Within days her frail body was pictured on the evening news while she screamed in continual pain. There was strong and measurable reaction. On the personal orders of British Prime Minister John Major, Irma, her father and sister, and dozens of other patients were flown to England for treatment. Reportedly, within a week, Irma had received twenty-five sacks of greeting cards, bushels of flowers, and many visits by well-wishers. Despite the care, Irma was left paralyzed from the neck down. She subsequently received plastic surgery. Meanwhile refugee aid donations poured in from many other countries. Irma later died from complications of her injuries. Undeniably this was a case of pictures causing an effect, but a very limited one with few positive results. Chris Cushing, a relief worker with the international aid organization Médecins sans Frontières, stated, "If you want to stop the Irmas, then you've got to stop the war." Neither Britain nor the other major powers supported any armed intervention in the crisis; that was not to come for several years. Other alleged cases of images affecting policy in wider arenas are harder to prove, and will be a subject of the case study chapters to follow.

Sites of Struggle

Finally, and most crucially for our purposes, icons of outrage share another quality: they are often sites of struggle for meaning. An example comes from the Vietnam War. Several Asian children run toward us along a road. In the background, we see soldiers and a cloud of smoke. When I showed this picture to my class, there was little recognition of it, but many did guess that it came from Vietnam. The young girl in the middle of the photo, naked and screaming, was guessed to have been suffering some sort of pain, probably fleeing, as one student put it, from her burning village. The picture was taken in June, 1972. The photo's primary subject was Phan Thi Kim Phuc, a nine-year-old girl. South Vietnamese planes dropped napalm in the area, intending to root out North Vietnamese forces nearby. Phuc was splashed by the chemical, which covered her right arm, burning her and forcing her to throw off her clothes. As she ran away, a *Life* magazine photographer took the picture, which was described in the magazine's pictorial retrospective as a "gut-wrenching photo which seemed to encapsulate the moral horror and military futility of this war—a conflict in which our forces and their allies often destroyed towns, as the phrase went, 'in order to save them.' A terrible gift to the anti-war movement, the picture played no small role in moving the U.S. toward a peace agreement 7 months later." The *Los Angeles Times* stated that this "savage image . . . with its anti-war theme . . . flashed around the world and came to symbolize, more than any other photograph taken in Vietnam, the atrocity of the war."[90]

Phuc was later taken to Cuba for medical treatment, where she became a "poster girl" for anti-U.S. propaganda. In recalling the incident, Phuc says, "I know that picture changed the world and it changed my life. I don't want to remember that day."[91] The photographer, "Nick" Ut, followed up on the subject of his image. He took her to the hospital, helped set up a bank account for her and tried to see that she got the best of care. Now, she is able to say, "I myself have seen other pictures of the war, but this is my picture."[92]

Of course, this is not everyone's reading of the photograph. General William Westmoreland, America's supreme commander in Vietnam from 1964 to 1968, claimed that the image was a fake, or rather that it failed to show what it claimed or what others had claimed of it. Speaking to a group of businessmen in Ft. Lauderdale in 1986, Westmoreland asserted that the girl actually had been burned in a hibachi accident at a family bar-b-que.[93] When the story achieved national prominence and reporters queried Westmoreland as to the origin of this differential interpretation, he claimed essentially that he had heard it somewhere but he wasn't sure where. Likewise, after the Tiananmen crackdown, the Chinese government publicly televised many trials of dissidents and even showed executions on national television. They did so to show their resolve to crush dissent, as a warning to those who would defy the authority of the state. The same pictures, however, were presented as evidence in human rights publications of the barbarity of the leaders of the People's Republic. That identical pictures can serve contradictory purposes shows how the image cannot be said to have a sole unambiguous meaning.

These then are the elements that have been attached to icons in general, and to icons of outrage in particular. They are not always coincident in the same picture, but no icon of outrage exists without assuming many such claims to notoriety and power.

ICONS IN ACTION

Images are meant to be seen and to be talked about, but too much abstraction mystifies the process through which discourse elites produce icons of outrage. It is better to examine how an individual news photograph entered the pantheon of photojournalism.

Consider Figure 1. The scene is a parched savanna, devoid of all but two objects. In the foreground is a black child—gender is indeterminate from the picture alone—bending over, face touching the earth. We cannot see his or her expression. On a diagonal, slightly in the background and to the left, is a vulture. Although the exact object of its focus is unclear from the picture, we might guess from the alignment of beak and haunch that it is looking at the child. In terms of photographic composition, the picture is unremarkable. The juxtaposition of the subjects, however, is striking. The two figures are not in direct conflict, but they are in positions we would expect from predator and prey, or rather scavenger and imminent corpse.

Only a handful of students in my class recognized this picture without the benefit of captioning. Almost all, however, speculated that it probably came from "Africa" or had to do with "hunger in Africa." Almost all as well described its essential visual and narrative elements as being a small (sick, hungry) child in danger from a threatening vulture. In fact, no one in the room declared having seen a vulture up close or seen an African child starving in personal experience. As Walter Lippmann commented, the origins of recognizing such objects are not from personal experience but the "pictures in the head" provided by news media.[94] Not only were these objects familiar through intertextual reference and cultural experience, the scene was easily imposable upon the stereotype of Africa as a land of starvation and despair. In other words, my students filed the picture in their mental category of what a scene of African famine (and wildlife) should look like.

They were, of course, correct. This image first appeared in the *New York Times* international section Friday, March 26, 1993, in a story about relief operations in the southern Sudan. A vicious civil war (and concurrent hunger and mass refugee crisis) was occurring in the country that only lately had gotten the full attention of relief operations. The caption offers the following description: "In a move meant to placate the West, the Sudanese Government is opening parts of the country's famine-stricken south to relief operations, but for some, it could be too late. A little girl, weakened from hunger, collapsed recently along the trail to a feeding center in Ayod. Nearby, a vulture waited."[95] The reporter makes no mention within the story itself of the young girl; she serves purely illustrative purposes. The news story describes a trip to the feeding center as an arduous journey taking many days.

The picture's status as an icon of outrage, according to our criteria, was achieved rapidly: celebrity through wide publication, laudation by discourse elites, metonymy, emotional reaction, and impositions of meaning beyond the event itself. The next year, it won the Pulitzer Prize in the Feature News photojournalism category. In response, the *New York Times* took out a full-page ad noting that the award was given "to the *New York Times*, for Kevin Carter's photograph of a vulture perching near a little girl in the Sudan, a picture that became an icon of starvation."[96] The *Sunday Mail* of London described the picture as "a truly iconographic image, it captured the full horror of the famine in Sudan— a starving child crawling towards a UN feeding station with a black and hooded vulture waiting patiently behind her. Journalism at its most potent, that one photograph prompted more bureaucratic action, more cash, medicine, and volunteers, and a sight more heartfelt understanding than words could or did."[97] John Marchese of the *Village Voice* described it as "a picture of a small starving child, naked but for tribal jewelry, collapsed on a dirt road as she struggles toward a feeding station. A plump vulture matter-of-factly stands behind her."[98] *Time* magazine said, "A child barely alive, a vulture so eager for carrion. Yet the photograph that epitomized Sudan's famine [*sic*]."[99] The *New York Times* itself described it later as a picture "of an emaciated girl collapsing on the way to a feeding center, as a plump vulture lurked in the back-ground."[100] In another piece, the *Times* claimed, "It was displayed in many other publications as a metaphor for Africa's despair."[101] The photograph was also described as "the picture that made the world weep." In a review of the picture and its aftermath, *Editor & Publisher* said that this was "a picture of a vulture eyeing a girl who collapsed while on her way to a feeding center."[102] Scott Simon of National Public Radio, commented, "the picture shows a vulture in the Sudan, sitting hungrily on its haunches, watching a young, hunger-weakened Sudanese girl, struggling to walk on legs that look frail as twigs as she crumples down to the parched, hard ground and rests, or it seems, waits to die."[103] Judith Matloff, a Reuters correspondent based in Johannesburg, and Kevin Carter's housemate and friend, described the image as a "well-fed vulture stalking a starving Sudanese girl."[104]

These verbal descriptions are revealing. In looking closely at the image—especially the grainy newspaper print version most viewers saw—there is actually less than some people seem to detect. The anthropomorphisms run rampant. The vulture does not look especially plump, nor is it perched, nor can we see its eyes focusing, nor read an expression of hunger on its "face." That the girl suffers from hunger and not disease; that she is on her way anywhere; that what she wears is tribal jewelry; even that she is in Africa is not directly seen in the picture, but inferred by what these writers have heard about the picture or the workings of stereotypes in their (and our) own heads. The rhetoric about the image, then, is more projection than inspection.

The image has also been appropriated for its commercial potential. The Save the Children Foundation used the picture in one of their advertising campaigns. A headline read, "Help stop a different kind of child abuse." Metaphorically the ad copy intoned "this abuse is merciless. It prays on innocent, fragile lives and brutalizes them with utter poverty . . . with constant hunger . . . with relentless diseases . . . with no hope for even a basic education." This ad and the symbolic value of the image is discussed in detail in former relief worker Michael Maren's exposé of the failure of foreign aid in Africa, appropriately titled *The Road to Hell*.[105] One of the Save the Children workers who was horrified at the use of the picture recalls that contacts in Africa felt especially disturbed by what they took to be the implications of the image, that "the message of all our advertising at Save was that Africans are too stupid and ignorant to take care of themselves. And if we don't do it, their parents and their government aren't responsible enough to do it." Furthermore, the image's use by the organization can be taken as a metonymic lie: Save the Children has no operations in the Sudan, does not provide famine relief, and does not work with war refugees. In short, as Maren adds bitterly, "No amount of money donated to Save was going to help that child or the thousands of others in the region." Jerry Michaud, the executive director of the End Hunger Network, Maren reports, was incensed at the use of the picture. He wrote to the head of Save the Children describing the ad campaign as a form of "hunger porn."

Another sign of the picture's iconic status was the focus in elite discourse on the story of the photographer and debates about the ethics of taking the picture. This dimension is often present in icons of outrage because many are pictures of human tragedies, and the ambiguous role of the photographer as observer is called into question. Although only in the rarest of times are we aware of it, pictures are taken by people; the lens is focused by a hand directed by a human eye. Professional photo-journalists operate within structured systems and codes of form and content as much as any other media workers, but as a particular image may rise above the mundane and become a star, at the same time the photographer may become almost a symbolic entity in her or himself.

Such was the case with photographer Kevin Carter. A few years after taking the famous picture, he committed suicide. In his suicide note, Carter remarked among other things, "I am haunted by the vivid memories of killings & corpses & anger & pain . . . of starving or wounded children."[106] Carter took the picture after covering the violence in South Africa and, according to one characterization, knew "he needed a break." At that time, he was working for the *Mail* of Johannesburg. He asked the paper to underwrite a trip to investigate stories of starvation during the civil war in Sudan. He was turned down and so, emptying his bank account, he financed his own trip. One of his first pictures, which he described as found rather than sought, was of the girl. Carter reported that he took the pictures and then sat under a tree smoking cigarettes and crying, only afterwards chasing away the vulture. An editorial piece published in the *New York Times* noting that the girl had survived was printed in response to reader criticism.[107] Afterward, the picture was taken as emblematic of the self-distancing of photojournalists. In an international forum on the ethics of photojournalism, the photo was cited by Japanese critic Mayo Issobe as the picture that defined the issue of whether photographers owed more to capturing a picture or to the subjects within the frame.[108] Why didn't the photojournalist help the girl? A friend of his reported that when he asked Carter "'what did you do with the baby?'" Carter "looked at me in bewilderment and said, 'Nothing, there were thousands of them.'"[109]

Carter's life before and after the picture was a checkered one. He suffered bouts of suicidal depression and alcoholism, endured unhappy relationships, and was fired from jobs. He was by all accounts an unstable young man. The winning of the Pulitzer did not change his life for the better remarkably. The quality of his work even declined, though it was more sought after. Several of his friends were killed while on assignment. His friend Joao Silva recalls, "After the Sudan, seeing what he'd seen, he'd been in bad shape." "What should he have done?" asks Chris Marais, another friend of Carter's and a photo editor. "All the journalists in that area had been instructed by the UN not to touch the local people because of the risk of disease. That night, when Kevin was telling me all this, he was sort of justifying himself, but then he stopped and said: 'I'm really, really sorry I didn't pick the child up.'"[110] A letter writer to *Time* magazine declared, "It is ironic that Kevin Carter won the Pulitzer for a photograph which to me is a photograph of his own soul and epitomizes his life. Kevin is that small child huddled against the world, and the vulture is the angel of death."[111]

The vulture and child picture, the story of Kevin Carter, and the discourse that surrounds the frame and the photographer are also indicative of some of the ambiguities that must be faced when trying to make sense of pictures in the press. First, while much of visual meaning is in the eye of the beholder, it is also true that pictures themselves show reasonably discrete situations which are not infinitely malleable; no caption could convince us that Carter's picture is not of a vulture and a child. But at the same time, photographers, editors, commentators, and historians try to direct us to an approved meaning.

The photo also typifies another paradox, and a key point of the investigations in this book. In the ten years prior to when Kevin Carter took the picture of the vulture and the girl, 1.3 million people in the Sudan died of hunger, disease or violence, largely stemming from a civil war between the Arab and Muslim-dominated government of the north, and the black and Christian and animist rebels in the south. According to the *Human Rights Watch Report on Southern Sudan*, and the *U.S. Committee for Refugees Report*, the government was guilty of indiscriminate aerial bombardment, policies of extermination and ethnic cleansing, summary torture and execution, placement of land mines in civilian areas and forcibly converting people to Islam.[112] Notably, among the other accusations was that the Muslim government purposely blocked or sabotaged relief efforts by refugee and humanitarian organizations in the south. In sum, the "hunger," whether visible or implied in the image, was an intentional result of a near-genocidal war.[113]

The year the picture was taken, 1993, was also the year that the Sudanese government, reacting to the American intervention in Somalia, became concerned that world attention would spur similar intervention in their country. Temporarily, therefore, they eased the ability of foreign aid organizations to assist the local population. The subsequent aid operation, called Operation Lifeline Sudan, provided an umbrella for support from many different non-governmental organizations, the United Nations and foreign nations. Aid workers estimated that 1.5 million Southern Sudanese were in need of "some form of assistance, with 800,000 requiring food assistance." Despite an inpouring of aid, the excess mortality rate in the south was still 220,000, and hundreds of thousands of displaced people flooded refugee centers. As the *Human Rights Watch/Africa Report* argues, the main culprit behind all the suffering was "violations of the rules of war." According to a report by the Center for Disease Control in March, 1993, "half the deaths in the preceding 12 months were attributed to starvation, with diarrheal disease the second most frequent cause of death. The team found that 40–44 percent of the children surveyed were 'critically undernourished' and the rates of severe under-nutrition were 'among the highest ever documented,' including in Somalia."[114]

Does this context affect our view of the picture? Does it make the whole world any more or less likely to weep when regarding an icon? Was Stalin correct that a vivid, personal anecdote is more compelling than statistics about the deaths of millions? Michael Schudson notes that it is not necessarily true that dry statistics will be overridden by a "captivating vignette."[115] Some news reaction research indicates that statistically-based stories are seen as more important than those that are more personal or visual.[116] This context illuminates another paradox of the icon of outrage: outrage may stir controversy, accolades, and emotion, but *achieve* absolutely nothing. Unlike Irma Hadzimuratovic, the little girl in Carter's picture was not plucked away by some special Western relief effort, nor did any intervention stem the causes of her suffering. Indeed, one can ask whether the metonymy projected onto this picture really has any relationship to the conflict from which it sprang. Far from a metonym, the photograph should be taken as an anomaly precisely because the human disaster of the Sudan, then as now, is largely ignored by Western media. In later reports from the southern Sudan (as this book was going to press), pictures similar to Carter's and those of the horrors from Somalia appeared again, with the declaration that 300,000 people were on the verge of starvation because of the civil war.[117]

Moreover, the Kevin Carter picture does not tell us who is really to blame for the girl's plight. Most commentators ascribe the evildoing to the vulture, or to starvation or civil war. The picture does not portray the human agency that caused her suffering; the actions of armies and politicians are absent from the frame. The forces of nature have little to do with the girl's pain. An animal that is only following a nature-driven program for eating food to survive is blamed in the place of the guilty humans whose lust for power is the real cause of human misery. In the end, the girl and vulture picture is a prime example of how an icon of outrage may have no more effect outside the world of discourse elites than any tourist photo of an exotic foreign land.

Finally, because most people know so little about the context and complexity behind the mask of the icon of outrage, it follows that the image is all the more prone to ideological manipulation, to almost any degree and in almost any direction. All men may be created equal, but most Americans, indeed most people of any nation, tribe, or kinship group value far more the lives of their own countrymen than the lives of the enemy or the unknown "other." Mass media frame issues of human suffering in similar dichotomy, making the distinction between the "worthy" victims who suffer through the machinations of anti-American powers and the "unworthy" victims who are depicted as agents of these powers.[118] Icons temporarily raise a few individuals to great importance yet, as noted, few icon dwellers reap much benefit from their exposure. In isolated cases, such as little Irma's, action is taken, though, as it turned out, too late to save her. However, nothing was done, no great aid was provided for the unnamed little girl from the Sudan. Dwelling in an icon can raise one's stock of worthiness, but only temporarily. This is the irony: the worthy victims, the suffering martyrs in the images of war, oppression, starvation, and genocide in the Sudan and, as we shall see, Tet, Tiananmen, and Somalia, gain almost nothing from the experience. An image's utility as a tool of discourse seems to far outweigh empathy for those who suffer; the two-dimensional impression on paper or video is more valuable than the flesh and blood life. While it is quite true that often individuals and sometimes governments are spurred to action by an image, it is more common that pictures only serve the machine of news production.

NOTES

1. See J. Neuman, *Lights, Camera, War: Is Media Technology Driving International Politics?* (New York: St. Martin's Press, 1996).

2. The reason for the banning of the painters and poets—though Plato admits his affection for Homer makes him "hesitate" to condemn—is that they too easily fool the senses, confusing reality with falsehood. Plato, *Republic*, Part X, 595c, 2nd ed., D. Lee trans. (London: Penguin, 1987[1955]).

3. In this arena, political leaders as well as ordinary people engage in the mass communication activity of surveillance. Such activity is one of Charles Wright's function/dysfunction dyads. The others are correlation, socialization, and entertainment. See C. Wright, *Mass Communication: A Sociological Perspective*, 3rd. ed. (New York: McGraw-Hill, 1986), pp. 4–5. The first three functions were originally drawn from H. Lasswell, "The Structure and Function of Communication in Society," in *The Communication of Ideas*, ed. by L. Bryson (New York: Institute for Religious and Social Studies, 1948), pp. 37–51.

4. J. B. Manheim, *All of the People, All the Time: Strategic Communication and American Politics* (New York: M. E. Sharpe, 1991), p. 130.

5. C. Robbin, "CIA's Guatemala Scandal Turns Up Pressure for Quick, Broad Reform of Intelligence Services," *Wall Street Journal*, April 11, 1995, p. A22.

6. Dan Rather, quoted in L. King, with M. Stencel, *On the Line: The New Road to the White House* (New York: Harcourt Brace, 1993), p. 18.

7. A. Devroy, "Commander-in-Chief Leaves Military Details to Pentagon," *Washington Post*, January 19, 1991, p. A26. See also J. Malone, "Firefighters Brave Bullets in Battle to Douse Flames [Clinton watches CNN]," *Atlanta Journal and Constitution*, October 5, 1993, p. A10.

8. S. Handelman, "Kremlin Growing Frustrated with Role of Outsider," *Toronto Star*, February 10, 1991, p. H4.

9. L. E. Gutstadt, "Taking the Pulse of the CNN Audience: A Case Study of the Gulf War," *Political Communication* 10 (October-December 1993): 399.

10. For general accounts of news production (including visuals) see E. J. Epstein, *News from Nowhere: Television and the News* (New York: Random House, 1973); G. Tuchman, *Making News: A Study in the Construction of Reality* (New York: Free Press, 1978). For specific descriptions of the importance of the visual in news, see M. J. Arlen, *Living-Room War* (New York: Viking, 1969), p. 113; M. W. Browne, "Viet Nam Reporting: Three Years of Crisis," *Columbia Journalism Review* 3 (Fall 1964): 4–9.

11. E. Girardet, "Public Opinion, the Media, and Humanitarianism," in *Humanitarianism Across Borders: Sustaining Civilians in Times of War*, ed. by T. G. Weiss and L. Minear (Boulder: Lynne Rienner, 1993), p. 51.

12. J. Lederman, *Battle Lines: The American Media and the Intifada* (New York: Henry Holt, 1992), p. 132.

13. D. Shaw, "News Often Has to Be Seen Before It Is Heard," *Los Angeles Times*, October 26, 1992, p. A16.

14. "Visualizing the News," *Newsweek*, April 14, 1997, p. 20.

15. E. J. Epstein, *News from Nowhere*; M. Mosettig and H. Griggs, Jr., "TV at the Front," *Foreign Policy* 38 (Spring 1980): 68–69; J. F. Larson, *Tele-*

vision's Window on the World: International Affairs Coverage on the U.S. Networks (Norwood, NJ: Ablex, 1984), p. 131.

16. T. Fenton, "Bringing You Today's War—Today," *TV Guide*, November 15, 1980, pp. 36–38; J. F. Larson, *Television's Window on the World*, p. 131.

17. A. Banks, "Frontstage/Backstage: Loss of Control in Real-Time Coverage of the War in the Gulf," *Communication* 13 (1992): 111–19.

18. S. Livingston and T. Eachus, "Humanitarian Crises and U.S. Foreign Policy: Somalia and the CNN Effect Reconsidered," *Political Communication* 12 (October-December 1995): 414.

19. J. Urschel, "Caution: Don't Base Policy on Emotions," *USA Today*, February 10, 1994, p. 10A.

20. L. A. Friedland, *Covering the World: International Television News Services* (New York: Twentieth Century Fund, 1992).

21. "Global Forum with Jimmy Carter, Part 8," CNN *News*, May 11, 1995.

22. D. Hoffman, "Focus on Yeltsin's Health: Colds, Lies and Videotape," *Washington Post*, September 1, 1996, p. A1.

23. D. Schwartz, "To Tell the Truth: Codes of Objectivity in Photojournalism," *Communication* 13 (1992): 95–109.

24. L. Morrow, "In Feeding Somalia and Backing Yeltsin, America Discovers the Limits of Idealism; The Cold War Is Over. Can America Manage the Peace?" *Time*, October 18, 1993, p. 36.

25. G. F. Will, "An End to Compassion," *Washington Post*, November 19, 1995, p. C9. Will doubted whether this was automatically the case.

26. T. Shales, "Television: On the Tube, Talk, Talk, Yak, Yak: The New Age of Blah," *Washington Post*, December 27, 1992, p. G1.

27. G. Kennan, "Somalia, Through a Glass Darkly," *New York Times*, September 30, 1993, p. A25. See also W. Goodman, "Inspiring Compassion, if not Action," *New York Times*, May 6, 1993, p. C22.

28. D. Williams, "U.S. Decides to Use Force on Serbs in Bosnian War," *Washington Post*, May 2, 1993, p. A1.

29. A. J. Bacevich, "Out of Touch: The U.S. Foreign Policy Elite in Crisis," *America* 171, December 10, 1994, p. 8.

30. As always, "man-on-the-street" interviews are provided to back such claims despite their dubious status as representative of wider public opinion.

31. H. Cleveland, "A Too-National Intervention," *Minneapolis Star Tribune*, December 13, 1992, p. 29A.

32. C. Toups, "Albright Cites 'Moral Imperative' for Bosnia Mission," *Washington Times*, December 13, 1995, p. A1.

33. B. Talbott, "Images Spur Gutierrez to Back Pullout," *Chicago Sun-Times*, October 8, 1993, p. 8.

34. W. Blitzer, "President Clinton Considers Action in Somalia," CNN *News*, October 5, 1993.

35. E. S. Povich, "House Ties China Reforms to Favored Trade Status," *Chicago Tribune*, July 11, 1991, p. 1C.

36. T.-K. Chang, *The Press and China Policy: The Illusion of Sino-American Relations, 1950–1984* (Norwood, NJ: Ablex, 1993), p. 8.

37. Ibid.; G. T. Allison, *Essence of Decision: Explaining the Cuban Missile Crisis* (Boston: Little, Brown, 1971). See also C. Cioffi-Revilla, R. L. Merritt, and D. A. Zinnes, eds., *Communication and Interaction in Global Politics* (Beverly Hills: Sage, 1987); B. C. Cohen, *The Press and Foreign Policy* (Princeton, NJ: Princeton University Press, 1963); M. Kern, P. W. Levering, and R. B. Levering, *The Kennedy Crises: The Press, the Presidency, and Foreign Policy* (Chapel Hill: University of North Carolina Press, 1983); S. Serfaty, ed., *The Media and Foreign Policy* (London: Macmillan, 1990).

38. T.-K. Chang, *The Press and China Policy*, pp. 246–47.

39. G. T. Allison, *Essence of Decision*, p. 144.

40. R. Weissberg, *Public Opinion and Popular Government* (Englewood Cliffs, NJ: Prentice-Hall, 1976), p. 3. See also the similar comments by Secretary of State Dean Rusk. Dean Rusk, "The Anatomy of Foreign Policy Decisions," *Department of State Bulletin* 53 (1965): 506–7. This strain of thought is commented on in depth in L. A. Kusnitz, *Public Opinion and Foreign Policy: America's China Policy, 1949–1979* (Westport, CT: Greenwood Press, 1984), p. 6.

41. R. E. Elder, *The Policy Machine: The Department of State and American Foreign Policy* (New York: Syracuse University Press, 1960); B. C. Cohen, *The Public's Impact on Foreign Policy* (Boston: Little, Brown, 1973); C. W. Kegley, Jr., and E. R. Wittkopf, *American Foreign Policy: Pattern and Process* (New York: St. Martin's Press, 1979).

42. R. Hilsman, *The Politics of Policy Making in Defense and Foreign Affairs: Conceptual Models and Bureaucratic Politics* (Englewood Cliffs, NJ: Prentice-Hall, 1987).

43. P. L. Geyelin, "The Strategic Defense Initiative: The President's Story," in *The Media and Foreign Policy*, pp. 19–32; S. H. Miller, "News Coverage of Congress: The Search for the Ultimate Spokesman," *Journalism Quarterly* 54 (Autumn 1977): 459–65; L. L. Kaid and J. Foote, "How Network Television Coverage of the President and the Congress Compare," *Journalism Quarterly* 62 (Spring 1985): 59–65.

44. T.-K. Chang, "The Impact of Presidential Statements on Press Editorials Regarding U.S. China Policy, 1950–1984," *Communication Research* 16 (August 1989): 486–509.

45. D. D. Perlmutter, "Visual Images and Foreign Policy: Picturing China in the American Press, 1949–1989," University of Minnesota, unpublished Ph.D. dissertation, 1996.

46. Richard Brody originally asked whether the "effect" was "a way of accounting for otherwise inexplicable rises in support for the president in the face of surprise and threat." R. A. Brody, *Assessing the President: The Media, Elite Opinion, and Public Support* (Stanford, CA: Stanford University Press, 1991), p. 58.

47. J. Hurwitz, "Presidential Leadership and Public Followership," in *Manipulating Public Opinion: Essays on Public Opinion as a Dependent Variable*, ed. by M. Margolis and G. A. Mauser (Pacific Grove, CA: Brooks/Cole, 1989).

48. R. A. Brody, "International Crisis: Rallying Point for the President?" *Public Opinion* 6 (1984): 41–43, 46; Sam Kernell, "Explaining Presidential Popularity," *American Political Science Review* 72 (1978): 506–22; J. E. Mueller, *War, Presidents and Public Opinion* (New York: John Wiley and Sons, 1973).

49. Z. Pan and G. M. Kosicki, "Framing Analysis: An Approach to News Discourse," *Political Communication* 10 (January-March 1993): 55–75.

50. R. M. Entman, "Framing: Toward Clarification of a Fractured Paradigm," *Journal of Communication* 43 (Autumn 1993): 52.

51. G. Tuchman, *Making News*, p. 193.

52. Z. Pan and G. M. Kosicki, "Framing Analysis," p. 59.

53. R. E. Denton, Jr. and R. L. Holloway, "Preface," in *The Clinton Presidency: Images, Issues and Communication Strategies*, ed. by R. E. Denton, Jr. and R. L. Holloway (Westport, CT: Praeger, 1996), pp. xiii–xiv.

54. A. Bayer, "Politics of Foreign Policy in Turmoil," *San Diego Union-Tribune*, May 14, 1995, p. A21.

55. D. Schorr, "Sam May Become the Deadbeat Uncle of Superpowers," National Public Radio, *All Things Considered*, April 5, 1995.

56. H. J. Gans, *Deciding What's News: A Study of CBS Evening News, NBC Nightly News, Newsweek and Time* (New York: Vintage, 1979); J. Galtung and M. H. Ruge, "The Structure of Foreign News: The Presentation of the Congo, Cuba and Cyprus Crises in Four Foreign Newspapers," *Journal of International Peace Research* 1 (1965): 64–90.

57. B. C. Cohen, *Foreign Policy in American Government* (Boston: Little, Brown, 1965), p. 194.

58. Paul Messaris has conducted similar experiments. Among undergraduates, he rarely found recognition of historical images exceeding 50 percent of the test subjects. See P. Messaris, *Visual "Literacy": Image, Mind, & Reality* (Boulder: Westview Press, 1994), pp. 176–80.

59. H. Schuman, R. F. Belli and K. Bischoping, "The Generational Basis of Historical Knowledge," in *Collective Memory of Political Events: Social Psychological Processes*, ed. by J. W. Pennebaker, D. Paez, and B. Rimé (Mahway, NJ: Lawrence Erlbaum, 1997), pp. 47–77. This issue is especially important in questioning how well people recall mediated news of events. See J. Stauffer, R. Frost and W. Rybolt, "The Attention Factor in Recalling Network Television News," *Journal of Communication* 33 (Winter 1983): 29–37.

60. One generation X-er, when asked if there were "seminal events for her generation—as say, Woodstock and Kent State were for Boomers?" answered, looking "puzzled, 'Well, we had the Gulf war, it seemed scary, but I got over it in two days.'" Quoted in M. Hornblower, "Great Xpectations," *Time*, June 9, 1997, p. 61.

61. F. E. Peters, *Greek Philosophical Terms: A Historical Lexicon* (New York: New York University Press, 1967), p. 51.

62. For discussions of the early use of icons and visual clichés in advertising, see R. Marchand, *Advertising the American Dream: Making Way for Modernity, 1920–1940* (Berkeley: University of California Press, 1985), pp. 235–84.

63. "Press Conference on Tiananmen Square Anniversary," Federal News Service, June 4, 1991.

64. S. D. Moeller, *Shooting War: Photography and the American Experience of Combat* (New York: Basic Books, 1989), p. 18.

65. Many researchers and journalists agree that the front page of a newspaper or magazine is the most influential and important location. See T.-K. Chang, *The Press and China Policy*, p. 91. See also C. Schettler, *Public Opinion in American Society* (New York: Harper, 1960), p. 210; L. Bogart, "The Public's Use and Perception of Newspapers," *Public Opinion Quarterly* (Winter 1984): 716–17.

66. R. Omaar, "Disaster Pornography from Somalia," *Los Angeles Times*, December 10, 1992, p. B7.

67. It is widely believed in photojournalism that the photographer with the single-shot still camera is less intrusive than the multi-personed, heavy equipment-laden video crew.

68. T. Hine, "Notable Quotables: Why Images Become Icons," *New York Times*, February 18, 1996, sec. 2, p. 1.

69. P. Messaris, *Visual "Literacy,"* p. 180.

70. G. Eppley, "While the Vulture Sat and Watched," [Cleveland] *The Plain Dealer*, April 15, 1995, p. 11B.

71. R. A. Hackett, "A Hierarchy of Access: Aspects of Source Bias in Canadian TV News," *Journalism Quarterly* 53 (1985): 253–65; W. L. Bennett, *News: The Politics of Illusion* (New York: Longman, 1983); D. L. Paletz and R. M. Entman, *Media, Power, Politics* (New York: Free Press, 1981); H. Molotch

and M. Lester, "News as Purposive Behavior: On the Strategic Use of Routine Events, Accidents, and Scandals," *American Sociological Review* 39 (1981): 101–12; H. J. Gans, *Deciding What's News*.

72. V. Goldberg, *The Power of Photography: How Photographs Changed Our Lives* (New York: Abbeville, 1993), pp. 156–60.

73. T. Shales, "Peace in Their Time," *Washington Post*, September 14, 1993, p. B1.

74. P. Guy, "Handshake Photo Worth 1,000 Words," *USA Today*, September 15, 1993, p. 8B.

75. R. Barthes, *Image-Music-Text*, trans. Steven Heath (New York: Noonday Press, 1988[1977]), pp. 140–41.

76. "Grim Images from Bosnia Shape Opinion," *St. Louis Post-Dispatch*, July 30, 1995, p. 3A.

77. D. D. Perlmutter, "The Vision of War in High School Social Science Textbooks," *Communication* 13 (1992): 143–60.

78. K. H. Jamieson, *Dirty Politics: Deception, Distraction, and Democracy* (New York: Oxford University Press, 1992). See also F. Biocca, "Organization of Codes and Discourses: Analysis of Semantic Framing," in *Television and Political Advertising: Signs, Codes, Meaning*, Vol. 2, ed. by F. Biocca (Hillsdale, NJ: Lawrence Erlbaum, 1991), p. 80.

79. T. Liebes and E. Katz, "Dallas and Genesis, Primordiality and Seriality in Popular Culture," in *Media, Myths, and Narratives*, ed. by J. Carey, pp. 113–25, (Beverly Hills: Sage, 1985).

80. P. Lester, *Photojournalism: An Ethical Approach* (Hillsdale, NJ: Lawrence Erlbaum, 1991), p. 7.

81. G. Clarke, "Freezing Moments in History," *Time*, December 28, 1981, p. 28.

82. J. Barron, "Crackdown in Beijing," *New York Times*, June 6, 1989, p. A16.

83. P. Wright, "Icon of the Revolution," [London] *Guardian*, June 4, 1992, p. 23.

84. M. Pedelty, *War Stories: The Culture of Foreign Correspondents* (New York: Routledge, 1995), p. 3; M. Massing, "When More Means Less," *Columbia Journalism Review* (July-August 1989): 43.

85. M. W. Browne, "Viet Nam Reporting."

86. D. Rieff, *Slaughterhouse: Bosnia and the Failure of the West* (New York: Simon and Schuster, 1995).

87. L. Monk, *Photographs that Changed the World: The Camera as Witness, the Photograph as Evidence* (New York: Doubleday, 1989).

88. C.D.B. Bryan, *The National Geographic Society: 100 Years of Adventure and Discovery* (New York: Harry N. Abrams, 1987), p. 439.

89. L. Johnson, "Bosnia-Hercegovina: Case of Wounded Girl Captures British Hearts," Inter Press Service [wire], August 11, 1993; N. Gowing, "Behind the CNN Factor," *The Washington Post*, July 31, 1994, p. C1; N. Gowing, "U.K.: Inside Story—Instant Pictures, Instant Policy," [London] *Independent on Sunday* [wire], July 3, 1994.

90. J. Coburn, "The Girl in the Photograph," *Los Angeles Times*, August 20, 1989, p. 8.

91. G. Judson, "Stepping Out from the Lens of History," *New York Times*, October 11, 1995, p. B1.

92. J. Coburn, "The Girl in the Photograph."

93. P. Shannon, "General Labels War Photo Fake," *Miami Herald*, January 18, 1986, sec. 1, p. 1.

94. W. Lippmann, *Public Opinion* (New Brunswick, NJ: Transaction, 1991[1922]).

95. D. Lorch, "Sudan is Described as Trying to Placate the West," *New York Times*, March 26, 1993, p. A3.

96. *New York Times*, April 13, 1994, p. A19.

97. P. Martin, "I'm Really Sorry I Didn't Pick the Child Up," [London] *Mail on Sunday*, October 16, 1994, pp. 40, 42.

98. J. Marchese, "Final Exposure: The Life, Violent Times, and Untimely Death of Kevin Carter," *Village Voice*, May 9, 1995, p. 29+.

99. S. Macleod, "The Life and Death of Kevin Carter," *Time*, September 12, 1994, p. 70.

100. B. Keller, "Kevin Carter, A Pulitzer Winner for Sudan Photo, is Dead at 33," *New York Times*, July 29, 1994, p. B8.

101. Ibid.

102. "Pulitzer Winner Commits Suicide," *Editor & Publisher*, August 13, 1994, p. 22.

103. S. Simon, "Tribute to Kevin Carter, Prize-Winning Photographer," NPR *Weekend Edition*, July 30, 1994.

104. J. Matloff, "The Legacy of Kevin Carter: Eye on Apartheid," *Columbia Journalism Review* 33 (November-December 1994): 57.

105. M. Maren, *The Road to Hell: The Ravaging Effects of Foreign Aid and International Charity* (New York: Free Press, 1997), pp. 157–58.

106. S. Macleod, "The Life and Death of Kevin Carter," p. 70.

107. Ibid.

108. Mayo Issobe, "Forum: Eye of the Beholder," [Japan] *Asahi Evening News*, n.d.

109. D. Beresford, "Dogged by Haunting Images," [Manchester] *Guardian*, August 22, 1994, p. T17.

110. P. Martin, "I'm Really Sorry."

111. J. C. Bonica, "Suicide of a Pulitzer Winner," [Letters], *Time*, October 3, 1994, p. 13.

112. M. Burr, *A Working Document: Quantifying Genocide in the Southern Sudan, 1983–1993* (Washington, DC: U.S. Committee for Refugees, October 1993).

113. J. Dreze and A. Sen, *Hunger and Public Action* (New York: Oxford University Press, 1991).

114. Human Rights Watch/Africa, "War in South Sudan: The Civilian Toll; Africa Watch Condemns Abuses by All Sides in the Conflict in South Sudan," *Africa Watch Newsletter*, October, 1993.

115. M. Schudson, *The Power of News* (Cambridge: Harvard University Press, 1995), pp. 115–16.

116. S. Iyengar and D. R. Kinder, *News that Matters: Television and American Opinion* (Chicago: University of Chicago Press, 1987), pp. 36–42.

117. "Tiny Victims," *Newsweek*, May 18, 1998, p. 44. In extreme close-up, a gaunt child, one hand upraised, squats on a barren savanna. It is just a picture with a caption; no news story of any length or prominence is attached, nor has anyone professed outrage enough to demand intervention.

118. N. Chomsky and E. S. Herman, *Manufacturing Consent: The Political Economy of the Mass Media* (New York: Pantheon, 1988).

Chapter Two

The "Magic Bullet" of General Loan: Tet, 1968

The [Saigon] execution was added to people's feeling that this is just horrible. This is just terrible. Why are we involved in a thing like this? People were just sickened by this, and I think this added to the feeling that the war was the wrong war at the wrong place.[1]

—John Chancellor

In reaction to the success of Allied propaganda in World War I, and the dazzling mass politics of the totalitarian regimes of the World War II era, many people saw communication "as a magic bullet that transferred ideas or knowledge or motivations from one mind to another."[2] Fallen into disfavor among researchers, the model nevertheless seemed to be embodied literally a generation later during America's war in Vietnam. A single, .38 caliber bullet was fired on the morning of February 1, 1968, outside a Buddhist temple, the An Quang Pagoda, in the capital of the Republic of Vietnam. It was a "shot televised 'round the world." Among those present were Eddie Adams, an Associated Press photographer, and Howard Tuckner, an NBC News correspondent and his three-man film and sound crew. Nearby as well were an ABC cameraman and a Japanese film crew. South Vietnamese marines pulled into view a young man, barefoot, wearing a loose, plaid shirt and black shorts, his hands bound behind his back. Adams recalled the next few seconds: "Some guy walked over—we didn't know who he was—and . . . pulled a pistol out. As soon as he went for his pistol I raised the camera thinking he was going to threaten him [the prisoner]."[3] Instead, the unknown man extended his arm and fired once into the right temple of the prisoner. It was at this moment that Adams pressed the shutter of his camera. [See Figure 2.] The NBC crew was filming as the man fell over backwards, blood spurting out of his head like a small fountain. At the instant of execution, however, someone walked in front of their camera. TV displayed the brief prologue and the grisly aftermath, but still photography captured the decisive moment of death.

The gunman was Brigadier General Nguyen Ngoc Loan, chief of the South Vietnamese National Police. After firing the shot he put his gun away, a small Smith & Wesson detective special. Then he faced the journalists and, in one reported version, stated: "Many Americans have been killed these last few days and many of my best Vietnamese friends. Now do you understand? Buddha will understand." Within a day, NBC *News* showed the film of the events on the *Huntley-Brinkley Report* to 20 million people. Eddie Adams's still photo appeared on the front page of most major newspapers; it was to be reprinted *ad infinitum* in magazines and books to the present day. The image won the Pulitzer Prize for Spot News photography. The iconic status of the picture was rapidly fixed and remains so to this day. It was and is presented as a symbol of the early months of 1968, when a maelstrom enveloped South Vietnam. A day previously, at the start of the Vietnamese New Year, Tet Mau Mau, National Liberation Front (Viet Cong) and PAVN (People's Army of North Vietnam) soldiers attacked most major cities in the south. Targets included police barracks, radio stations and military headquarters; more ominously, the insurgents carried out a campaign of assassination against "puppet elements," mostly government officials.

What became known as the Tet offensive, then, was a "Big Story," perhaps the decisive battle and the most analyzed event of the war.[4] In many places, like the ancient capital of Hue, which was almost overrun, the enemy did not follow traditional hit-and-disappear guerrilla tactics; they held the city for 26 days. The grounds of the American embassy in Saigon were penetrated by a Viet Cong sapper team whose members all died in a fiery, six-hour siege. The offensive itself lasted until the end of March; follow-up strikes continued throughout the year. The effects seemed clear. By the completion of Tet, American public opinion polls showed that for the first time, a majority were dissatisfied with the conduct of the war. General William Westmoreland, commander of the Military Assistance Command-Vietnam (MACV) 1964–1968, was, according to most interpretations, "kicked upstairs" to Washington in response to his perceived inadequacy. Secretary of Defense Robert McNamara, his disenchantment with the war growing to a point of severe depression, was fired and replaced. The "wise old men," the brain trust of senior business, political, and military advisers that President Johnson counted upon for a consensus about how to run the war, had become bitterly divided. Incoming Secretary of Defense Clark Clifford produced a report counseling against escalation of the war effort. Many among the elites who surrounded Lyndon Johnson were telling him that the war was a failure. Johnson announced that he was not seeking another term as president in the wake of Senator Eugene McCarthy's strong showing in the New Hampshire presidential primary. In addition, and perhaps most decisively, Johnson announced that there would be no great new commitment of American troops to Vietnam and there would be a scale-back in the bombing of North Vietnam. In the words of a legion of later historians and commentators of the time, Tet was the watershed, the turning point, the beginning of the end of America's war in Indochina. Most important, many of the results of Tet have been suggested as arising from the portrayal of the events in the mass media, especially the sensational, bloody, kinetic visual images—such as that of the Saigon execution—that appeared in American newspapers and magazines and on television screens. However, the questions Peter Braestrup, in his massive review of press coverage of the Battle of Tet, asks remain relevant to this day:

What *information* did the photograph actually convey? That a brave but over-wrought South Vietnamese police director, with a history of emotional insta-bility, inexcusably shot an enemy taken in civilian clothes in the heat of battle? That our South Vietnamese allies were atrocity-prone? That Asians value life cheaply? That South Vietnam was a brutal police state?[5]

Tet was also important because the struggle to define it was the crucial debate of the Vietnam War. The most common dyad was the juxtaposition of the notion that Tet was a military victory for the United States and its allies, but at the same time was a psychological and political defeat.[6] Many in the United States military and in the Vietnam-based intelligence and administration services felt that they had been "robbed" of a victory. This might be summed up as the "lost victory hypothesis" that has permeated conservative, military, scholarly and political commentary on Vietnam.

The foundation for such thinking was laid even before Tet began. Sensing that some sort of major enemy action was pending, General Westmoreland, in a Washington trip in November 1967, predicted to journalist Neil Sheehan that current fighting would lead to "the beginning of a great defeat [for the enemy]."[7] The defeat he had in mind was on the North border, at the hilltop fortress of Khe Sanh, where Westmoreland hoped to fight a set-piece, World War II-type battle. General Earle Wheeler, chairman of the joint chiefs of staff, also predicted that "there may be a communist thrust similar to the desperate effort of the Germans in the Battle of the Bulge," where Hitler, despite initial success, had exhausted his nation's last military resources.[8] On December 20, 1967, speaking to the Australian Parliament during a Far East tour, President Johnson foresaw a "kamikaze" attack by the North Vietnamese Army, most likely at Khe Sanh.[9]

Indeed, there is a strong case that Tet was objectively a military defeat for the Communist forces, but was not framed as such by press and home front observers.[10] A CIA liaison in the White House at the time of Tet recalled in an interview in 1982 that "Tet was one of the great ironies of history. Tet was very similar to the Battle of the Bulge. . . . It was the largest defeat that the Communists ever suffered in the field and was the greatest political victory externally."[11] Robert Komer, the head of the pacification programs—the attempt to build a supportive infrastructure at the hamlet level for the Republic of Vietnam—in 1967–1968, noted that "we in Saigon, to a man, at least in the Com-mand, agreed that Tet was a big victory for us."[12] The enemy suffered an estimated 37,000 killed in the first month of battle. Only at Hue was any ground captured and held, and even then only briefly. The damage done to the pacification program proved to be minimal. Most important, *no national "general uprising" occurred*, as the northern government and southern Liberation Front leaders had hoped, predicted, and called for.[13] The enemy, Westmoreland concludes in his memoirs:

had achieved in South Vietnam neither military nor psychological victory. . . . Had it been the same for the American people, had President Johnson discerned the same support behind him that [South Vietnamese President] Thieu did behind him, and had he acted with forcefulness, the enemy could have been induced to engage in serious and meaningful negotiations.[14]

By this rationale, the battle was won in Vietnam, but lost in Washington and, as Westmoreland claims, lost by the biased accounts of the press.

Whatever its merits, the lost victory hypothesis has entered post-Vietnam political debate as well. Ever the astute reader of the public mood, presidential candidate Ronald Reagan in 1980 told a convention of the Veterans of Foreign Wars: "For too long, we have lived with the 'Vietnam Syndrome.' . . . It is time that we recognized that ours was, in truth, a noble cause."[15] Reagan's secretary of defense, Caspar Weinberger, in a speech to a veterans group, expressed the often-to-be-repeated sentiment that we did not "intend" to win the Vietnam War.[16] Prior to the start of the overwhelming bombing campaign against Iraq in the Gulf War, George Bush told a national audience that "no hands are going to be tied behind backs [as in Vietnam]." At the end of the conflict, Bush proclaimed, "The spectre of Vietnam has been buried forever in the desert sands of the Arabian peninsula."[17] The lost victory thesis also has wide resonance in the public. In 1979, a poll by the Harris organization found 73 percent of respondents agreeing with the statement that: "The trouble in Vietnam was that our troops were asked to fight in a war which our political leaders in Washington would not let them win."[18] Veterans, as well, joined this consensus. As Stanley Karnow relates, according to a 1980 poll conducted for the Veterans Administration, 82 percent of veterans who were classified as "heavy combatants" in Vietnam thought that "the war was lost because they were not allowed to win." Karnow adds, with the appropriate adverb, "astonishingly, 66 percent indicated a willingness to fight again, presumably under fewer limitations."[19]

The people charged with losing the victory are either political leaders in Washington, the press, or both. The strategic and personal failings of political and military leaders during the Vietnam War may be endlessly debated, but the culpability of the U.S. press can and has been carefully analyzed. For the most part, people who say that "the media did it" tend not to be media researchers but either participants in the events or non-media historians. The evidence presented by those who studied the media representation of Tet is far less damning. Peter Braestrup, for example, despite his often scathing critique of the press coverage, squarely lays at the door of the Johnson administration and its "vague," "incoherent," and generally lethargic response to Tet any blame for its policy implications.[20] In other words, in line with observations made about the strong potential power of the presidency to shape opinion, Braestrup argues that Johnson left a vacuum by sitting out the fight. Such is also the verdict of William M. Hammond, a military historian at the Pentagon, who produced the official U.S. government history of press–military relations in Vietnam.[21] In addition, Daniel Hallin, in his comprehensive *"Uncensored War": The Media and Vietnam*, concludes that the media did not "lose the war."[22] More important, he links media behavior to the state of society and the level of consensus in the political structure. Hallin points out, "It may be one of the many ironies of Tet coverage that it gave the public a more accurate view of the overall course of the war through the *inaccurate* view it gave of the outcome of the particular battle."

FRAMING THE "MAGIC BULLET"

Understanding the struggle to define what Tet was, and what the premier icon of Tet connotated, reveals the kinds of debates that still divide American culture. The assumed power of the Saigon image is clearly revealed when some of the historical discourse about it is surveyed. [See Appendix A.] In this compilation, speakers and writers ranging from hawks (supporters of the war) to doves (its opponents)— soldiers, poets, historians, journalists, Americans and Vietnamese— attest that the shooting was "shocking" to the public and the body politic. The descriptions of content and ascriptions of meaning range from the sober to the lyrical. Statements that the image was important are simple enough, though they are also self-confirming. Denoting the metonymy of the image is debatable. Most revealing, and most tenuous on a factual basis, are the words that assign to the image a universal, uniform reaction from the mass audience: "impact," "shocked the world," "turning point of the war," "world-wide furor," "confirm the suspicion that this was a 'wrong war' on the 'wrong side,'" "extraordinarily powerful," "one of the most searing spectacles of the whole war," "shocked and troubled millions of Americans," "the American public was repulsed," "captured what was most disturbing about the war to many Americans," "scarred the American psyche," "Americans . . . said to themselves 'that's enough, we've had it,'" "people were just sickened by this."

And so on. But on what evidence can such claims be grounded? No picture is an island. Facts or quotes chosen for commentary, and captions or narrations about the image, are frames meant to affect its meaning. Conversely, what we are not told, frames not offered, may be as revealing as the dominant frames. The Saigon execution photo is an example of the subtle process of such discourse. To understand the picture, we must examine how it was presented to the public, that is, ask questions about its subjects, form, and context. Such investigations will prove to undermine assertions of universalistic "shock" and "repulsion."

Who Was Nguyen Ngoc Loan?

Wallace Terry, *Time* magazine's deputy bureau chief in Saigon from 1967 to 1969, recalled that shortly prior to the execution he sent a Vietnamese reporter to the An Quang Pagoda to cover the fighting in the area. When the reporter returned to the office, he did not mention the shooting. Terry remarks: "[Later] I heard that General Loan had executed a Viet Cong soldier, with no trial, he had just been captured, he'd executed him on the spot in front of American television and Eddie Adams's camera. When I asked [the Vietnamese reporter] why didn't he tell me what had happened, [he] said, 'Ah, Mr. Terry, General Loan does that all the time. That's not news.'"[23] In every appearance of the picture at the time of the incident, the shooter is identified as General Loan. He was a prominent figure in South Vietnamese politics and the war effort, yet in essence he is treated like an unknown. Eddie Adams, in one recollection of the events, states that when the general arrived on the scene "we didn't know who he was [and] I had no idea it [the shooting] was going to happen."[24] In retrospect, this is an amazing admission. Adams was not new to Vietnam; he had arrived to cover the landing of the American Marines at Da Nang, in March of 1965.[25]

Loan was one of the most famous faces and names in the country. The lack of recognition, however, is less surprising when we consider it in light of the fact that throughout the war American media coverage of the South Vietnamese Army was almost nonexistent.[26] In virtually all stories Loan is identified by his rank and jurisdiction, but we learn nothing of his family, his records, the impression of those around him, both Vietnamese and Americans. One of the *only* descriptions given of Loan at the time of the shooting was by Roger Peterson of ABC, who characterized the general as "the embarrassed and angry man in charge of police and defending the capital."[27] This reading of mood is wholly, we may assume, a projection of the reporter; Loan is shown and described by all present at the Pagoda to be "impassive," a man of *sang froid*. In short, newspaper and newsmagazine readers and television viewers of the time—and most people viewing the image today—would know almost nothing about the man with the gun in the famous icon except that he was South Vietnamese and an officer.

The context of Loan's identity, however, has relevance to the icon. The general was 37 years old at the time of Tet '68. Born in North Vietnam, he had originally served in the army as a paratrooper. Loan was made director of the military security service in 1965, director general of the 72,000-man national police force in October of the same year, and then head of the Central Intelligence Organization in April 1966. His career was checkered with incidents and actions that suggested a far more complex man than just a street corner thug. He had a reputation for being involved in corruption: historian Frances FitzGerald alleged that he had "all but cornered the extortion racket in Saigon"[28] and was a man with "few scruples."[29] Although Loan was supposed to be spearheading anti-corruption efforts, these produced nothing but a few show arrests and trials. Loan's second trait, in the eyes of the Americans who knew him or knew of him, was fierceness; he was, after all, head of the secret police in a country engaged in a civil war. William Lederer, in the author's note of his book on America's failure in Vietnam, claims, "Many people—some in Vietnam and some in the United States—have helped me write this book. Unfortunately I cannot thank my Vietnamese friends by name. If I did this they might receive a midnight visit from General Loan's men."[30] Loan was also extensively involved in internal South Vietnamese politics. He was accused of election corruption in rounding up votes for his patrons in the army and the political leadership. Even before Tet, he became notorious for crushing several Buddhist uprisings.

A less visible facet of Loan was shown in his tense relationship with the American intelligence services, especially the Pacification and Phoenix Programs. Much of his role has only recently been revealed in interviews with American advisers and managers. "Phung Hoang," the Phoenix Program, was an American effort to uproot Communist infra-structure and personnel in South Vietnam, with projects ranging from water well construction to assassination. Its structure was to be managed by the Americans but enforced in cooperation with the South Viet-namese.[31] As Stanley Karnow relates, the program generated outcry in the United States, where it was dubbed a wholesale massacre by the anti-war movement, and in Vietnam it gathered a reputation for corruption, bureaucratic infighting, and incompetence.[32] This view of the program, however, changed for Karnow after the war when Viet Cong veterans told him that the program had not only cost them thousands of their men, but the fear and suspicion it aroused had severely undermined the revolution in the south. Because of his influence in the government and with police forces, Loan was intimately involved in the planning of Phoenix. However, at each step of the way, he was a voice of caution and of implementing the program very slowly, apparently feeling that it infringed on Vietnamese sovereignty. In responding to one phase of the operation, Loan declared to an American adviser, "You join us; we won't join you."[33] In other words Loan, however sinister his reputation, was no puppet of American interests.

Conversely, another possible frame unimposed was that Loan was the South Vietnamese *hero* of Tet.[34] Despite warnings about a coming Communist offensive, many in the South Vietnamese government and military did not adequately prepare for an onslaught. President Thieu, for example, went to his wife's family's village in the delta to celebrate the Tet holiday. Likewise, many units of the army were severely understaffed, having been ordered to "stand down" days before the attacks.[35] The Americans were no less ill-prepared for the scope and intensity of the struggle to come. In his memoirs, General Westmoreland recounts that one of his senior generals explained, "Even had I known exactly what was to take place, it was so preposterous that I probably would have been unable to sell it to anybody."[36] Loan's chief nemesis in the struggle with the American intelligence community, Robert Komer (who was managing the Pacification Program), allegedly advocated demilitarizing important checkpoints into Saigon to improve the flow of commerce. One American Phoenix operative noted, "Loan was saying that there was a massive influx of VC into Saigon . . . but Komer was calling it light, and Hart [another of Loan's American enemies in the Phoenix program] backed him. . . . Komer opened up all the avenues which led to Tet."[37] The U.S. intelligence apparatus characterized "Loan's warnings as crying wolf."[38] Yet, it was the general who ordered police units to stay on duty despite the holiday, he who, against orders from the high command, kept elite marine and paratrooper units at the ready; the police forces were practically the only government presence visible in the capital during the first days of Tet.[39] According to Nguyen Cao Ky, vice-president of South Vietnam in 1968, Loan had 85 percent of the police forces available when the Communists attacked.[40] When the offensive began, Loan was a one-man fire brigade, roaming the city in his oversized American flak vest, rallying South Vietnamese units and organizing attacks on guerrilla-held points. According to laudatory intelligence appraisals, the military defeat of the Viet Cong in the capital was due largely to Loan's foresight and aggression.[41]

What did Loan Say?

Journalists deploy quotations to frame news images; these quotes are rarely in themselves subjects of disputation. Eddie Adams in one version of the story says that Loan waved other people back as his only communication before the shooting. The word "summarily" is employed by many writers, a discourse cliché to describe an event that all those on the scene registered as being sudden. General Loan did not linger to question the captured man, he simply shot him. Adams recalls, "Just then Loan walked in out of nowhere and I saw him load his pistol"; the camera and the gun shot simultaneously. Howard Tuckner maintains, "General Loan took one look at him [the prisoner] and knew he was going to get no information out of him. Loan had been through this with many prisoners. There was not one word. Loan did not try to talk to him nor to scare him. He did not wave his gun at his face or his head. He did not put the gun to his temple. He just blew his brains out."[42] Wallace Terry recalled his correspondent noting that it happened very fast without much talking.[43] This is the portrayal repeated in the other major publications as well. In Tuckner's narration for the NBC presentation he leads up to the moment of firing with a terse introduction of Loan: "A South Vietnamese officer held the paper taken from the enemy officer. The chief of South Vietnam's national police, Brig. Gen. Nguyen Ngoc Loan, was waiting for him [single loud shot]." In almost every newspaper or magazine account examined for this book, the suddenness of the execution is either stated or implied by the sentence structure. The narrative is simple: Loan appeared, then shot. No one has claimed that the captive said anything.[44]

The quotes attributed to Loan after the shooting are also revealing.

Adams recalled that the general faced all the reporters and stated, "They killed many of my men and many of your people," then walked away.[45] Tuckner reported that Loan walked up to him and said: "Many Americans have been killed these last few days and many of my best Vietnamese friends. Now do you understand? Buddha will understand."[46] Already, a discrepancy exists: whom did Loan address? His English was clear, but here are two seasoned reporters recording the quote very differently; one version seems a prosaic explanation, the second more personal and philosophical. In the reporting of the time, the quotes were either excluded (as was the case in the NBC film) or their wording varied in the reporting of February 2 and 3. The AP Log reads, "Impassively, Loan put his pistol in his holster and walked over to where we were standing. He said softly in English, 'They killed many Americans and many of my men.' Then he walked away." The *New York Times* offers another variation: "They killed many Americans and many of our people." Other major papers and magazines, such as the *Atlanta Constitution*, the *New York Daily News*, and *Newsweek* did not include the quote in their first showing of the image. The *Chicago Daily News*, the *Los Angeles Times*, and the *Washington Post* reported Loan's statement as, "They [the Viet Cong] killed many Americans and many of my people." Because of its publication schedule, *Time* magazine did not show the picture until February 9, when it noted that Loan said, "They killed many Americans and many of our people." Reprinting the picture later in the month, (February 23) *Time* changed the quote without explanation: "Many Americans have died recently . . . so have many of my best friends. Buddha will understand—do you?" In *Life* magazine, published on March 1, the picture was shown to accompany an editorial by Shana Alexander. "The smoking revolver still in his hand, Loan discovers U.S. newsmen behind him and says, 'Many Americans have died recently. So have many of my best friends. Buddha will understand. Do you?'"

In trying to comprehend the framing of the image by the American press—that is, what American viewers and readers were told about the picture—Loan's quote is important. Of course, audiences frame pictures through their own prejudices as much as discourse elites try to impose frames on those pictures. It suggests a rationale, a defense that might have been acceptable to many Americans. Learning that this "Viet Cong" killed Americans and/or killed "his men" or "our people" would have been a vital frame that audiences would have employed to interpret the image. In the later section on public reaction to Tet and to the Saigon execution picture, I argue that there is strong evidence that the shooting of "an enemy" would not have produced outrage in the American public. Experimental designs might test this hypothesis on a limited basis. In one study I conducted, I gave half the students in a 40-person class a copy of this picture, which had the caption: "Street execution, Saigon, 1968." The other 20 students were given the same image, but with a caption identifying the time and place and giving Loan's full quote, "Many Americans have been killed these last few days and many of my best Vietnamese friends. Now do you understand? Buddha will understand." In the first group, the one without the quote, when asked to discuss the picture, the students concentrated most of their writing on the expression of the man they assumed was "about to be shot" and on the impassivity of the shooter. On the other hand, the group that did read a version of Loan's words reacted to those words, or rather interpreted the image in their light, discussing the justifications for the shooting, some quite positively. The problem with such experiments, of course, is that they do not recreate real–world audience reception environments, but these results should be kept in mind in light of the paucity of information that audiences were provided to understand the picture.

Who Was the Man Killed?

The American media provided even less information about the man killed, and little of it was positive. If General Loan is a shadowy figure, of whom the presenters of the icon thought viewers need know only the barest details, then the man Loan shot is a completely two-dimensional cipher. In the major news accounts [See Appendix B] immediately after the execution, American audiences would have learned that the man was a Viet Cong suspect, but also captured in connection with terrorist actions such as the killing of others, including Americans. Of course, even the use of the word "suspect" does not necessarily impose a neutral frame on a picture's subject. A news photo of a man hustled in handcuffs into a jail accompanied by a caption or a voice-over that informs us that he is a suspected or alleged child molester does no favor to the accused. Whatever the fine print of the U.S. Constitution, the heinousness of a crime tends to obscure technical assumption of innocence until guilt is proven. Thus, for many in the American viewing and reading public, the label "Viet Cong" was a trigger for a negative judgment, especially when contrasting pictures of Americans killed at Tet were printed and televised.

In subsequent historiography the divisions between "suspect" and confirmed VC become more divided. Robert Kennedy, in a speech shortly after the events, dubbed him a "Viet Cong suspect," as did Don Oberdorfer in the first history of the Tet struggle. Oberdorfer, however, specifically informs the reader that the man "had been armed with a pistol, usually the mark of an officer, but wore no military insignia or garb, helmet or body armor—just a checked shirt and black shorts."[47] He is admitted by the new regime in Hanoi to have actually been a commando.[48] Most historians of Tet and Vietnam brand the man a "suspect," but generally do not follow up with further investigation on him.[49] Some sources, however, try to do more than simply label the man. Former war protester David Harris, in a memoir, attempts to humanize the prisoner, noting that "the general seemed the slicker, the commando more homespun, like half of Mr. and Mrs. Saigon, plucked off any of the city's street corners."[50] Yet, what is interesting about subsequent descriptions of the man is that ideology does not spur interest in exactly who he was. Only rarely in the historiography of Vietnam is the man's name—Bay Lop—recorded.[51] In sum, no mainstream reporter, nor most historians, felt the inclination to go beyond the two dimensions of the picture. He was a body and a face in a photograph; no *human* interest was attached to him. That many of the same people would say that the man's death incensed and shocked them is one of the paradoxes of the icon of outrage.

If little was said about who the man was, more was potentially inferred by audiences about what he did. Overwhelmingly, the words and images implied a connection with, if not outright responsibility for, atrocities committed by the Viet Cong in the battles in Saigon. In the NBC broadcast, Howard Tuckner's piece on the shooting is introduced by John Chancellor as follows:

[In Saigon] There was awful savagery. Here the Viet Cong killed a South Vietnamese colonel and murdered his wife and six children. And this South Vietnamese officer came home during a lull in the fighting to find the bodies of his murdered children. There was awful retribution. Here the infamous chief of the South Vietnamese National Police, General Loan, executed a captured Viet Cong officer. Rough justice on a Saigon street as the charmed life of the city of Saigon comes to a bloody end.

The *Times* also gives space to a picture of a South Vietnamese officer holding a child, "His Family Slain By Vietcong; A South Vietnamese officer carries the body of one of his children from his home. Terrorists overran the base of his unit in Saigon, beheaded an officer, and killed women and children."[52] Viewers of both pictures, then, could have easily assumed that the two were a sequence, with Loan avenging the dead child. The hawkish *Chicago Daily News* judged, "there is not much point now in going queasy over a picture of one man shooting another, there is worse to come." The *Chicago Tribune* accompanied pictures of the suspect—the caption does not use an "identified as" or "alleged" modifier but states he was a "Viet Cong officer"—being led up by soldiers, shot by Loan, and the general putting away his pistol, with the comment, "Communist bands, in addition to gunning for allied military personnel, had staged several executions since the outbreak of the fighting here Wednesday. Wives and children of Vietnamese officers were among the victims."[53] The *Washington Post* added, "Communists had staged several executions since fighting broke out in the capital, and the relatives of government officers had been among their victims." The *New York Daily News* reported in Runyonesque prose: "There are a couple of facts we should bear in mind, however, about the picture: (a) the executed Vietcong was out to kill as many people on our side of this war as he could; (b) so are all his surviving pals. This gives you an idea of how perilously idiotic are the demands of our doves for a one-sided allied pause in bombing Red North Vietnam." In short, the executed man, in the context of the discourse provided by news captioning and voice-overs, is fixed as a villain, not a worthy victim. Regardless of the suffering registered on the man's face, the reading and viewing audiences' interpretation of the image would be colored by notions of "rough justice" avenging murdered children. It is very probable that millions of Americans, influenced by their own prejudices and the framing of the picture, looked at the Eddie Adams image of the executed prisoner and shrugged, "He got what he deserved." This was the sentiment of the *only* letter to the editor regarding the picture published in *Time* magazine in February of 1968.[54]

Finally, another aspect of the shooting should be examined: was it un-American? The picture's ascribed metonymy may have had some basis in fact. If we accept that summary executions like this one were carried out in Vietnam "all the time" by General Loan and his counterparts in the National Liberation Front, was it deviant behavior for us? This was the way the war was often fought. Did we have a right to be shocked? The evidence is strong, from much anecdotal testimony by soldiers and government investigations, that what Loan did was practiced in Vietnam by all sides, including Americans, and was common in previous wars as well.[55] The "search and destroy" strategy coupled with the pressure for body counts, anger over buddies lost in ambushes and traps, as well as in some men a lust for blood, created a "kill everything" ethic in many ground troops.[56] The North Vietnamese regulars and Viet Cong cadres seemed to understand that almost certain death awaited them after capture. "If they were wounded, they literally—whether they were VC or NVA—believed that we would kill them anyway," recalled one G.I.[57] In Vietnam, as very likely in all wars, prisoners died, as another G.I. put it, because "the kids were damn angry."[58] Other pictures of similar atrocities existed; the assumption that it was "part of the war" was widespread.[59] Peter Arnett, for example, recalls: "Someone remarked at the time that the Geneva Conventions were never translated into Vietnamese and that is why no one observed them."[60]

Later, when more stories of rough justice emerged, an American adviser to the South Vietnamese units provided perhaps the simplest rationalization:

We usually kill the seriously wounded Viet Cong for two reasons. One is that the hospitals are so full of our own soldiers and civilians there is no room for the enemy. The second is that when you've seen five-year-old girls with their eyes blindfolded, their arms tied behind their backs, and bullets in their brains, you look for revenge. I saw two little girls that dead [*sic*] yesterday. One hour ago I shot a Viet Cong.[61]

This reaction was evinced by those in the American armed forces as well. An AP story quoted an anonymous U.S. Army sergeant as commenting, "If I had my way, we would execute on the spot every Viet Cong and Viet Cong suspect we catch."[62] General Earle Wheeler argued that the incident resulted from "a flash of outrage rather than 'in cold blood.'"[63] Picking up on the other Tet image of horror, the South Vietnamese officer proffering his dead child, as even more gruesome, Wheeler noted that it was a "sickening indictment of our enemy's real nature."[64] Such comments and assumptions must have percolated among viewers predisposed to thinking that rough justice was actually just desserts. Veterans of previous wars especially may have understood through personal experience that "these things happen."[65] In this light,

Eddie Adams's verdict must be considered:

Everyone condemns Loan for shooting this guy. But I tell everyone: "If you were General Loan and there was a war going on, and your people were getting killed, how do you know *you* wouldn't shoot him, too?" Cold-blooded execution? Bullshit. He was doing what he was there for—to win the war. I just happened to be there. How many times did this happen that we *didn't* see?[66]

The spoken, written, and visual discourse attached to the shooting did not support condemnation of Loan. While the events at the An Quang Pagoda were variously interpreted, there was much less than meets the eye to have provided fuel for public outrage.

MEASURING PUBLIC REACTION

The Loan shooting may be interpreted as a spectacular frame whose power is in drawing our attention, as: "Wow, great picture!" There are, however, serious difficulties in supporting the idea that the picture would have had strong impact on the American public. Sympathy, after all, arises mainly from either group affiliation or personal connection. There is a reason why the makers of disaster films spare us from the special effects for a few moments to detail the poignant life stories of the characters about to be crushed, burned, or eaten by giant spiders. Likewise, journalists add human interest to any tragic story by telling us about the victim's life. The reporting from Tet provided no human interest elements about the man who shot and the man who died. There was nothing to which an American audience could feel any linkage, no American in the scene as perpetrator or victim. The incidental framing of this event was that a South Vietnamese officer was shooting a Viet Cong terrorist. Devoid of any other details, is it reasonable that millions of Americans were shocked and outraged at what they saw? Can we assume that the image simply confirmed prejudices about Asians and about the violence inherent in war? That one person is our ally and another our enemy may be said to have little relevance. Few Americans, from in-country soldiers to midwestern civilians, had high regard for the Vietnamese, South or North.[67] Nguyen Cao Ky, Loan's patron, commented, "The other side, the Communists, always treated us as a puppet of America. But then the American people themselves also considered us as a puppet of America, not as true leaders of the Vietnamese people."[68]

Public Opinion Surveys

No one conducted a national survey of attitudes about the Saigon execution photo or news film. Yet people do not react to a news photo independently of everything else they know or have heard about the situations presented or the vast number of other contextual factors. Photographs are simply forms of data that are incorporated into belief systems; it is rare that they overturn them. To understand reaction to a photograph, then, one must examine the belief system.

In the early 1970s, John Mueller compared American attitudes about its previous "limited war" in Korea with those expressed on Vietnam.[69] Mueller wanted to explain an interesting phenomenon: support for the Korean war dropped very early and then decreased steadily, while in Vietnam, it declined gradually over time. In trying to isolate a major cause for the scale, timing, and trends of opinion, Mueller looked at factors such as the locale, limitations of the battlefield, popular justifications of the war, domestic presidential politics, the ways the wars began and how they ended, the economy at the time, and mortality rates. What he found was that the number of American deaths was the single most important influence on public opinion. The disparity between Korea and Vietnam was that in the former conflict, the death rate was extremely high in the first year, especially during the Chinese intervention at the end of 1950. As peace talks commenced in mid-1951, the death rate declined. In Vietnam, as Mueller argues, "The costs were accumulated at a more gradual rate."

Crucially, the Tet period was the time of "peak" U.S. mortalities. The total number of Americans killed in Vietnam surpassed the Korean total in March 1968. Public support for the war decreased by about 15 percent every time U.S. Vietnam-related deaths increased by a factor of 10. Mueller also argues against the idea that television had a major role in affecting support for the war effort. He notes, "The poll data used in this study do not support such a conclusion. They clearly show that whatever impact television had, it was not enough to reduce support for the war below the levels attained by the Korean war, when television was in its infancy, until casualty levels had far surpassed those of the earlier war." The Vietnam War, as compared to Korea, had gone on too long, and was beginning to cost too much in the one coin the American people cared most about: the blood of their young men.

Another major study of opinion during the Vietnam War, by Jeffrey Milstein, largely corroborates Mueller's findings.[70] Support for the war was strongly negatively correlated with the number of U.S. deaths in the war. Milstein also argued that the mortality level affected the popularity of President Johnson and his job approval rating. He concludes, "The most significant costs to the American people were the number of American 'boys' killed and wounded in Vietnam. . . . The more casualties incurred, the more the public disapproved of the president and his Vietnam policy." The sharpest decline in support of the Vietnam War occurred between February and August of 1966. This was during the beginning of anti-war demonstrations and the Fulbright hearings on Vietnam.

Finally, a more focused study by Samuel Kernell also indicated that U.S. deaths were the most important factor in affecting public opinion about the war.[71] Kernell examined *monthly* rates as opposed to cumulative figures. He found, in the case of Korea, a negative correlation (-0.68) between these rates and the popularity of President Harry Truman. In Vietnam, the average monthly figure of 478 Americans killed correlated with a 1.5 percent drop in Lyndon Johnson's popularity. The preciseness of the "mortality factor" is remarkable. Early in the conflict an American Congressman predicted, "We can take 1 casualty [war-related death] per congressional district. We can maybe even take 10. But if it gets to be 100, Congress will stop it [the war]."[72] In fact, by 1972, the year of closure for America's direct involvement in Vietnam, deaths of U.S servicemen reached 100 for each congressional district.[73]

These findings support the idea that the Saigon execution photo might very well not have had a striking impact on the beliefs of ordinary Americans.[74] Reaction to Tet, thus, must be measured as indicative of other factors, most importantly the suffering of American soldiers, even though they are not shown in the Saigon photo or the film. They are an off-camera frame that would have been filled in by a nativist, sensitive public. The deaths of American servicemen reported in the press or known through acquaintances or experienced in their own families was the major factor in causing Americans' support for the war to decline. For example, in July, 1967, Louis Harris Associates asked people to rank what they felt were the "most troubling aspects of the Vietnam war."[75] Thirty-one percent of the total respondents said they were most concerned with "the loss of our young men/casualties/loss of lives/killing." The second highest response was "we are not making any apparent progress/should escalate/taking so long to end" with 12 percent. This was followed by 9 percent being most troubled by "don't understand the war/why are we fighting?/It's a senseless war." Interestingly, only 6 percent of respondents were most troubled by "killing innocent people/women and children." In other words, the death of Americans was a tragedy; the death of others, even civilians, was peripheral. Again, in this light, Americans would be unlikely to feel outrage over the death of a "Viet Cong suspect."

Direct Reaction to the Pictures

Another way to infer reaction to the Saigon execution is to look at demonstrable public reaction to its showing on television or in print. We are lucky in this regard to have the classic study by researchers George Bailey and Lawrence Lichty.[76] Their focus was on the mechanics and rationale of the decision by NBC to air the film of the shooting. They also, however, gauged viewers' reaction to the image. Again, the viewing audience that saw the *Huntley-Brinkley Report* the night the Saigon execution film was shown was estimated at *twenty million.* In response to this icon of outrage, this image that supposedly shocked and sickened the nation, and possibly overturned public opinion, Bailey and Lichty report, NBC received 90 letters. The majority of these, 56 letters (62%) accused the network of "bad taste" in showing the film, presumably at the dinner hour. After this the criticism most cited was concern that "children might have seen the film." Indeed, more than thirty of the letters "were from parents of young children." Bailey then sent out a questionnaire in April, more than a month after the events and the screening. Sixty-nine of the letter writers responded. These people reported themselves to be more politically active than the American average. In other words, those closer to the status of discourse elites were also the most likely to attempt to be heard by media, so it is likely that even these 90 were not a representative slice of the audience.[77] Bailey and Lichty conclude, "Interestingly few persons referred to the Vietnam War in their letters or in responding to the questionnaire. Only four said that the film showed a 'true picture' of the war but no one questioned the truthfulness of the NBC film." In sum, whatever public reaction there was to the image, it did not manifest itself in action or in an outpouring of outrage, at least to the NBC film, which was after all the more gruesome scene.[78]

THE "RELEVANCE" CONTEXT OF TET

Finally, we must ask a larger question about the possible impact of the image on ordinary Americans, and that is what else might have competed with the Saigon execution picture for the public's attention. Asked another way, would this image have had any relevance in the life of ordinary viewers?[79] The first context is economic. In the 1930s Abraham Flexner charged "no nation is rich enough to pay for both war and civilization. We must make our choice; we cannot have both."[80] As part of his policies, President Lyndon Johnson wanted to check Communism in Asia, to win, as he so often put it, *his* war, with *his* guns, and *his* boys. He also, however, sought victory in his war on poverty. His motivation to grasp for both guns and butter was as follows:

If I left the woman I really loved—the Great Society—in order to get involved with that bitch of a war on the other side of the world, then I would lose everything at home. All my programs. All my hopes to feed the hungry and shelter the homeless. All my dreams to provide education and medical care to the browns and the blacks and the lame and the poor. But if I left that war and let the Communists take over South Vietnam, then I would be seen as a coward and my nation would be seen as an appeaser and we would both find it impossible to accomplish anything for anybody anywhere on the entire globe.[81]

As it was, Johnson, to continue his colorful analogies, tried to support both his "women" on a fixed salary. As late as 1966, in his State of the Union Address, he reassured the nation that it was wealthy enough and "its people are strong enough to pursue our goals in the rest of the world while still building a Great Society here at home."[82] He refused to raise taxes to support either the war or the great society. Taxation was as unpopular as ever at that time; 70 percent of respondents to a Gallup poll in 1967 opposed raising any taxes to pay for Vietnam.[83]

Yet, as expenses rose, Johnson continued to delay dealing with the situation, often resorting to asking Congress for supplemental funding for "unexpected" increases in war costs.[84] In the summer of 1967, the first concessions to the tide were made; a gigantic 10 percent surcharge was levied against corporations and individuals. That same year, Johnson found himself cutting money from the social welfare portion of the budget. By the next year, the year of Tet, the budget deficit jumped to $25.2 billion, the greatest increase since World War II. The economic side effects were disastrous: increasing inflation, decreasing productivity, rising labor costs, falling consumer demand, and fluctuating real income for workers. The costs were also notable to elites; deficits and erosion of the nation's gold reserve were hurting the value of the dollar, causing concern for domestic and international bankers. The situation worsened so that by January 24, a few days before Tet, Johnson was warned by the chairman of the council of economic advisers that a "world depression" was a real possibility. Thus, another context that may have framed images from Tet was that the international financier reading the *New York Times* as well as the steel worker watching NBC *News* would increasingly have understood that the war was hurting him or her in the pocketbook.

But we need not search only for such macro-causes that may have either obscured or affected the interpretation of the events from Vietnam. An important example of social contexts comes from a study done of evidence of the impact of the Tet offensive in "Middletown" Muncie, Indiana, the famous "most studied town" in America.[85] Historian Anthony Edmonds examined coverage, commentary, editorials and letters to the editor about the war in three local newspapers. He also reported on oral history interviews done in the period and later. He found a diversity of reactions, from those sympathetic to the war protests, to those who supported the president, to those who favored vigorous escalation. Edmonds claims that "more common, however, were sentiments of bewilderment, disappointment and concern over the real possibility of a protracted war and stalemate." Other national news in the local paper augmented a sense of loss of control of America's destiny: the Pueblo incident, the growing trade deficit, difficult dealings with France's president Charles de Gaulle.

Most revealing, even among those who called for continuing the war, there was little support for the war as it was being fought. A "win or get out" attitude seemed to sum up the views of many middletowners. Edmonds argues that there was no consensus in Muncie. He notes, however, and probably this is his most important finding, that by mid-February, local issues dominated the press. Citizens, interviewed as part of an oral history project about the Vietnam War, never even mentioned the Tet offensive. Indicative of this is an editorial cartoon that appeared in a local paper. A group of "'world problems,' prominently featuring Vietnam, stands outside a locked door labeled 'Indiana.' A sign hanging from the door warns, HOOSIER HYSTERIA: Do not disturb." These middle Americans were not therefore unconcerned with the Vietnam War or indifferent to its costs, but for them, unlike for the policy and press elites of Washington and Saigon, it could not remain an object of daily fascination. Compared to college basketball and rising home mortgage rates, perhaps Tet was not that big a story after all.

MANUFACTURING TET

With Vietnam in mind, historian Michael Walzer has noted, "Every war is fought twice—first militarily and then, especially among the losers, politically and intellectually."[86] Some 58,169 American soldiers died in Vietnam, and the conflict provided none of the traditional indicators of a victory: we made no plot of foreign soil forever ours, restored no friendly government to power, liberated no occupied innocents, threw down no great dictators. Instead we withdrew slowly, tortuously, and watched as our allies and client states in Laos, Cambodia, and South Vietnam were swallowed up in utter defeat. This unassailable fact—that the war did not end at the time of our wishing and in the outcome of our favor—has created divisions within American society that remain to this day. In the wake of the fall of Saigon in 1975, there was a lull in the argumentation over Vietnam. President Ford, in a speech given shortly before the end, suggested that Americans could not regain their sense of pride by "refighting a war that is finished."[87] This proved to be the calm before the typhoon; beginning in the late 1970s and continuing—even increasing—to the present day, a torrent of historical studies, articles, novels, memoirs, and films have attempted to renew or revise the fundamental issues of Vietnam. The legacy of the war and what it meant for the United States is an unclosed chapter. Understanding the struggle to define what Tet was reveals the kinds of debates that probably will linger forever.

Tet came at a time when many basic forces other than simply media were eroding public, press, and elite opinion-maker faith in the administration's prosecution of the Vietnam War. These pressures range from the chronic (U.S. casualties, the length of the war), the acute (economics, the Pueblo, race problems) to the idiosyncratic (Hoosier basketball). Tet did not occur in a vacuum; extramedia reality, related to the war in general but to Johnson's leadership in particular, affected the hearts, minds, and pocketbooks of all Americans. The vision of Tet should be reviewed in such a light. There is little evidence of "strong effects" by news media on people's minds, at least in the first weeks of the offensive. Support for the war did decrease in later months—perhaps a sleeper effect—but it had been doing so for years anyway, only interrupted by late 1967 public relations efforts by the administration predicting better times in Vietnam.

Moreover, as many writers, from all stances of support or opposition to the war agree, President Johnson's retreat from advocacy, his surrender of the bully pulpit, his unwillingness to rally opinion to either a greater war effort or an immediate pullback, created a vacuum of leadership. As George Gallup noted, "Inaction hurts a President more than anything else."[88] When the president does not try to rally the people to action, the people can hardly be expected to support his policies; the Vietnam conflict was a case of indecision making by the commander-in-chief. The impression was of a forever war, a stalemate, indecisively directed by weak leaders.[89] Steady decline could be the only result when the "number one foreign policy opinion maker" shows little faith or extends tepid support for his own positions.

Yet, despite a credibility gap, the Johnson administration still could have rallied public confidence, at least temporarily, in a stepped-up war effort. The president, still under the fraying umbrella of the cold war consensus, had a great deal of power to influence public opinion in the area of foreign policy; Congress did not curtail any Vietnam programs until 1969. Lyndon Johnson frittered away that power with compromises, misstatements, and half-truths. He lost his credibility with the people and with the elites whom he needed to gather support to enact and sustain any policy, and eventually, it is clear, he lost even his own self-assurance. The polling data suggest that if, in early February, instead of sitting back and gathering advisers to consider his moves, Johnson had boldly gone before the American people, cried "Pearl Harbor" (or more reasonably, "Battle of the Bulge"), and ordered a full war commitment to Vietnam, a majority of the public would have rallied to his side, if only temporarily.

But why, with so many other factors at work, was the shooting seized upon by discourse elites as a metonym for the war? Why the assumption of great and powerful effects? What seems to be at work is a variation of what is known as the third person effect.[90] Traditionally, third person effect research has examined how people represent themselves in relation to "others."[91] According to one definition, "people will tend to overestimate the influence that mass communication have on the attitudes and behavior of others."[92] In previous work, the disparity between self-assessment of, for example, media effects and the estimation of the effects on others has ranged from 35 percent to 69 percent.[93] We might assume that other people are more affected by mass media than us; they are more vulnerable to deception, more likely to be dupes, to become violent, to swallow falsehoods. One basis of this comparison is perceived as correctness and breadth of knowledge, what we think we know in contrast with what we estimate that others know.[94] On the other hand, some questions may be framed as not based on knowledge but a measurement of "moral virtue," and in these as well self-evaluation may differ markedly from the description of the "other."[95]

In the case of the Saigon execution photo there is a *first person effect*—other people will react to a mass media product the same way as I. The picture was talked about among elites, so they assumed the public shared their fascination and concerns. Why? In this case, ego involvement and moral virtue are part of the equation. Many third-person effects revolve around perceived *deleterious* influences of media, e.g. engendering a tendency to violence. Here, the people who wrote about the Loan shooting and attempted to frame it—the discourse elites—see shock, outrage, ascription of importance, assumption of wisdom, and of turning against the war as being beneficial effects; that is, the picture, for all its outrageous content, made people see an essential truth clearly. In parallel, even supporters of the war and defenders of General Loan still assumed the picture was important because they and other discourse elites, even in the opposing political camp, said it was; they in turn worried that the public would be influenced by the negative interpretation. Moreover, people who think they have found revealed truth will want to impose it upon others. Since we rarely challenge the veridicality or verisimilitude of news photographs, we assume that the concern they cause and the effects they produce are universal. In other words, if I see a meaning in an image, then others must too; if I feel shock, or perhaps because in my peer group it is "correct" to express such outrage, then that outrage is to be projected on the millions who also engaged the icon. In this process, icons of outrage are born and made great, since their power is assumed to be intrinsic. Magic bullets need not prove their impact since they only exist in the minds of the beholders.

Yet, there is no evidence that, as one writer put it, "The American public was repulsed by what was perceived as the blatant barbarity of its South Vietnamese ally."[96] In the first person effect, it is almost as if elites rationalize as follows: *Of course the Saigon execution photo is a "great" image—just look at it. Of course it's shocking; aren't you shocked? Of course it "sums up" the brutality of the war; isn't that obvious? And, consequently, aren't you affected by it? Who wouldn't be?* These are all false assumptions, or rather they are personal views, or opinions shared in a peer group of like-minded media elites or intelligentsia, imposed onto greater publics. If so, could not the execution photo's "meaning" have been forcefully redirected? To connect leadership, visual journalism, and policy, the shooting of a Viet Cong child-killer could have been employed as a rallying icon. What would have happened if a hard-voiced, angry President Johnson had, after the first days of Tet, demanded an escalation of the war, an all-out fight to a decisive victory? What if he had held up the photo and said, "We need a thousand more General Loans?" Or what if, in answer to a reporter's asking him if there were summary executions being conducted of Viet Cong suspects, Johnson had retorted with a Texas sneer, "Not enough!"? Would not tens of millions have agreed with him out of disdain for the Viet Cong our enemy, and with an eagerness to "win"? The president did not attempt to lead the nation in that direction, but he could have, and many would have followed. The ambiguous icon of outrage could have served the war effort and the peace movement equally well.

NOTES

1. Quoted in *Newsreels to Nightly News: Episode IV*, History Channel, 1997.
2. W. Schramm, "The Nature of Communication Between Humans," in *The Process and Effects of Mass Communication*, ed. by W. Schramm and D. Roberts (Urbana: University of Illinois Press, 1971), pp. 6–11.
3. Interview with Eddie Adams, November 22, 1987, in S. D. Moeller, *Shooting War: Photography and the American Experience of Combat* (New York: Basic Books, 1989), p. 378.
4. P. Braestrup, *Big Story: How the American Press Reported and Interpreted the Crisis of Tet 1968 in Vietnam and Washington*, Vol. I. (Boulder: Westview, 1977), pp. 461–62.
5. P. Braestrup, *Big Story*.
6. R. Buzzanco, "The Myth of Tet: American Failure and the Politics of War," in *The Tet Offensive*, ed. by M. J. Gilbert and W. Head (Westport, CT: Praeger, 1996), pp. 231–57.
7. Quoted in J. Prados, *The Hidden History of the Vietnam War* (Chicago: Ivan R. Dee, 1995), p. 133.

8. Quoted in P. Braestrup, *Big Story*, p. 60.

9. J. Prados, *The Hidden History of the Vietnam War*, p. 136.

10. The objectives of the "general offensive, general uprising" are discussed in J. J. Wirtz, *The Tet Offensive: Intelligence Failure in War* (Ithaca, NY: Cornell University Press, 1991); Hoang Ngoc Lung, *The General Offensives of 1968–1969*, Indochina Monographs (Washington, DC: U.S. Army Center of Military History, 1981); Van Tra Tran, "Tet: The 1968 General Offensive and General Uprising," in J. S. Werner and Luu Doan Huynh, eds., *The Vietnam War: Vietnamese and American Perspectives* (Armonk, NY: M. E. Sharpe, 1993), pp. 37–65.

11. Interview with George Carver, March 11, 1982, in M. Lorell and C. Kelley, Jr., with D. Hensler, *Casualties, Public Opinion, and Presidential Policy During the Vietnam War: A Project Air Force Report* (Santa Monica, CA: Rand, 1985), p. 52.

12. Interview with Robert Komer, March 11, 1982, in M. Lorell and C. Kelley, Jr., with D. Hensler, *Casualties*, p. 52.

13. One line of speculation is that it was in the interests and thus was the intention of the northern government to sacrifice and politically neutralize National Liberation Front forces through a suicidal offensive. See W. S. Thompson and D. D. Frizzell, *The Lessons of Vietnam* (New York: Crane, Russak, 1977), pp. 100–101.

14. W. C. Westmoreland, *A Soldier Reports* (Garden City, NY: Doubleday, 1976), pp. 333–34.

15. D. E. Bonior, S. M. Champlin, and T. S. Kolly, *The Vietnam Veteran: A History of Neglect* (New York: Praeger, 1984), p. 75.

16. PBS, *Frontline*, June 12, 1983.

17. Quoted in *Washington Post*, January 17, 1991, p. A10.

18. Louis Harris and Associates, *Myths and Realities: A Study of Attitudes toward Vietnam Era Veterans* (Washington, DC: U.S. Government Printing Office, 1980), p. 61.

19. S. Karnow, *Vietnam: A History* (New York: Penguin, 1983), p. 15. Note that this was before the Reagan 80s and the reclamation of Vietnam as a lost crusade.

20. P. Braestrup, *Big Story*, p. 709.

21. W. M. Hammond, *Public Affairs: The Military and the Media, 1962–1968* (Washington, DC: Center of Military History, U.S. Army, 1988).

22. D. C. Hallin, *The "Uncensored War": The Media and Vietnam* (Berkeley: University of California Press, 1986). Quotes that follow are on pp. 212–13, 173.

23. Speaking on *Vietnam, The Camera at War*, History Channel, 1997. This is a revealing statement, though it is not completely clear whether Terry was explaining his astonishment that something so patently deviant from the norm of American life occurred at all, that it had become routine in Vietnam, or that it happened in front of cameras. In any case, Terry, as did the AP, NBC, and thousands of other news organizations, made a framing decision that the photo was news, front page deviance, worthy of attention.

24. Interview with Eddie Adams, November 22, 1987, in Moeller, *Shooting War*, p. 378.

25. Neither was Tuckner, and Tuckner had a Vietnamese crew. The Vietnamese ABC cameraman did not film the execution because he was "afraid of General Loan." P. Braestrup, *Big Story*, p. 465; ABC *Evening News*, February 2, 1968. See Appendix XL, Vol. II, for a study of how the Saigon execution film was edited.

26. Ibid., p. 445. As Braestrup notes (p. 447, f1), only a single American journalist, a *Newsweek* stringer, specialized in monitoring the ARVN. See also C. R. Wyatt, *Paper Soldiers: The American Press and the Vietnam War* (New York: W. W. Norton, 1993), p. 139; A. J. Joes, *The War for South Viet Nam, 1954–1975* (New York: Praeger, 1989), p. 94.

27. P. Braestrup, *Big Story*, p. 465.

28. F. FitzGerald, *Fire in the Lake: The Vietnamese and the Americans in Vietnam* (Boston: Little, Brown, 1972), p. 312.

29. Ibid., p. 289.

30. W. J. Lederer, *Our Own Worst Enemy* (New York: W. W. Norton, 1968), p. 7.

31. D. Valentine, *The Phoenix Program* (New York: William Morrow, 1990).

32. S. Karnow, *Vietnam*, pp. 601–2.

33. D. Valentine, *The Phoenix Program*, p. 121.

34. The exception was Walter Cronkite. In his famous broadcast, *Who, What, When, Where, Why: Report From Vietnam*, February 27, 1968, he speculated that Loan was one of those who had warned the government that an offensive was to take place at Tet.

35. T. L. Cubbage, III, "Intelligence and the Tet Offensive: The South Vietnamese View of the Threat," in *The Vietnam War as History*, ed. by E. J. Errington and B.J.C. McKercher (Westport, CT: Praeger, 1990), p. 106; W. C. Westmoreland, *A Soldier Reports*, pp. 388–89; D. Oberdorfer, *TET! The Turning Point in the Vietnam War* (New York: Da Capo, 1984), p. 150.

36. W. C. Westmoreland, *A Soldier Reports*, p. 321. He also asserts that "The North Vietnamese decided, in effect, to go for broke, to mount a co-ordinated general offensive throughout South Vietnam, designed to achieve that objective peculiar to Vietnamese Communist insurgency, the general uprising. Ironically, Secretary McNamara was in Saigon manipulating a decrease in even my 'minimum essential' troop request at the same time the North Vietnamese were making their big decision." (p. 311)

37. D. Valentine, *The Phoenix Program*, p. 148.

38. Ibid.

39. Hoang Ngoc Lung, *The General Offensives of 1968–1969*.

40. Nguyen Cao Ky, *Twenty Years and Twenty Days* (New York: Stein and Day, 1976), p. 162.

41. D. Valentine, *The Phoenix Program*, pp. 148–49.

42. Quoted in G. A. Bailey and L. Lichty, "Rough Justice on a Saigon Street: A Gatekeeper Study of NBC's Tet Execution Film," *Journalism Quarterly* (Summer 1972): 222.

43. Interview in *Vietnam, The Camera at War*, History Channel, 1997.

44. The sole exception was *Newsweek*, which on February 12, 1968, claimed that, "Unable to make the suspect talk, Loan took out his revolver, calmly pointed it at the prisoner's head and shot him dead," (p. 28). This is probably a misinterpretation of Tuckner's comments.

45. Interview in K. Willenson, *The Bad War: An Oral History of the Vietnam War* (New York: New American Library, 1987), p. 186.

46. G. A. Bailey and L. Lichty, "Rough Justice," p. 223.

47. D. Oberdorfer, *TET!*, p. 164.

48. Van Tra Tran, "Tet: The 1968 General Offensive and General Uprising."

49. See, for example, S. Karnow, *Vietnam*, p. 447.

50. D. Harris, *Our War: What We Did in Vietnam and What It Did to Us* (New York: Times Books, 1996), p. 91.

51. Lac Hoang and Viet Mai Ha, *Why America Lost the Vietnam War* (self-published, 1996), p. 72.

52. *New York Times*, February 2, 1968, p. I-1.

53. *Chicago Tribune*, February 2, 1968, p. 3. Headline: "Execution in Saigon." Credit: "Saigon, Vietnam, Feb. 1 (AP)."

54. J. S. Carson, M.D., "Letters," *Time*, February 23, 1968, p. 5.

55. See discussion about the prevalence of killing prisoners in previous wars in J. Keegan, *The Face of Battle* (New York: Penguin, 1988[1976]), pp. 47, 48, 84–85, 108–12.

56. J. W. Gibson, *The Perfect War: Technowar in Vietnam* (Boston: Atlantic Monthly Press, 1986), pp. 146–47, 207.

57. Terry Musser, quoted in J. R. Ebert, *A Life in a Year: The American Infantryman in Vietnam, 1965–1972* (Novato, CA: Presidio Press, 1993), p. 281.

58. Sergeant Gerry Barker, quoted in J. R. Ebert, *A Life in a Year*, p. 283.

59. Malcolm Browne, quoted in P. Arnett, *Live from the Battlefield: From Vietnam to Baghdad, 35 Years in the World's War Zones* (New York: Simon and Schuster, 1994) p. 134.

60. P. Arnett, *Live from the Battlefield*, p. 134.

61. "U.S. Cautioning Saigon on Captives' Treatment," *New York Times*, February 5, 1968, p. A14.

62. "Viet Cong, Allied Atrocities Reflect Bitterness of War," *Baltimore Sun*, February 4, 1968.

63. Letter, Wheeler to Henry S. Reuss, February 3, 1968, Directorate of Defense Information, Tet Offensive (7) file; W. M. Hammond, *Public Affairs*, p. 352.

64. W. M. Hammond, *Public Affairs*, p. 352.

65. Or, General Loan was the most careless officer in the Allied armed forces, or perhaps, in the heat of the offensive, he didn't think it worth his time to play the game of bluff and duplicity that MACV had played for so long.

66. Interview in K. Willenson, *The Bad War*, p. 187.

67. The image could, in this fashion, have contributed to the unpopularity of the American war effort by simply confirming the idea that the South Vietnamese were no better than the North. Conversely, the picture is in many ways stereotypical of Western perceptions of the "orient." Thus, it is quite possible that Americans looked at this picture and thought, "Well, that's what those Asians do." James Ebert, in his study of the one-year rotation of American GIs in Vietnam, concluded that, "American soldiers also viewed the Vietnamese government and its armed forces with contempt. It was a government that most soldiers believed to be corrupt and hardly worth defending, which prompted GIs throughout the war to wonder why they were enduring all that they were." See J. R. Ebert, *A Life in A Year*, p. 234. See also results of surveys of Vietnam era persons, including veterans, in E. Frey-Wouters and R. Laufer, *Legacy of a War: The American Soldier in Vietnam* (Armonk, NY: M. E. Sharpe, 1986).

68. M. Maclear, *The Ten Thousand Day War: Vietnam, 1945–1975* (New York: St. Martin's Press, 1981), p. 148.

69. J. E. Mueller, *War, Presidents, and Public Opinion* (New York: John Wiley and Sons, 1973). Quotes are from pp. 37, 167. See also J. E. Mueller, "Trends in Popular Support for the Wars in Korea and Vietnam," *American Political Science Review* 65 (June 1971): 358–75.

70. J. S. Milstein, *Dynamics of the Vietnam War: A Quantitative Analysis and Predictive Computer Simulation* (Columbus: Ohio State University Press, 1974). Following quote is on p. 55.

71. S. Kernell, "Explaining Presidential Popularity," *American Political Science Review* 72 (1978): 506–22.

72. C. V. Crabb, Jr. and P. M. Holt, *Invitation to Struggle: Congress, the President and Foreign Policy*, 3rd ed. (Washington, DC: Congressional Quarterly, 1989), p. 139.

73. Ibid.

74. Images of violence might have heightened the impression that the total number of U.S. casualties had increased. One Vietnamese killing another does not confer this impression, although it certainly might suggest that Vietnam was a dangerous place for the American soldier.

75. Louis Harris and Associates, Inc. Study 1734, questions #6, #20C, July 1967.

76. G. A. Bailey and L. Lichty, "Rough Justice."

77. In any case, 61 percent also reported opposing the war in Vietnam. Bailey does not report how this question was framed. However, he notes that this is exactly the percentile of Americans who also stated opposition to the war in the May, 1968 Gallup Poll.

78. Caroline Page, a British researcher, claims that the reaction in the U.K. was stronger. See C. Page, *U.S. Official Propaganda During the Vietnam War, 1965–1973: The Limits of Persuasion* (New York: Leicester University Press, 1996), pp. 223–24.

79. Daniel Sperber and his colleagues have advanced our understanding of communications processes by keying in on this notion of relevance. See D. Sperber and D. Wilson, *Relevance: Communication and Cognition* (Cambridge: Harvard University Press, 1988).

80. A. Flexner, *Universities: American, English, German* (New York: Oxford University Press, 1930), p. 11.

81. D. Kearns, *Lyndon Johnson and the American Dream* (New York: Harper and Row, 1976), pp. 251–52. See also I. Bernstein, *Guns or Butter: The Presidency of Lyndon Johnson* (New York: Oxford University Press, 1996).

82. P. Geyelin, *Lyndon B. Johnson and the World* (New York: F. A. Praeger, 1966), p. 291.

83. P. E. Converse and H. Schuman, "Silent Majorities and the Vietnam War," *Scientific American* 222 (1970): 24.

84. As Kolko, one of the few historians to appraise the economic effects of Vietnam, relates, this created a wholly unexpected budget deficit, putting pressure on Congress to raise money by taxation for both the war on poverty and the war in Vietnam. G. Kolko, *Anatomy of a War: Vietnam, the United States, and the Modern Historical Experience* (New York: New Press, 1994), pp. 197–98, 288. See especially Chapter 22.

85. A. Edmonds, "The Tet Offensive and Middletown: A Study in Contradiction," in *The Tet Offensive*, ed. by M. J. Gilbert and W. Head, pp. 135–42.

86. M. Walzer, "Review of *America in Vietnam* by Guenter Lewy," *The New Republic*, November 11, 1978, p. 31.

87. S. Karnow, *Vietnam*, p. 667.

88. K. J. Turner, *Lyndon Johnson's Dual War: Vietnam and the Press* (Chicago: University of Chicago Press, 1985), pp. 160–61.

89. W. Cronkite, *A Reporter's Life* (New York: Alfred A. Knopf, 1996), p. 249. See also D. Kearns, *Lyndon Johnson and the American Dream*, p. 282; J. Reston, "A Mystifying Clarification from McNamara," *New York Times*, January 29, 1964, p. I–32; J. Reston, "Blabbermouth Approach to Vietnam," *New York Times*, March 1, 1964, p. IV–8; D. Halberstam, *The Powers That Be* (New York: Alfred A. Knopf, 1979), p. 510; R. S. McNamara, with B. VanDeMark, *In Retrospect: The Tragedy and Lessons of Vietnam* (New York: Times Books, 1995); K. J. Turner, *Lyndon Johnson's Dual War.*

90. R. M. Perloff, "Ego-Involvement and the Third Person Effect of Televised News Coverage," *Communication Research* 16 (April 1989): 236–62.

91. J. Cohen and R. G. Davis, "Third-Person Effects and the Differential Impact in Negative Political Advertising," *Journalism Quarterly* 68 (Winter 1991): 680–88; J. Cohen, D. Mutz, V. Price, and A. Gunther, "Perceived Impact of Defamation: An Experiment on Third-Person Effects," *Public Opinion Quarterly* 52 (Summer 1988): 161–73. See also A. C. Gunther, "What We Think Others Think: Cause and Consequences in the Third-Person Effect," *Communication Research* 18 (June 1991): 355–72.

92. W. P. Davison, "The Third-Person Effect in Communication," *Public Opinion Quarterly* 47 (Spring 1983): 3.

93. Ibid.; A. C. Gunther, "What We Think Others Think." See also A. C. Gunther, "Overrating the X-Rating: The Third-Person Perception and Support for Censorship of Pornography," *Journal of Communication* 45 (Winter 1995): 27–38; L. E. Atwood, "Illusions of Media Power: The Third-Person Effect," *Journalism Quarterly* 71 (Summer 1994): 269–81.

94. C. Antaki and A. Lewis, eds., *Mental Mirrors: Metacognition in Social Knowledge and Communication* (London: Sage, 1986).

95. G. R. Goethals, D. M. Messick and S. T. Allison, "The Uniqueness Bias: Studies of Constructive Social Comparison," in *Social Comparison: Contemporary Theory and Research*, ed. by J. Suls and T. A. Wills (Hillsdale, NJ: Lawrence Erlbaum, 1991), pp. 149–76.

96. L. Monk, *Photographs That Changed the World: The Camera as Witness, the Photograph as Evidence* (New York: Doubleday, 1989), p. 42.

Chapter Three

The Consensus of Outrage:
Tiananmen, 1989

I was so moved today by the bravery of that individual that stood alone in
front of the tanks rolling down, rolling down the main avenue there. And
I'll tell you, it was very moving. And all I can say to him, wherever he
might be or to people around the world is we are and we must stand with
him.[1]

—President George Bush

In the spring of 1989, world media attention focused on increasingly
large student demonstrations in the People's Republic of China. The
saga became instantly identifiable by the name of a square in the heart of
Beijing: Tiananmen. The movement, led by attractive, ardent young
people, and resplendent with colorful festivities, stirring speeches, and
visual symbols and slogans that appealed to American and Western
ideals, was eventually crushed by the tanks and police squads of the
Chinese government. As at Tet, it has become a commonplace that the
media's role in the events was profound and influential. Probably at no
time in the history of American journalism was so much coverage
dedicated to a foreign affairs story in which the United States had no
presidents, soldiers, or hostages involved. The role of mass media in
general, and the visual image in particular, in shaping the events has
been cited even by scholars of China traditionally more interested in
social, political, and economic contexts. Elizabeth Perry, for example,
introducing a recent work on Tiananmen, asserted that the images from
China in the spring of 1989 drew worldwide attention, "alternately
inspiring and horrifying audiences and changing forever the way they
thought about China."[2]

One of the images Perry, and a host of other journalists, politicians,
pundits, and historians identify as having the most lasting impression
and most profound impact was also the one that my students most
associated with the Tiananmen events: a man blocking a column of tanks
on a wide street. [See Figure 3.] At least three still photographers and

several video crews recorded this key icon of Beijing Spring. In each image, the same incident played itself out. A column of tanks rolled down East Changan Boulevard unopposed. Then a young man—later identified by the name Wang Weilin—in dark pants and a white shirt, carrying a jacket and a satchel (or a shopping bag) but no weapons, stood in their path for several minutes. He yelled, "Why are you here? . . . You have done nothing but create misery. My city is in chaos because of you."3 The tanks tried to maneuver around the man, but like a bold matador he blocked their every move. He climbed on top of the lead tank and tried to persuade the commander to turn back. Finally, friends ran onto the scene and pulled the young man away. All this was witnessed by many watching the drama from the windows of the Beijing Hotel.4 And the scene is still reviewed and replayed today. In 1998, *Time* magazine voted him "the unknown rebel," one of the "top 20 revolutionaries and leaders of the twentieth century."5 The young man thus became, as writer Pico Iyer maintains, "the unknown soldier of a new republic of the image."

Tiananmen itself seemed a perfect venue for visual media attention. The events were highly dramatic, colorful, and exciting to watch. Each day brought some new plot development: protest marches, conflicts with police, the raising of statues, rallies, infighting within the government, hunger strikes. All of these were visually alluring to the camera—lots of bodies, flags, and tension. The dramatis personae were also well cast for visual display: old, "evil" reactionary leaders clinging to power through brutality and lies, and young, slim, appealing students willing to brave prison and endure hunger strikes for "freedom" and "democracy." While the students and their leaders probably did not become household names in the West, some, such as China's premier Li Peng and student leader Chai Ling, became archetypes. The former was dark overlord; the latter became a sympathetic and "magnetic presence for the foreign cameras."6 American policy makers, from the president to members of the House and Senate to local mayors and alderman of all political stripes, made public statements in reaction to the conflict. News pundits and commentators discussed the events in daily programming and many TV and print special reports.7 This attention was not due simply to the aesthetics of the incidents. China was an important trading partner of the United States and for almost half a century has been one of the main concerns of American foreign policy.8 While the United States had no direct stake in the conflict, the crisis could be construed as legitimately appealing to U.S interests.

Yet, such reasons are tautological; any news story can be justified as being important *ex post facto.* Only now, years later, and only among the pages of academic books, are ambiguities about the events that the "whole world watched" arising. As several China scholars have recently noted, in tracking the evolution of thought about Tiananmen, "The initial 'unanimity on the issue of China' . . . now appears to have been little more than widespread agreement that the Chinese government's crackdown and subsequent campaign of arrests and disinformation were abhorrent acts."9 Some further questions seem revisionist: Was there really a massacre at Tiananmen? Did the student leaders intentionally set out to provoke a violent reaction by the government? Were foreign journalists instigating events, as the Chinese government charged, not just covering them? Was there really one Tiananmen, or was there a variety of complex experiences? Or, even more perversely, did Tiananmen as we saw it occur, or was it simply, on a vast scale, what Daniel J. Boorstin called the "pseudo-event," made for the camera, where everyone, protesters and police, reporters and little old ladies, was part of the cast? Did Tiananmen have any significance beyond its media status? Was Tiananmen really an example of mass media sound and fury that had little or no lasting impact except on its survivors and victims?

Because of its status as a major event in media history, Tiananmen has also been the focus of considerable attention by mass communication researchers.[10] Typically, such studies have been content analyses of verbal and visual coverage in Chinese, Western, and other sources. The framing paradigm, the question of how the coverage of Tiananmen was presented with attached interpretations and emphases, has been the goal of much of the more comprehensive of these studies. The findings are remarkably similar and, as shall be described below, also coincide with the observations of the most recent historiographical examinations of the events.[11] Essentially, Tiananmen was framed through Western eyes. The drama that the American public witnessed was selected, edited, and presented with accompanying commentary and captioning by reporters very much interested in translating into easily understood units of discourse the often complex occurrences of the spring of 1989. Elites of journalism, politics, the academy, and others all colluded to make "the man against the tanks" image the icon representing the events in immediate and subsequent commentary and memory.

These observations must be weighed in comparison to the relative scale of saturation coverage that Tiananmen received. In an op-ed piece in the *New York Times*, Simon Leys points out that the incidents at Tiananmen were the latest but also the least of various bloodlettings in terms of body count in China's history: "Chinese communism could liquidate more than a million Tibetans—yet this fact never seriously impaired China's prestige and international credit. Why? There were no television cameras on the spot."[12] Is Tiananmen an example of a sort of binary nature of reality in a mediated world: what is shown exists, is "on," what is not shown does not exist, is "off?" For these reasons, this chapter will examine not only what was shown in the coverage about China in the spring of 1989, but also what was *not* shown, and what was not provided in the discourse that elites employed to frame the images they presented to us.

Such queries about inconspicuous absence of pictures and of explanatory discourse are crucial to understanding the ambiguous and constructed nature of the icon. The case studies in this book are investigations of how icons are created; at the same time it is instructive to ask why some icons do not exist, why some pictures do not rise to iconic status, why some events do not become famous in the popular and elite sense, and why some news is not visually revealed. Infants cry in hunger, dissidents rot in jail, and rivers run with the blood of victims of genocide every day unaccompanied by Western photography and commentary. Much of the propaganda apparatus of the news industry is dedicated to assuring us that we are well informed, so that we, by committing only a few minutes a day to mass media, will know our planet intimately. As with everything else concerning television, the promise is much less than the reality, but the promise, powered by the news photograph, passes itself off as the totality.

TWO NON-ICONS OF TIANANMEN

The first non-icon of Tiananmen is not even a visual image, except in the imagination. Chai Ling, a student leader in the protests, gave a press conference on June 4, 1990, the first anniversary of the Tiananmen events. At one point she was asked about the status of the young man who stood against the tanks. Chai answered that she did not know, but added, "However, I know of a young woman, and [sic] the evening of June 3rd did exactly the same thing. She stood in front of a tank with one arm on her hip and the other arm waving in the sky trying to stop a tank, and the tank ran right over her. Even though she did the same courageous thing as [the man] but no—she didn't have the opportunity to be recorded by film or by photograph."[13] In an interview later that year with *MS* magazine, Chai again brought up the young girl's story, pointing out that "no journalist, no photographer recorded her act. I don't even know her name."[14]

Second, there is the case of an event visualized but framed as being unrelated to Beijing Spring: the first major student protests in China in 1989. According to one of the few reports, "thousands of Chinese" marched through the streets of the city of Nanjing near the Hehai University, where the violence and protests first began.[15] Ostensibly, the student protesters had one object of anger as reported by Nicholas Kristof of the *New York Times*: "The latest troubles started when two African men brought Chinese dates to a Christmas Eve dance in the eastern city of Nanjing, touching off a brawl that has led to racial confrontations in at least four cities." *Newsweek* reported the students chanting "'Kill the black devils!'" while "attack[ing] the Africans' dorm, smashing windows, destroying possessions and shouting." In their analysis of the events, news writers said that the demonstrations were partly due to traditional Chinese xenophobia, but were also indications of the resentment felt by the Chinese towards foreigners who were accorded special status and who received additional funding from the government. Kristof explained that the riots indicated a disenchantment with foreigners among many Chinese, concluding, "Chinese are fed up with seeing foreigners [including Americans] . . . treated as gods."

Neither of these events produced icons or had icons imposed on them. Just as news industries frame what is and what is not connected to an event, historians of society and of media decide what should be part of the complexity they claim to more thoroughly analyze.[16] Neither did the incidents become major news stories covered in a variety of publications, prominently, with frequency, or as the subject of commentary by discourse elites. Some attention was paid, but in the measure of amount of words and images, and its prominence in telecasts, newspapers and magazines, it was a minor story. In other words, in journalism and subsequent historiography, these events were not *framed* as being relevant to the Tiananmen events as they occurred, or even in retrospect. That they should have is not unreasonable to suggest. The question is why so many people, including historians and reporters, failed to create associations between these incidents and the Tiananmen events. Why didn't the tank-crushing-delicate-young-girl image become an object of focus, or fame, of celebrity, or outrage? And why weren't the *first* major student demonstrations in China of 1989 linked to the larger eruptions a few months later? By suggesting answers to these questions, I will outline some of the mechanics of icon creation.

Of Chai Ling's story there is no independent corroboration, though it is certainly possible, given the widespread testimony and the frequency of protester/government clashes in the final days, that this event did occur. We can only speculate how it would have looked in a photograph. A picture, taken from the same angle and with the same clarity as the more famous man-with-tank image, would have had iconic potential. The outrage that so many Westerners claimed to feel at the famous image would perhaps have been even more clearly expressed toward an image of a young girl run down by the "forces of oppression." The pale young woman as victim has a strong history as a generic icon, especially within propaganda posters that purport to display the barbarity of an enemy.[17]

That this girl's story, if it occurred, is not one of the great icons of Tiananmen is an indication that although visual images may not have strong, direct, and unambiguous effects on elites and publics, still the visual image itself is a useful, but not absolute, precondition for outrage. In an interactive fashion, those events which gain the attention of discourse elites are also those which have the most cameras trained on them, and thus are likely to produce icons. But even in those cases—and Tiananmen was one par excellence—many pictures are not taken. The demand of the marketplace of news is for the strong visual; any incident that does not provide such a visual is inherently less newsworthy.[18] Secondly, as noted, one of the criteria of the icon of outrage is instantaneousness. "Great" news photos emerge immediately, without delay. If, from the camera of some dissident, smuggled out of China years after the fact, a picture of a girl being crushed by a tank emerges, would it become an icon?

Why the anti-African riots and protests were minor incidents in U.S. news and the historiographical framing of 1989 is less obvious. Any written work describing the protest of Chinese students of 1989 should logically begin its first chapter with these, the first protests. However, the anti-African demonstrations were, by the standards of news values, a minor story in the news stream. The events occurred in a distant land, not in the capital but in a region not immediately accessible to Beijing-based Western correspondents.[19] The riots waxed and waned quickly;

their results included property destruction but not death, and the pictures were all after the fact. The issues at hand did not seem to hold any pressing concerns for ordinary Americans or U.S. foreign policy makers. Indeed, it is revealing that the "lessons" of the riots that Nicholas Kristof draws for the readers were an attempt to connect the events to Western interests.

More important, in the West, most writers who empathized with the student protesters, even those claiming objectivity and a critical (if not unsympathetic) stance toward them, chose to completely ignore this prologue. Their reasons are understandable. As will be discussed below, most China observers (including journalists) felt strong kinship with the marchers in the spring of 1989. They would no doubt claim that the anti-African riots, although perhaps symptomatic of students' frustrations about the status quo, were not related to the democracy protests arising a few months later.[20] Beginning a book intended for a Western audience on a protest movement by describing Chinese students as rioting xenophobes whose actions were more reminiscent of the American south in the 1920s than Berkeley in the 1960s would be to create a negative frame for the reader. The protests to come, full of their positive associations with American and Western ideals of democracy, freedom, tolerance, and opposition to tyranny, would be undermined by the association with racism, hatred, and persecution.

It is also revealing that in apologias by the Chinese government and its allies for its actions on June 4 against the larger body of protesters, nowhere do they refer to the earlier protests. It is perhaps part of the poor public relations skills of the Chinese government that they did not more readily use a tool of defamation so popular in the West, accusing one's enemy of racism. The absence of this charge is also probably due to the government's view that these incidents were not important at all, and because part of its strategy was that the students were tools of foreigners. It would thus be a contradiction to claim that the movement was born of opposition to foreign presence and influence. Also, the general propaganda line of the Chinese government was that the democracy protests of the spring were anomalies. Reducing the sense of repetitive disorders throughout the year was imperative.

THE MAN AND THE TANKS

In the years since its enactment and creation, the image of the man blocking the tanks has become the supericon of Tiananmen—the "icon of the revolution," claimed the London *Guardian* of June 4, 1992—and one that, at least in the eyes of most Western observers, is a natural sign of the outrages perpetrated by the hard-line, Communist government of the People's Republic of China. The similarities between it and the Saigon execution photo are notable. In both cases, the same incident was captured by multiple visual journalists working for different media. Charles Cole of *Newsweek*, Jeff Widener of the AP, and Stuart Franklin of Magnum took still pictures of the incident from the same location, the Beijing Hotel. ABC and BBC news crews also filmed the incident. In both Saigon and Beijing, the icon contained no Americans; the conflict portrayed was of natives against each other, a seeming violation of the rule that American news is about what Americans do. However, a man and a column of tanks on a diagonal photo and video of a wide, empty boulevard—of such simple elements icons may be born. Whereas the Viet Cong suspect faced away from General Loan, here the young man confronts the force of movement and nemesis. In the Saigon execution frame, from screen left are thrust the vectors of force of the action, the outstretched arm and the gun. In the Tiananmen image, the active force comes from screen right. In the former image, the power of the state with a gun is victorious; the blocking object is literally blown away. In the icon of 1989, the blocking agent is victorious, but *only in the icon*, for minutes later, as the man was hustled away, the tanks passed, and, of course, the government crackdown proceeded.

Both pictures have that essential simplicity of opposing forces that seems to appear in many icons of outrage. Both icons also arrived at times that made them available for the news cycle of major events. Like the Saigon picture which appeared just as the first "shocking" news of Tet arrived, the man and tanks incident appeared on the big news day from Tiananmen, just after the crackdown, while most other sources of pictures via satellite feeds had been cut off.

The icon's celebrity and prominence were indisputable. It is instructive to look at a few of its manifestations to understand how it was employed as an emblematic icon of Tiananmen and how journalists (and the president of the United States) framed its significance and connotation.[21] Like all icons as well, the picture is not a solitary object, but rather surrounded by discourse. Some of this discourse is directly associated with it: the words that we hear on the telecast or see on the printed page upon which the icon is presented. Some of the discourse context is what we have heard or read before the encounter with that image. Other discourse contexts arise from cultural associations and perhaps even primordial human archetypes. In addition, icons must be judged in relation to the pictures that surround them in the immediate text in which they appear, but also those images that anticipate and precede them. The man defying the tanks appeared on June 5, the day following the Chinese government's crackdown. Western viewers of this image, then, were previously shown pictures suggesting the brutality of the authorities (scenes of wounded and dead protesters, troops marching through a burning city), and told of the thousands of deaths that occurred at Tiananmen Square. These prior contexts offer all the more reason why a picture of a man successfully blocking a row of tanks would seem more resonant and impressive.

On CNN's June 5 broadcast, correspondents in Beijing phoned in reports that fighting was spreading outside the city and that other army units would attack those at the Square because of their "outrage" at the civilian deaths. CNN reporter Mike Chinoy's closing words over several still pictures of chaos in Beijing were: "It's a strong indication that many in the Chinese army are as appalled at the carnage caused by certain elements of the army as the population is as well." In short, the defiance of the man before the tanks was primed on CNN to be an example of a consensus of public rebellion, possibly including elements of the Chinese army itself. Even though the man stood alone, he had the support of the masses on his side; also, the tank commander hesitated to take violent action. Susan Brooke, in the CNN studio, continued, "China's civilian population has been confronting military force with courage and little else. Although it is still dangerous in the streets, Beijing's residents continue to defy the occupying forces today. CNN's Tom Mintier reports that often this defiance came in the face of overwhelming odds."

Tom Mintier began his narration by noting: "It was yet another night of defiance by the civilian population of Beijing." These comments were expressed over still photographs of troop movements through wrecked cars and burning buses. Mintier continued, "And another attempt by the army to snuff out all forms of resistance with guns and bullets. Buses were turned into flaming roadblocks, but military tanks cut through them like a knife through butter." Then the famous sequence begins at the moment the vehicles rumble up in confrontation. Mintier narrates: "But the world witnessed a daring act by one man against insurmountable odds. Armed with only courage, standing in the middle of the street facing more than a dozen tanks bearing down on him, he refused to move. He demonstrated the will to resist beyond any words that could ever be spoken." We watch as the lead tank shifts screen left, trying to go around the man in the white shirt, but he jumps and shuffles to the side to block the maneuver. "Several times the tank attempted to go around the man, only to be confronted once again, then climbing on top of the tank to look directly into the eyes of the driver." At this point, Mintier falls silent as he allows, as promised, the pictures to go beyond words.

Mintier comments without a hint of irony, but it is rare on network news for any pictures to be allowed to speak for themselves for even the briefest time. Interestingly, we are not allowed to watch the full extent of the drama. The tape is interspersed with jump cuts, where obviously a studio editor decided that watching more than 10 seconds of the man on top of the tank would bore the American audience. All icons are thus abbreviated. We rarely see the still photos taken before and after a well-known picture; and even the "decisive moment" is often cropped. Likewise, the full-length video of a famous scene is seldom played out.22 This, as in the case of the Rodney King video (which was nearly always abridged), may affect interpretations of the image's meaning. We do not see what is behind icons; what happened before and after them is often edited from our view. This is a convention of visual journalism; given the brief time devoted to most news packages or stories it is also considered a necessity.

As the video continues, in the background we hear apparently supportive and concerned shouting and whistling. It is not clear if this comes from the street or from reporters and others in the hotel. Mintier resumes: "Despite the sound of gunfire, the man refused to allow the tanks to pass." The edited video proceeds as the man climbs down from the tank; the tanks try to go forward, he stops them again. There is another, this time very noticeable, jump cut, and suddenly other civilians stand around the defiant man, and in a still picture sequence we see him taken away. Mintier continues: "Finally, several other people ran into the street carrying a white flag and dragged the man to safety. The column of tanks continued down the street."

After this, completing the immediate discourse frame, there are other scenes of captured military vehicles, people stoning army trucks, wounded participants and observers, students flashing the "V for victory" sign, while Mintier tells us that the death toll will surely run into the thousands. He concludes: "But the images of the past few days will never be forgotten, by people around the world, but most importantly by the people of China, who have watched in horror as their own army launched a slaughter of immense proportions."

The June 5 NBC Special Report, *China In Crisis*, begins with the statement by George Bush that opens this chapter. Then the screen dissolves to the video of the man outmaneuvering the swiveling tank. Bush continues as a voice-over to these images. Tom Brokaw, after a montage of other images from Tiananmen, begins: "That was President George Bush, in a Washington speech tonight, describing the most poignant scene of the day in the turmoil which is now China." The anchorman enacts NBC's similar discourse frame around the images that we have just seen by also reporting—what would only later be revealed as completely false stories—that Chinese premier Li Peng was wounded in an assassination attempt and that other military units converged to attack those who had crushed the student movement. Later in the broadcast, we see the man and tank images again, overlaid by the commentary of correspondent Keith Miller, who notes that the Tiananmen area is considered sacred to the Chinese. "And so those brave, or foolhardy, citizens who now confront the army at risk of their lives do so with an outrage that comes from their understanding of what it is to be Chinese."

In the same vein, ABC uses the man and tanks image as an introduction to the June 5 *Nightline*. For three or four seconds, there is no commentary as we watch the man confronting the tank, as Chinese instrumental music plays over the scene. Correspondent Jackie Judd narrates: "At an intersection, a protester suddenly ran into the middle of the street, and in front of the oncoming tanks. The tanks stopped, and the lead tank tried moving to one side and then to the other side to avoid hitting him. But the protester kept running in the same pattern." The image wipes to a funeral procession through the streets of Beijing. Ted Koppel then reports the stories of Li Peng being shot in the leg, of Deng Xiaoping's rumored death, and of a possible civil war developing. Koppel, demonstrating a more natural caution than many of his colleagues, notes that many of these stories "may have more of a basis in wishful thinking of angry demonstrators than in any reality." The broadcast then shows a compilation of scenes from Beijing including many of destruction, and of wounded and dead people in hospitals. Jackie Judd again narrates: "Shortly before noon Monday, Beijing time, a column of tanks moved out of the Square and they began heading east in the direction of the Beijing Hotel." She repeats the above narration, but this time her full report is aired, and she concludes:

Finally the lead tank, the rest of the convoy naturally stopped [*sic*]. And when the convoy finally did stop moving, the protester suddenly climbed on top of the tank. He stayed there for about 15 to 30 seconds. When I saw that moment, I knew what it meant when the protesters had said they were willing to die for their cause, because what he did was such a remarkable and bold and brazen[23] act of defiance. After that 15 to 30 seconds, he climbed down off the tank. At that point, these protesters, these other protesters . . . who were watching this incredible scene from the sides of the road, they rushed onto the center of the street and pulled this fellow away, out of harm's way.[24]

The picture also was replicated prominently and frequently in news publications. It appeared on the front page of the *New York Times* of June 6. The caption read: "A drama within a drama on the streets of Beijing. An unarmed Chinese civilian halting the progress of a tank convoy heading for Tiananmen square yesterday. He later climbed on the lead tank and spoke to its crew before being hustled away by friends." A commentator also argued that the image showed that "one man can make a difference" and "in its quiet way, this little confrontation seemed to symbolize the fragility of the Government's position."25

In *Newsweek*, the picture was shown on June 19, where the process of iconization was already evident in the caption: "'A single student standing in front of a tank': Among the indelible images of the upheaval in Tiananmen, a lone demonstrator blocks an armored column on Changan avenue." The picture is repeated, across a two-page spread in the end of year issue of December 12, 1989, beginning a "People of the Year" roundup. The caption, alluding to the book by John F. Kennedy, reads, "In Beijing, a lone youth showed a profile in courage." In a block of text about the changes and upheavals in the world that year another comment reads: "One after another, the images defied belief: Near Tiananmen Square, a lone man armed only with courage faced down a column of tanks."

The picture appears four times in *Time* magazine in 1989. First, on June 19, it is the cover image, captioned "Revolt against Communism: China, Poland, USSR." Inside, illustrating a special section written by Strobe Talbott, titled "Defiance," the picture appears in a two-page spread. The actual image is a different one, showing the man with his hands at his sides. An extended caption, which also introduces the section, reads:

One man against an army. The power of the people vs. the power of the gun. There he stood, implausibly resolute in his thin white shirt, an unknown Chinese man facing down a lumbering column of tanks. For a moment that will be long remembered, the lone man defined the struggle of China's citizens. "Why are you here?" he shouted at the silent steel hulk. "You have done nothing but create misery. My city is in chaos because of you." The brief encounter between the man and the tank captured an epochal event in the lives of 1.1 billion

Chinese: the state clanking with menace, swiveling right and left with uncertainty, is halted in its tracks because the people got in its way, and because it got in theirs.

The previous cover appears in miniature again in *Time* of July 10, in the letters column. Sonny King of Mesa, Arizona provides a new caption, "The People's Liberation Army has finally saved the People's Republic of China from the people." A sidebar, titled "Hero of the Year," notes that "the lone Chinese protester who faced down a column of tanks has already garnered 35 votes from our readers for *Time's* Man of the Year for 1989." Finally, as in *Newsweek*, the picture, this time Stuart Franklin's photo of the man with his arms at his sides, appears as the first image in the "Year in Pictures" section. The introduction to the section, which is also the caption for the picture, reads: "Images: a revolutionary year produces visions of freedom, defeat and resolve. Though distant and grainy, this photograph of a Chinese man standing down a tyrannical regime is the most extraordinary image of the year. It is flesh against steel, mortality against the onrush of terror, the very real stuff of courage."

As is evident, especially from the language of *Time* and *Newsweek*, the iconization of the picture was solidified almost immediately. As a final laurel in its crown, the picture was featured as the cover photo in *Life* magazine's "Year in Pictures" section. "Who can fathom such bravery?" queried *Washington Post* columnist Richard Cohen, a few days after the events.26 A senior AP photo editor said it was one of those few photos that was able "to distill an entire event into one image."27 Another writer claimed it showed "one lone man against the nation state . . . with the whole world watching."28 "It was a magnificent gesture of defiance," commented the *Washington Post*'s media critic Tom Shales.29 While photographs rarely speak for themselves, what is attributed to still images and video of the man before the tanks by this range of commentators is dramatic and even lyrical. Discourse elites instantly imposed a consensus that the image was powerful and evocative of universal ideals and aspirations. It would be superfluous to dissect the metaphors and the potent descriptive language they employ. What is clear is that almost everyone reporting or commenting on the news of June 5 wanted to symbolically stand with that man, and predicted that his actions would affect political developments to come.

POST–TIANANMEN VIEWS

The metonymic imposition of the news reports is that the image *was* Tiananmen; this was the picture that "captured an epochal event in the lives of 1.1 billion Chinese." Only in retrospect have questions been asked about what exactly this image stood for, what it represented, and whether the original, unambiguous framing was the only possible way to understand it. If the picture summed up Tiananmen, and indeed summed up the revolts against Communism throughout the world in 1989, we can ask what exactly was summed up about them. If it was "une scène emblematique," as French journalist Alain Peyrefitte argued shortly after the events, we can ask, of what? This question is relevant because no meanings are *naturally* tied to any pictures and no image is born a metonym. How did later commentary frame the picture and incident?

In subsequent popular culture and histories, others have thrust greatness upon the moment. In a PBS documentary on Tiananmen, the narrator intones: "On the morning of June 5th there was a moment that would come to symbolize all that had happened during those spring days. He disappeared into the crowd afterwards and no one knows where he is now. No one is even certain of his name. But for the millions who saw this scene all over the world, its meaning was clear. Here was human hope and courage challenging the remorseless machinery of state power."[30] It has been described as "the image many Westerners think of first when they remember the Tiananmen massacre."[31] As previously noted, Thomas Hine, the multimedia editor for *Bartlett's Familiar Quotations Expanded*, included the image on a CD-ROM because "it was a striking image of the individual confronting power."[32] Andy Grundberg, the photography critic of the *New York Times*, wondered which had more impact, the still photos of the man and tanks or the news film. He concluded that the video images "had an emotional immediacy that still burns in the mind."[33] The picture was the cover image for Time-Life's book *Massacre in Beijing: China's Struggle for Democracy*, published only a few months after the incidents.[34] An eyewitness report on the "Peking massacre" published in Taiwan contains the image and captions it, "Behold him, single in the field, tearfully facing a column."[35] In 1994, Jacques Andrieu claimed in a French magazine investigation of the role of journalists at Tiananmen that in his country very few people recalled anything about the events save that one image.

The picture is also cited as an icon within discourse across the political spectrum, from presidents to analysts to protesters. President Bush commented at a White House news conference that the defiance of the dissident and the "restraint" of the tank soldiers convinced him that "the forces of democracy are going to overcome these unfortunate events in Tiananmen Square."[36] He also predicted, "That image, I think, is going to be with us a long time."[37] These remarks are revealing. Kathleen Hall Jamieson has argued, "The eloquent president is both historian and herald who has a talent for making concise, memorable phrases of the raw consensual stuff in the rhetorical environment."[38] The icon of outrage, however, is available to all those who seek to associate their words with images, not just the eloquent. Bush, like any member of the discourse elite, understood the stuff of which icons are made, and felt compelled to reply to the pictures other elites were citing, but he also served as an *icon* herald.[39] This was not a conspiracy, but rather the recognition of shared conventions of what a striking image arriving at the right moment in the news cycle can be subjected to. The picture, then, has been and will be with us for a long time, because Bush and other elites chose for it to be.

Other political figures at the time and since used the icon as an illustration of their political arguments. When a week after the crackdown, the Chinese vice consul in San Francisco defected, he later stated, "One thing I carried with me everywhere was a series of pictures of the man in front of the tank in Beijing. They were an inspiration to me, and more important than my luggage."[40] Andrew B. Brick, a policy analyst with the Heritage Foundation's Asian Studies Center, declared in a speech that, "Nothing captures this spirit of Tiananmen better than the brief encounter between the man and the tank. There he stood, implausibly resolute in his thin white shirt, an individual facing down a column of armor. For a moment that will be long remembered, that lone man defined the struggle of China's citizens."[41] While visiting Argentina, the president of China, Yang Shangkun, was greeted with protesters showing the man with a tank image.[42] In December of 1990 a Chinese trade delegation to Seattle was met with pro-Tibet demonstrators waving "the famous photograph of a man blocking a column of tanks on a Beijing street last year."[43] On the World Wide Web the picture is employed at several sites, either with human rights concerns or for dissidents in China. On one site run by "Support Democracy in China" and "Christus Rex et Reemptor Mundi" ["Christ is King and Redeemer of the World"] a pictorial history of Tiananmen events begins with the icon and asks: "Can a single human being make a difference? Can he or she stop the forces of evil dead in their tracks? A courageous young man captured the imagination of the whole world, when he single-handedly stopped the advance of a tank column by standing in its way."[44]

The importance of the image is also accorded by historiography about China in 1989, much of it remarking on the power of media. It is the "one quintessential moment" named by China historian Orville Schell as "perhaps the most enduring image of the whole seven weeks [of protests]."[45] Craig Calhoun, in his analysis of the student movement, writes, "One gesture of resistance from these days stands out . . . etching the image of defiance into international memory."[46] In another history of the events the author comments: "China's youth spoke . . . to fellow Chinese and to all people with peaceful protests whose images, caught by foreign print and television journalists, transfixed the world: three student representatives kneeling to offer a petition; hunger strikers lying weak and nearly motionless under a blazing sun; and the lone figure blocking a column of tanks from advancing."[47] Another writer proclaims that it "would become one of the lasting images of the rape of Beijing."[48] In a similar view, the young man was the "one person the whole world remembers."[49] Kwan Ha Yim, in his survey of Deng Xiaoping's rule over China, called it "an isolated incident that was widely portrayed by the Western media as a symbol of the entire upheaval in the capital."[50] In his history of Tiananmen, Timothy Brook deems it "the most memorable piece of defiance."[51] Likewise, others argue that it was "a dramatic event [that] crystallized the defiance of the students."[52]

The image has several possible primordial and cultural associations that are often struck with icons. Orville Schell saw in the young man a "Horatio-at-the-bridge."[53] Indeed, the picture can be made to tap into many deep-seated Western ideals and slogans such as the triumph of the individual and the dignity of the human spirit. Depending on one's cultural realm of knowledge, other allusions can be imposed. Certainly, the man can stand for David, and the tanks as the modern heirs of Goliath of Gath; or, as Schell alludes, here is Horatius Cocles at the Sublician bridge defending Rome from the chariots of Etruria. Here is Roland—with satchel instead of horn—among the rear guard of Charlemagne's army, standing against the Moorish legions. Here is King Arthur, standing his ground in the face of the hordes of Mordred. Here is Leonidas of Sparta, in the battle that saved Western culture, standing among his few picked men against the might of Persia. Fans of Jack London may see Ernest Everhard fighting the oligarchs in *The Iron Heel.* Or, perhaps more visually resonant, here is the hero of a thousand western movies, confronted by ranks of evildoers: one man, standing alone at high noon on the city street.54 The icon can also suggest another familiar theme in Western culture—the human fighting the mechanical monster. Do we see Charlie Chaplin's struggles with the great machine of industrial capitalism in *Modern Times*, or innumerable science fiction films where humans confront mechanical monsters? Does it trigger the Luddite impulse to a revolt against the iron world of machines that rule our lives? Icons of outrage such as the man facing the tanks at Tiananmen, therefore, are seen to hold power because they are ready vessels for the attachment of deep cultural and historical allusions.55

A consensus exists in the West that the picture was important, well known, and influential, and that the event was a metonym of Beijing Spring; but is no other interpretation possible? If everyone agrees an image means something, then must they be correct? Are the meanings of images arrived at by majority discourse, or pluralities, or is unanimity required to avoid any trace of ambiguity? In dictatorships where only one approved meaning is attached to an event, but people, in their own minds, may refute the official story, how may we judge the consensus of truth?

Consider that this image, so neatly fitting into an icon of outrage in the West, is employed as a *counter-myth* by the government of the PRC, that is, "presented as 'proof' of the enormous restraint that the military showed under stress."56 Premier Li Peng was considered one of the hard-liners at Tiananmen. He was a Party man, born to a martyr of the revolution, and raised in the family of Zhou EnLai. His allies in the hierarchy have always been among the most staunchly Communist of the old guard. In 1992, he was interviewed by French journalist Alain Peyrefitte, who told the premier that French public opinion, while long sympathetic to China, had turned hostile in the wake of Tiananmen. Peng answered by arguing,

But it is exactly because these modern techniques exist that the truth was gravely contorted. You have no doubt seen the sequence where a man, when a tank bears down on him, stands and persuades it to stop. That image indicated to President George Bush that that man was truly extraordinary, to have been able, all alone, to stop a column of tanks. But there is another explanation. If one examines this scene objectively, doesn't it show the humanity exhibited by the

Chinese Army, the orders to act gently issued by its commanders? As if one man could stop a tank by himself![57]

Likewise, Che Muqi, a pro-government Chinese academic, wrote the revealingly titled *Beijing Turmoil: More than Meets the Eye* shortly after the events, and interpreted the metonymy of the image contrary to most Western assumptions:

This man stood in front of the tanks. When the first tank turned to one side trying to dodge him, he also went to that side to block it. The tank did not crush him, or open fire on him. No matter how the American media distorted the facts by using this photo, any one with any common sense would wonder how a man with nothing in his hands could stop a column of tanks. Isn't this proof that the martial law troops had exercised great restraint?[58]

In an interview, a Chinese government press official expressed a similar sentiment:

It's all in how you look at it, and what you want to see. . . . That famous picture of the student standing in front of the tank is seen around the world as the courage of one individual against military might and force. We see it differently. To me it is a symbol of the tolerance of the Army. The soldiers were very tolerant during most of the six weeks of the uprising until provoked in the streets at the very end.[59]

On PBS's *Front-Line*, another official of the Chinese government argued that, "Anyone with common sense can see that if our tanks were determined to move on, this lone scoundrel could never have stopped them. This scene recorded on videotape flies in the face of Western propaganda. It proves that our soldiers exercised the highest degree of restraint."[60] At first glance, it seems almost incredible to make such a claim. "Deux versions incompatibles," Peyrefitte notes, then asks: "Quelle est la bonne?"[61] Is this incompatibility a sign of contradictions in truth, the failure of an icon to show the contradictions, or that pictures are often able to accept contradictory interpretations?

WHO WAS THE MAN?

The identity of the man also has relevance. A *Time* magazine report of 1990 claimed he was a 19-year-old student and "son of a factory worker" and stated that he was "sentenced to ten years' imprisonment for his nonviolent intervention."[62] More recent reports say he was a 26-year-old printer. In an interview, Chinese premier Zhang Zemin reported that the man had probably been executed,[63] but later, in direct contrast, stated, "I think never killed." Interestingly, the man is rarely identified by name. His body and action have made him generic and his personality is stripped; such is the fate of most icon dwellers. Why is his name unimportant, but who he is in terms of social class, age, and profession so vital that such details are almost always provided? Why do we not know if he was married, or how many sisters and brothers he had, or what part of China he came from, or, more important, his present location? Like General Loan to some extent and the Viet Cong suspect and the Sudanese girl completely, the main subject of an icon of outrage, especially if not American, is largely left to be a cipher. Indeed, in understanding what metonymic allusions were chosen for the image, the identity of the man should be very relevant.

Why was he initially deemed a student? Why is he still portrayed and framed as a symbol of the student uprising and not of, for example, the frustration of Beijing residents and workers over economic destabilization brought on by increasing corruption and the nascent Western-style market economy? The answer, of course, was that this was a student movement, and thus it only made sense that the icon that defined it should include the impersonal symbols of the state and the personalized embodiment of the student protesters. Being a worker instead of a student makes his role somewhat problematic, but only if the context of Tiananmen is better understood. His worker status could have been selected as an *ironic* encapsulation of the ambiguous role of ordinary non-student Chinese during Beijing Spring. Subsequent scholarship has suggested that this is an "untold" story.[64] There was a great deal of tension and little communication between the student and worker communities, at least until the last days of the movement. On many issues, a gap which neither group seemed eager to close appeared between students and workers.[65] The origins of the rift are multi-contextual. In the changing economy of China, students and intellectuals seemed to be the group with the most to lose in the transition to a market-based system. Students and teachers have traditionally held a place of honor in China; intellectuals in general often saw themselves as natural leaders of the people. The worker-student split may have been more conscious and intentional on the part of the students who saw themselves as a class apart from ordinary laborers and craftsmen.[66]

Contributing to this elitism may be an officious interpretation of Communist doctrine that valued highly the role of a vanguard of intellectuals. In most Communist seizures of power such cohorts, while giving ritualistic deference to the ideal of worker-led revolution, formed the main block of the party apparatus leading the people to their "own best interests." In his Tiananmen memoirs, Michael Duke, who is wholly sympathetic to the dissident movement, quotes a student arguing that it was the duty of "elite intellectuals" to lead the way for the people.[67] Indeed, much post-Tiananmen scholarship has suggested that the "Democracy" movement was elitist in character, not seeking strong bonds with ordinary workers. Anita Chan and Jonathan Unger claimed that the entire student movement was characterized, until the last weeks, by a tendency to keep the workers at arm's length.[68] In one case it was reported that students actually linked arms and hands to stop workers joining them.[69] In many student speeches, the connection to workers was ignored or accorded marginal value.[70]

American news media, focusing on the students, tended to ignore the role of the workers in the uprising, especially in its crucial last weeks.[71] As is often the case in historiography, the students and the intellectuals were also the ones most accessible, most likely to speak English, most likely to know how to provide quotes ("give me liberty or give me death") and symbols (the Statue of Liberty) which were easily transferred across borders. Workers—and certainly peasants—were less likely to be vocal, or to know how to speak to foreign journalists. Nevertheless, many workers seemed eager to help when they could, engaging in labor strikes, and actually fighting against the army in the final days. One observer concludes, "Considering the lack of student initiative, the extent of worker participation was really rather remarkable."[72] Moreover, despite all the attention and strident public appeals made on the students' behalf, it was the workers who suffered the greatest indignities and persecution after Tiananmen.[73] By one investigation, at least eight times as many workers and other civilians were killed as students.[74] In any case, the absence of a worker-student alliance—and indeed almost any reference to the vast rural peasantry—suggests that the student movement had much more limited aims than those imposed on them by some in the West. That an *ironic* frame was not imposed on the man vs. tanks image reveals how strongly biased were Western media.

Finally, the latest developments (as this book was going to press) further confuse the situation, but create a strong parallel with the case of the Sudanese girl and the Viet Cong suspect. It is now clear, according to recent news reports and testimony from Chinese dissidents and others, that we know even less about "Wang Weilin" than ever. Some stories claim that this name was a fiction, and that the man remains unidentified. It has never been confirmed, apparently, whether he was a factory worker or a student. A Hong Kong-based human rights group has announced that "Wang" is in hiding and was never arrested. Reportedly, the Chinese government undertook a specially-directed search for him in the post-Tiananmen roundups, but of 400 people listed with his name, none could be identified as the man who stood in front of the tanks. Other activists, however, report that he has been executed extrajudicially, and thus was not on any roster of arrestees. Yet "Wang" is still listed by Human Rights Watch/Asia as a political prisoner in China. The U.S. State Department *Country Reports on Human Rights Practices for 1990* did not confirm whether he was arrested, in hiding, or dead. Of such indeterminacy and debate are icons made.[75]

WHO (IN THE WORLD) WAS WATCHING?

That Tiananmen was a spectacular media event is unquestionable. It seems incontrovertible that the events proceeded as the "whole world watched." Yet, as in the case of Tet and General Loan, this may be a projection—the first person effect—where discourse elites watching the Tiananmen events assumed that everyone else watched as well, and reacted in the same way. Certainly, the phrase "the whole world is watching" seemed a familiar one in discourse, both contemporary and historical, about Tiananmen. Jonathan Alter wrote, "If TV's presence doesn't actually aid democracy, it may make the cruelest of repressions harder to inflict. Eventually, the whole world will see."[76] Ed Bark of

Dallas Morning News argued: "The video messenger seemingly sees all. Pro-democracy students are crushed by China's army at Tiananmen Square on live television, earning China universal condemnation. China's attempts at damage control are thwarted by the indelible global video memory of a defiant man standing alone and unarmed before a column of tanks."[77] Another writer suggested, "Like the anti-Vietnam war protesters in Chicago during the Democratic National Convention in 1968, the students in Tiananmen Square were aware that 'the whole world is watching.'"[78] Frank Tan, in discussing the impact of the events on Chinese journalism, asserted as well that the "the whole world was watching via the eyes of the foreign press corps."[79] Historian Craig Calhoun recalls viewing a protest march on May 4:

I watched brigades of students from the main universities marshal in northwest Beijing, carrying banners and signs, a few wearing sashes or headbands bearing slogans. . . . [S]tudents knew that "the whole world was watching," and they sported signs in French ("Vive la liberté") and English ("Give me liberty or give me death") to attract the television cameras and communicate with citizens in Europe and the United States.[80]

But did China earn universal condemnation? This will be explored below. In one work, several China scholars agreed that the student hunger strike "aroused the sympathy of the whole nation and the whole world; even the government was forced to make conciliatory moves behind the scenes."[81] A Western witness to Tiananmen, Robin Munro, perceived that reporters were affected by their assumption that "the whole world was watching, and reporters often saw themselves as guarantors of the students' safety."[82]

Many of these premises were, in retrospect, unwarranted. The attention the media gave to Tiananmen was much greater than the attention paid by the public. Lynn E. Gutstadt, vice-president for audience research at CNN, has noted that, in tracking the ratings of various types of news events over time: "The high-interest news events, those that make the performance line jump, all were either domestic U.S. events, such as earthquakes, hurricanes, or hijacking of U.S. aircraft, or they were international events where American lives or interests were at risk. The international events that many might consider critical, even historic, such as the Tienamen [*sic*] Square massacre or the fall of the Berlin Wall, get a relatively small increase from the domestic audience."[83] The Tiananmen events reached a ratings high of approximately 2.3. In contrast, the San Francisco earthquake received a rating of 4. In other words, when Americans are not involved, the public tends to tune out. As suggested in the analysis of the Tet image, the American public is not necessarily interested in what news elites find important.[84] The "many" Gutstadt refers to are, of course, her cohort or reference group. The ratings share was so low that it could very well have been entirely composed of elites: people in media themselves, those in the academy and people in business and the political structure who are the group identified by political scientists as being interested in foreign affairs.

The elite world—those who made up the cohort that write about China or foreign policy (or news pictures)—was watching. The shock, drama, and conflict of Tiananmen, thus, did not seem to attract a new audience to the screen; the usual suspects were probably watching. In short, there is evidence that the whole (wider) world *could* have watched Tiananmen—it certainly was shown on all channels and print sources— but there is no evidence that they did. A TV rating of 2.3 does not represent "the world." There is greater evidence that the whole world was watching when it was revealed that Kristin shot J.R. on *Dallas*. To cite another example, the closing arguments of the O.J. Simpson murder trial had a 4.5 share on CNN. This is not to say that the general public ignored or was unaware of what was occurring at Tiananmen; rather that those events were more likely to be of greater and keener interest to discourse elites.

Another problematic issue that undercuts the alleged "power" of the man and tanks image is that the military, as the Chinese government claims, displayed no brutality. While there are many photographs of dead people, both civilians and soldiers, from Beijing in early June, the omnipresent Western video cameras missed the slaughter, if there was one. My students recalled seeing bloody clashes of tanks and civilians, but in reality none were ever shown on American television.[85] If anything, the absence of Western journalists at the Square—most had retreated to nearby hotels—occasioned a *mea culpa* by some. John Simpson of the BBC argued: "Someone should have been there when the massacre took place. . . . We filmed as the lights in the square were switched off at four a.m. They were switched on again forty minutes later, when the troops and the tanks moved forward to the Monument [of People's Heroes statue group] itself, shooting first in the air and then, again, directly at the students themselves, so that the steps of the Monument and the heroic reliefs which decorated it were smashed by bullets."[86] Others noted, "The problem with this [Simpson's] report is that the Monument and the entire lower half of Tiananmen Square are hidden from view from the Beijing Hotel, half a mile away."[87] There, many American journalists, including camera crews from all three networks, watched the proceedings that were in their field of vision. "Once the shooting began, the camera crews were ordered back to the cover of the Beijing Hotel. The equipment was simply too unwieldy for anyone to operate while under fire," explained ABC producer Kyle Gibson, who went to Tiananmen Square and kept his network informed with walkie-talkie.[88] It was "television without pictures" from the "bunker" of the hotel, recalled ABC correspondent Jackie Judd.[89] Pictures in some cases emerged from Tiananmen through the phone lines, via image-scanning "pixelator" devices; the image of the man standing against a column of tanks was wired to NBC in New York in this way.

Interestingly, one characteristic of most icons of outrage is that the parasocial distance between the image and the viewer is often restricted. Getting up close has always been the professional *sine qua non* of news photography. Robert Capa, the legendary war photographer, once noted that if a picture wasn't good enough, it's because you weren't close enough. This dictum is still a sacred tenet in photojournalism courses; it is hard to name more than a few long-distance icons. However, every picture of the great defining icon of Tiananmen, "the most extraordinary image of the year," was taken at an extreme distance from hotel windows and balconies. We can, perhaps, regard this as a failure to get "up close" to the subjects of Tiananmen. This is a discourse frame that was *not* imposed on the man-and-the-tanks picture. To have done so would have been to nullify the basic premise of the "we bring you the world" mantra of the news industry.[90]

Finally, this question of the journalists' distance may have had an unforeseen outcome. One possible scenario is that the worldwide press coverage of the students' protests, of earlier incidents of government troops being turned back, of police being disarmed by ordinary people, by the seeming powerlessness of the Chinese state to exert control over its own children, had caused the authorities to lose face, to be embarrassed in the sight of the rest of the world. What if journalists had been standing right there at the edge of the street in full view of the tank commander? Would the outcome have been the same? Would the tanks have held back and waited for the man to be pulled away? Or would the similarities between the Saigon shooting image and the pictures of the man and the column of tanks at Tiananmen have merged in the closure of the incident as well? Would the great defining icon of Tiananmen have been a man, not successfully defying the iron chariots of state authority, but, like the young girl of the alleged incident of the day before, crushed in order to send a message to the world that the government was in charge? In this sense, it is possible that the invisibility of the journalists may have contributed to the outcome of the incident. On the other hand, the reverse is possible; the "restraint" of the tank commander may have been assisted by his knowing that the Beijing Hotel was studded with zoom lenses.

And what of the effect of the cameras on the man himself? Chinese government authorities used Western news (and confiscated tourist) photographs and video of the protests to identify "hooligans" and "roughnecks" (their designation for the protesters).[91] Even if he was not uncovered from such sources, and "Wang Weilin" was in fact arrested, it was the icon that sealed his fate. At any rate, even from a great distance, the presence of the journalists may have influenced the events observed; no icon is immaculately conceived.

MANAGING OUTRAGE

As the first pictures of the crackdown on June 4 arrived on TV, President George Bush was vacationing at his estate in Kennebunkport, Maine. Marlin Fitzwater, his press spokesman, found the president in the main house and told him, "You've got to see this." Both men walked down to the Secret Service Command post which was the only building on the grounds that received cable television.[92] There, Bush, his guards, and his immediate staff watched the violence at Tiananmen, and the pictures of the man and tanks. That morning, Fitzwater recalled, "We were the first government to respond, labeling it an outrage and so forth, and it was based almost entirely on what we were seeing on television." But Fitzwater sensed that press reaction to his comments was tepid: "You couldn't devise words to match the images. There was no word too 'hot.' For example, we were saying words like 'outrage' and 'brutality'—pretty tough words—and they were just being dismissed as not caring. We needed words like 'bloody,' 'guts' and 'murder,' just to break through the perception that was created by those pictures." Similarly Margaret Tutweiler, then press spokesperson for the State Department, insisted that her boss, James Baker, also watch the CNN coverage.[93] According to one report, CNN was the news source for much of the government (and the other Washington-based news media) on the nights of June 4 and 5.[94]

What Fitzwater suggests by his observations is that pictures in the press, especially those which are perceived by the press and political elites to be significant and important, may influence the scope and the tone of foreign policy debates and discourse. One "effect" of icons of outrage, therefore, may be not to spur action but to impose a language of description, a sort of *compassionspeak* or *denialspeak*, or if the occasion warrants, *outragespeak* that seems apropos. By this reckoning, the Bush administration was much more successful in managing Tiananmen than the Johnson presidency in handling Tet. His initial "patience and forbearance" may have infuriated those who desired stronger language, but eventually Bush spoke the words of outrage and rhetorically stood by the man with the tank. Even this reaction was criticized as too "muted."[95] Yet, he, unlike President Johnson, succeeded, once the icons had faded, in enacting his policies regardless of Congressional or public "outrage."

In short, there is no doubt that among many discourse elites the images from Tiananmen reinforced a negative view of the government of China. As Gadi Wolfsfeld has suggested, all antagonists in a political struggle operate in a "competitive symbiosis" with the news media.[96] At Tiananmen one side "won" the media battle, that is, garnered all the press' sympathy and decisively influenced the frame that the press enacted around the images of the event. The other side "lost" that battle. This evaluation of the "losing" Chinese government was, in addition, shared by both ends of the political spectrum, the right through traditional concern for Taiwan and anti-Communism, the left through traditional concern for human rights issues. Conservative Senator Jesse Helms (R-North Carolina) and liberal Representative Stephen J. Solarz (D-New York), joined hands to call for tougher sanctions against Communist China. "We need to stand with these young people who are trying to achieve freedom," stated Helms.[97] All the ingredients cited for a break in foreign policy were in place; all the conditions for pictures in the press to affect the course of foreign affairs decision-making were met. At first, it seemed that a new era of a tougher China policy had arrived. On June 5, President Bush announced a series of measures taken in reaction to the events. All were framed by the administration as being strong, decisive, and intended to communicate American outrage at the bloodletting in Beijing and elsewhere. Among the sanctions were:

- freezing commercial exports and imports of military equipment
- freezing sales of high technology goods to China
- blocking all further World Bank loans to China
- ceasing all "high level contact" between the United States and China, especially that between military leaders

In addition, medical assistance through the Red Cross was offered to help those injured, and visas of Chinese students in the United States were to be examined sympathetically for extension. Further, in a June 8 news conference, Bush stressed that his administration could not restore normal relations until China started to "recognize the validity" of the democracy movement. "I think it is very important that the Chinese leadership know it's not going to be business as usual," Bush declared.[98]

This reaction came in response to outrage expressed by commentators, editorialists, and some in Congress. Yet, soon thereafter, a United Airlines jet crashed and Hurricane Hugo and the San Francisco earthquake struck. The latter two events, of course, received substantially greater TV ratings than the Tiananmen protests. As public attention shifted, American foreign policy was steered quietly back onto its previous trajectory. Deputy Secretary of State Lawrence Eagleburger and National Security Adviser Brent Scowcroft led a secret American delegation to Beijing. Afterwards, although the mission was described as underlining the American administration's disapproval of the Tiananmen events, the renewal of negotiations surely signaled to the Chinese leadership that, though not all was forgotten, eventually all would be forgivable. On May 29, 1990, President Bush formally notified the Congress of its intention to renew China's "Most Favored Nation" status.[99] Bush offered reasons for his move (which were later reiterated by the Clinton administration). First, China was simply too important a player in the world to push into isolation. Second, the restrictions imposed on China after Beijing Spring apparently in no way moderated the actions of the Chinese government. Later in the year another reason for wooing China was presented: support in the United Nations Security Council against Iraq's invasion of Kuwait.[100]

Indeed, in the ritual that renewing China's MFN status has been for years, such reasons are always offered. They are the reasons of expediency. In the Senate Foreign Relations Committee Hearing a few days after the first anniversary of Tiananmen, administration officials reported that they had inquired about the man who stood before the tanks, but they were given no "clear" answer. Assistant Secretary of State Richard Solomon also stated that "the administration believes it would be counterproductive to halt trade with China as a means of showing disapproval." Later that year, Bush vetoed a proposal that would have allowed 40,000 Chinese students studying in the United States to extend their stays up to four years, if they feared political persecution in returning home. A series of other concessions and relaxations of the original sanctions continued over time.[101] The simplest indicator of the results of Tiananmen on China's status in the world—the only coin of the international realm that really counts—is trade. In 1988, China's balance of trade with the United States was favorable: China exported to America 3.5 percent more goods than it imported. In 1989, this surplus almost doubled. In 1990, it increased to 10.4 percent. As of 1994, U.S. imports from China exceed exports to that country by 29.5 percent. In short, since Tiananmen, China's favorable economic balance with the United States has increased by almost ten times.[102] When the MFN issue was raised once again in 1997, *USA Today* of May 20 reran the AP picture of the man with the tanks, and an administration run by liberal Democrats, facing a Congress run by Republicans, again intoned that we could not break with China. The game continued, but with one exception: the Clinton administration proposed that China's MFN status become permanent so as to avoid the "bloody battles" each year that greet its annual renewal. In general, Clinton followed the line of the previous administration: a pro-trade China policy that "Votes For Business."[103]

In sum, the Tiananmen events and incident of the man facing down a column of tanks would seem to be prime evidence that pictures can affect policy, but only marginally. The image's aesthetic power was greater than its political power. The losers of the media battle won on the ground, and some eight years later have triumphed in all areas of their foreign policy interests save the capturing of the Olympic Games for Beijing in the year 2000.[104] Further, the irony is that if the Chinese government had been *more* totalitarian and simply expelled all foreign journalists, and closed international phone lines, it could have quietly dispensed with the demonstrators at Tiananmen Square. While there would have been an international reaction, that reaction would not have had icons of outrage around which to coalesce. The suggestion is that a "powerful" picture in the press can have an effect on foreign policy structure. At the same time, the opinions of the president, the number one foreign policy decision maker, can work against such pressures. Despite their ubiquity, icons of outrage do not have the ability to end-lessly and repetitively stir the same degree of outrage and reaction, even among those who initially claim to be moved. They can provoke some action, or rather discourse elites use them to provide evidence for the actions they propose. For those elites who wish a contrary course of action, these icons enforce a ritual of speaking words of compassion, denial, or outrage. The qualities that we impose on them, however, may wear thin as the events themselves fade in memory and in context, and new horrors supplant them in our immediate visual environment. This is what might be called icon fatigue.

Second, the reaction to images in the press may be strong, but also shallow, because few political elites are willing to expend their total political capital and influence on reacting to the outrage, especially that from a foreign land, and not directly involving the lives of Americans. Certainly, the Tiananmen events, as reported and shown by Western media, and commented upon by a host of discourse elites, dramatically influenced American public opinion about China. Throughout the 1980s, China's favorable rating in polls fluctuated between about 65 and 72 percent, while its unfavorable rating never rose above 28 percent. After the crackdown, the unfavorable rating in polls rose to a high of 58 percent and the favorable rating dropped to a low of 16 percent.[105] In contrast, sympathy for the protesters was very high.

At the same time, George Bush and every member of Congress knew that there was no strong pro- or anti-China *vote* in America. Polls showed little support for a complete break in relations. Respondents to an ABC-*Washington Post* poll taken June 15–19 supported suspension of military sales (92%), but a majority (54%) also felt the president's response to Tiananmen was "just about right."[106] Simply put, the Tiananmen events were not in themselves watershed political issues. The journalists cared, the senators and representatives cared, the American public cared, fleetingly, about what happened at Tiananmen; or at least they felt it was important to go on the record as expressing words of sympathy and even anger. Other powers-that-be, such as major American corporations that had a stake in continuing the forty billion dollar a year trade with China, those within the diplomatic bureaucracy who saw no need to break relations permanently with one of the major powers of the world, and presidents who came to believe that some sort of "constructive engagement"—i.e. business as usual—was the best China policy, in the end had more sway. Despite the mass of discourse supporting the man against the tanks as one of the premier icons of outrage of the late twentieth century, the fact is that within a few years after the event's picture, "Wang Weilin," the "courageous man" who "defied tyranny" while "the whole world was watching," lingers in prison, remains in hiding, or is dead, the victim of a summary execution. Meanwhile, Tiananmen Square once again is a tourist attraction; China's trade with America is stronger than ever; and China has reabsorbed Hong Kong amidst tumultuous nationalistic celebrations. It follows that although Bush was criticized for not using more vitriolic language and taking harsher actions against China,[107] his "measured response" was more politically astute than has been credited. Token words and deeds were enough. The icon may endure, but the effects are fleeting; "China's heroes," as they were framed, were not forgotten but were made irrelevant.[108]

NOTES

1. Quoted in "China In Crisis," NBC *Special Report*, June 5, 1989.

2. E. J. Perry, "Introduction: Chinese Political Culture Revisited," in *Popular Protest and Political Culture in Modern China*, ed. by J. N. Wasserstrom and E. J. Perry, 2nd ed. (Boulder: Westview Press, 1994), p. 3.

3. What he said to the tank commander is no longer a matter of record, or rather the record has changed.

4. The tanks were actually *leaving* Tiananmen Square.

5. P. Iyer, "The Unknown Rebel," *Time*, April 13, 1998, p. 192.

6. G. Black and R. Munro, *Black Hands of Beijing: Lives of Defiance in China's Democracy Movement* (New York: John Wiley and Sons, 1993), p. 235.

7. Mikhail Gorbachev visited China at the height of the protests, bringing even more media into the area and registering the global importance of the events. This was another case of political elites by body or by word pointing to an event to signify to media that this was important. See discussion of the role of the leader's body in a televisual age in R. Hariman, "Decorum, Power, and the Courtly Style," *Quarterly Journal of Speech* 78 (May 1992): 149–72. Gorbachev did not set the agenda, but he did assist in shaping it. Much Tiananmen literature cites the importance of Gorbachev's visit in relation to political events and media coverage. See C. Calhoun, *Neither Gods nor Emperors: Students and the Struggle for Democracy in China* (Berkeley: University of California Press, 1994), pp. 67–69; J. N. Esherick and J. N. Wasserstrom, "Acting out Democracy: Political Theatre in Modern China," in *Popular Protest and Political Culture in Modern China*, p. 32; C. Johnson, "Foreword," in *The Broken Mirror: China after Tiananmen*, ed. by G. Hicks (Chicago: St. James Press, 1990), p. xi; Nan Lin, *The Struggle for Tiananmen: Anatomy of the 1989 Mass Movement* (Westport, CT: Praeger, 1992), pp. 83–84, 148–49; F. Michael, "China and the Crisis of Communism," in *The Broken Mirror*, p. 454; O. Schell, *Mandate of Heaven: The Legacy of Tiananmen Square and the Next Generation of China's Leaders* (New York: Touchstone, 1995), p. 88.

8. A major interest is one of vital importance; a peripheral interest is one not given consideration in policy decisions. See D. Buhite, "'Major Interests': American Policy toward China, Taiwan and Korea, 1945–1950," *Pacific Historical Review* 47 (1978): 425–51.

9. J. Wasserstrom, "History, Myth, and the Tales of Tiananmen," in *Popular Protest and Political Culture in Modern China*, pp. 273–74.

10. See L. A. Friedland and Zhong Mengbai, "International Television Coverage of Beijing Spring 1989: A Comparative Approach," *Journalism & Mass Communication Monographs* 156 (April 1996): 1–60. See also D. D. Perlmutter, "Journalistic Norms and Forms of Crossnational Imagery: How American Newsmagazines Photographed Tiananmen," in *International News Monitoring*, ed. by M. Griffin and K. Nordenstreng (Boston: Hampton Press, 1998, forthcoming); Yanru Chen, "Marketing China after Tiananmen: Marketing Mix as Applied to the Promotion of International Tourism," *Asian Journal of Communication* 3 (1993): 75–93; L. K. Fuller, "Tiananmen as Treated by the *Christian Science Monitor*," *Political Communication and Persuasion* 8 (April-June 1991): 79–91; Zhou He and Jianhua Zhu, "The 'Voice of America' and China: Zeroing in on Tiananmen Square," *Journalism Monographs* 143 (February 1994): 1–45; C. C. Lee and J. M. Chan, "The Hong Kong Press Coverage of the Tiananmen Protests," *Gazette* 46, (November 1990): 175–95; L. Li, "Opening the Pandora's Box: Were the American Media Guilty of Negligence in Disclosing Tiananmen Protestors' Identities?" *Gazette* 52 (November 1994): 209–22.

11. C. Calhoun, *Neither Gods nor Emperors*; R. V. Des Forges, Luo Ning, and Wu Yen-Bo, eds., *Chinese Democracy and the Crisis of 1989: Chinese and American Reflections* (Albany: State University of New York Press, 1993); J. N. Wasserstrom and E. J. Perry, eds., *Popular Protest and Political Culture in Modern China*.

12. S. Leys, "After the Massacres," in *The Broken Mirror*, p. 159. See also S. W. Mosher, *China Misperceived: American Illusions and Chinese Reality* (New York: Basic Books, 1990); P. Hollander, "Soviet Terror, American Amnesia," *National Review* (May 2, 1994): 28+.

13. "Remarks of Chai Ling, Chinese Student Democracy Movement Leader—First Anniversary of the Tiananmen Square Massacre," National Press Club, Washington, DC, *Federal News Service* [wire], June 4, 1990.

14. "Elsewhere in the World," *USA Today*, September 25, 1990, p. 4A.

15. Accounts and quotes drawn from M. Beck (with D. Elliott), *Newsweek*, Jan. 9, 1989, p. 35; N. Kristof, "China's Burst of Rage," *New York Times*, January 8, 1989, sec. 4, p. 3; S. Burton, "Beat the Black Devils!" *Time*, January 9, 1989, p. 37; D. Southerland, "China's Long-Held Image of Foreigners Fuels Racial Conflict," *Washington Post*, January 3, 1989, p. A8.

16. L. A. Friedland and Zhong Mengbai, "International Television Coverage." See also D. D. Perlmutter, "Journalistic Norms and Forms of Crossnational Imagery."

17. Such imagery was a staple for World War I and II posters. In every case, the girl is young, pale, slender, and attractive. See examples in P. Paret, B. I. Lewis, and P. Paret, *Persuasive Images: Posters of War and Revolution from the Hoover Institution Archives* (Princeton, NJ: Princeton University Press, 1992); S. Keen, *Faces of the Enemy: Reflections of the Hostile Imagination* (San Francisco: Harper and Row, 1992); Anthony Rhodes, *Propaganda: The Art of Persuasion in World War II* (Secaucus, NJ: Wellfleet, 1987).

18. The interesting exception is the publicity campaign by the government of Kuwait and, tacitly, the U.S. government, to build sympathy for the plight of Iraqi-occupied Kuwait. [See Chapter Five.]

19. Tiananmen is used as shorthand by many writers, but there was considerable activity outside Beijing. The focus of press attention, however, was in the capital. See C. Calhoun, *Neither Gods nor Emperors*, p. 146.

20. This is notable in the language of reporting and even in the language that I am employing in this book. Words can betray sympathies: Chinese students *rioted* against blacks, but *protested* for Democracy?

21. These video excerpts are not all the images that were shown, but rather a selection from among them.

22. However, in one history of the Tiananmen events published by a human rights group, the pictures by Stuart Franklin are shown in sequence, from the initial confrontation to when the young man was pulled away. See Human Rights in China, *Children of the Dragon: The Story of Tiananmen Square* (New York: Collier Books, 1990).

A series by Magnum photographer Stuart Franklin. The picture captions read as follows:

Caption 1: "A worker pauses in the middle of Changan Avenue, as tanks roll out of the square . . ." (p. 189).

Caption 2: "The tanks approach . . ." (p. 190).

Caption 3: "And a confrontation develops . . ." (p. 191).

23. Judd's words are somewhat unclear in the video. The closed captioning reads that she says "brave," but it sounds more like "brazen."

24. As Judd speaks, the video continues. We do not see still shots; we watch the man being hustled off to the side of the street.

25. J. Barron, "Crackdown in Beijing," *New York Times*, June 6, 1989, p. A16.

26. R. Cohen, "Witnessing Grand History Via Television," *Bergen County Record*, June 9, 1989, p. B11.

27. P. Guy, "Handshake Photo Worth 1,000 Words," *USA Today*, September 15, 1993, p. 8B.

28. B. Partlow, Gannett News Service [wire], June 29, 1989.

29. T. Shales, "Keeping Open the China Gate," *Washington Post*, June 9, 1989, p. C1.

30. PBS, *Frontline,* June 4, 1996.

31. R. L. Moore, "U.S., China See Past in Sharp Contrasts," *Orlando Sentinel,* January 29, 1995, p. G1.

32. T. Hine, "Notable Quotables: Why Images Become Icons," *New York Times,* February 18, 1996, sec. 2, p. 1.

33. A. Grundberg, "Blurred and Shaky Images That Burn in the Mind," *New York Times,* January 14, 1990, sec. 2, p. 35.

34. D. Morrison, ed., *Massacre in Beijing: China's Struggle for Democracy* (New York: Warner Books, 1989).

35. *The Peking Massacre: A Summary Report of the 1989 Democracy Movement in Mainland China* (Taipei: Kwang Hwa, 1989), pp. 52–53.

36. J. Barron, "Crackdown in Beijing," p. A16.

37. T. Shales, "Keeping Open the China Gate," p. C1.

38. K. H. Jamieson, *Eloquence in an Electronic Age: The Transformation of Political Speechmaking* (New York: Oxford University Press, 1988), p. 97.

39. See discussion of Bush's leadership style and substance in R. J. Barilleaux and M. E. Stuckey, eds., *Leadership and the Bush Presidency: Prudence or Drift in an Era of Change?* (Westport, CT: Praeger, 1992).

40. A. Lynch, "Diplomat's Life After Defection," *San Francisco Chronicle,* July 13, 1990, p. B3.

41. A. B. Brick, "China Two Years After the Pro-Democracy Demonstrations," *Heritage Foundation Reports, The Heritage Lectures,* no. 306, March 29, 1991.

42. "China Asks Argentina to Reset Debt Terms," *Journal of Commerce,* May 30, 1990, p. 1A.

43. T. Brown, "Protesters' Messages Made Clear," *Seattle Times,* December 2, 1990, p. B1.

44. Http://www.christusrex.org/www1/sdc/Tiananmen.html.

45. O. Schell, *Mandate of Heaven,* p. 163.

46. C. Calhoun, *Neither Gods nor Emperors,* p. 143.

47. Minzhu Han and Hua Sheng, eds., *Cries for Democracy: Writings and Speeches from the 1989 Chinese Democracy Movement* (Princeton, NJ: Princeton University Press, 1990), p. xvii.

48. G. Thomas, *Chaos Under Heaven: The Shocking Story of China's Search for Democracy* (New York: Birch Lane Press, 1991), p. 300.

49. P. Li, S. Mark, and M. Li, eds., *Culture and Politics in China: An Anatomy of Tiananmen Square* (New Brunswick, NJ: Transaction Publishers, 1991), p. 35.

50. Kwan Ha Yim, ed., *China Under Deng* (New York: Facts on File, 1991), p. 289.

51. T. Brook, *Quelling the People: The Military Suppression of the Beijing Democracy Movement* (New York: Oxford University Press, 1992), p. 177.

52. Yi Mu and M. V. Thompson, *Crisis at Tiananmen: Reform and Reality in Modern China* (San Francisco: China Books and Periodicals, 1989), p. 94.

53. O. Schell, *Mandate of Heaven,* p. 163.

54. W. Wright, *Six Guns and Society: A Structural Study of the Western* (Berkeley: University of California Press, 1975).

55. For example, in Wim Wenders's film *Until the End of the World,* it is 1999, the government of China has been overthrown, and a gilded statue of the man who faced down the tanks has been erected in Beijing.

56. J. N. Wasserstrom, "History, Myth, and the Tales of Tiananmen," in *Popular Protest and Political Culture in Modern China,* p. 297.

57. A. Peyrefitte, *La Tragedie Chinoise* (Paris: Fayard, 1990), p. 240. [Original in French; text is my translation.]

58. Che Muqi, *Beijing Turmoil: More than Meets the Eye* (Beijing: Foreign Languages Press, 1990), p. 39.

59. C. Snow, Jr., "First Impressions Can Be Wrong," *World Paper*, April, 1990, p. 15.

60. PBS, *Frontline*, June 4, 1996.

61. A. Peyrefitte, *La Tragedie Chinoise*, p. 12.

62. "Chinese Protester," *Orlando Sentinel Tribune*, December 16, 1992, p. A3. See also T. Brook, *Quelling the People*, p. 177.

63. B. Walters, "A Smile, and Eyes That Go Cold," *New York Times*, May 18, 1990, p. 31. See also N. D. Kristof, "China's Untold Story: Who Died in the Crackdown?" *New York Times*, June 3, 1990, p. 20.

64. E. J. Perry, "Casting a Chinese 'Democracy' Movement: The Roles of Students, Workers, and Entrepreneurs," in *Popular Protest and Political Culture in Modern China*, pp. 74–92. This is the source for many of the citations that follow.

65. Ibid.

66. E. A. Gargan, *China's Fate: A People's Turbulent Struggle with Reform and Repression, 1980–1990* (New York: Doubleday, 1990), p. 296.

67. M. S. Duke, *The Iron House: A Memoir of the Chinese Democracy Movement and the Tiananmen Massacre* (Layton, UT: Peregrine Smith, 1990), p. 37.

68. A. Chan and J. Unger, "China after Tiananmen," *Nation*, January 22, 1990, pp. 79–81. See also H. Rosemont, Jr., "China: The Mourning After," *Z Magazine*, March, 1990, p. 87. Rosemont maintains that "the workers were no less unhappy than the students in the Square, but the two groups were unhappy about different things." He argues that one motivation for keeping distant from the workers was that the students rightly perceived that the government felt more threatened by a workers' uprising than a student protest.

69. F. Lee, *China Rising: The Meaning of Tiananmen* (Chicago: Ivan R. Dee, 1990), p. 203.

70. Mok Chiu Yu and J. F. Harrison, eds., *Voices from Tiananmen Square: Beijing Spring and the Democracy Movement*, (Montreal: Black Rose Books, 1990), pp. 111, 112.

71. G. Black and R. Munro, *Black Hands of Beijing*, pp. 234, 235.

72. E. J. Perry, "Casting a Chinese "Democracy" Movement," in *Popular Protest and Political Culture in Modern China*, p. 84.

73. Minzhu Han and Hua Sheng, eds., *Cries for Democracy*, pp. 354–55; C. Calhoun, *Neither Gods nor Emperors*, p. 141.

74. H. Rosemont, Jr., *A Chinese Mirror: Moral Reflections on Political Economy and Society* (La Salle, IL: Open Court, 1991), p. 22. See also G. Black and R. Munro, *Black Hands of Beijing*, p. 234, who claim that the real massacre of workers and Beijing citizens occurred not in Tiananmen Square but elsewhere.

75. See P. Iyer, "The Unknown Rebel," *Time*, April 13, 1998, p. 192; "Chinese Man Who Stood in Front of Tanks in 1989 Still at Large," Deutsche Presse-Agentur [wire], April 6, 1998; P. Wright, "Icon of the Revolution," [London] *Guardian*, June 4, 1992, p. 23; Hearing of the Asian and Pacific Affairs Subcommittee, the Human Rights and International Organizations Subcommittee, and the International Economic Policy and Trade Subcommittee of the House Foreign Affairs Committee, Federal News Service [wire], May 29, 1991.

76. J. Alter, "Karl Marx, Meet Marshall McLuhan," *Newsweek*, May 29, 1989, p. 28.

77. E. Bark, "International Diplomacy: Television Style," *Orlando Sentinel Tribune*, December 23, 1990, p. 61.

78. "China and the Power of the Tube," *Broadcasting*, June 26, 1989, p. 34.

79. F. Tan, "The *People's Daily* and the Epiphany of Press Reform," in *Chinese Democracy and the Crisis of 1989*, p. 276.

80. C. Calhoun, *Neither Gods nor Emperors*, pp. 53–54.

81. P. Li, S. Mark, and M. Li, eds., *Culture and Politics in China*, p. 80.

82. R. Munro, "Remembering Tiananmen Square: Who Died in Beijing, and Why," in *China's Search for Democracy: The Student and the Mass Movement of 1989*, ed. by S. Ogden, K. Hartford, L. Sullivan, and D. Zweig (Armonk, NY: M. E. Sharpe, 1992), p. 394.

83. L. E. Gutstadt, "Taking the Pulse of the CNN Audience: A Case Study of the Gulf War," *Political Communication* 10 (October-December 1993).

84. Gabriel Almond estimated that between 70 and 90 percent of the American public pay little or no attention to foreign affairs and "participate in policy-making in indirect and primarily passive ways." G. A. Almond, *The American People and Foreign Policy* (Westport, CT: Greenwood, 1977).

85. T. Brook, *Quelling the People*, p. 152.

86. G. Black and R. Munro, *Black Hands of Beijing*, p. 247.

87. Ibid.

88. "In Beijing, a Month of Living Dangerously," *New York Times*, June 25, 1989, sec. 2, p. 29.

89. Ibid.

90. Interestingly, in a design and informational sense, the long shot was the better picture. An extreme close-up of a man framed against the bulk of a tank would not have been such powerful fodder for righteousness and metonymy. The long shot emphasizes the presence of a column of tanks, the relative small-ness of the man, the solitude of his struggle, and the "High Noon" dynamic of the confrontation.

91. L. Li, "Opening the Pandora's Box," pp. 209–22.

92. T. J. McNulty, "World politics: Made in America," *Chicago Tribune*, July 14, 1996, p. 1C.

93. W. Henry, III, "Man of the Year: History as it Happens," *Time*, January 6, 1992, p. 25. See also L. A. Friedland, *Covering the World: International Television News Services* (New York: Twentieth Century Fund, 1992), pp. 5–6.

94. *Turmoil at Tiananmen: A Study of U.S. Press Coverage of the Beijing Spring of 1989*, Joan Shorenstein Barone Center on the Press, Politics and Public Policy, Harvard University, John F. Kennedy School of Government, June, 1992, p. 188.

95. See R. L. Stanfield, "Muted Outrage," *The National Journal* 21, July 1, 1989, p. 1719; W. Schneider, "Bush Too 'Professional' about China?" *The National Journal* 21, July 1, 1989, p. 1722.

96. G. Wolfsfeld, "Media, Protest, and Political Violence: A Transactional Analysis," *Journalism Monographs* 127 (June 1991): 1–61.

97. CNN *Prime News*, June 4, 1989.

98. *Washington Post*, June 6, 1989, p. A19.

99. "Excerpts from Bush's News Session on China's Trade Status with U.S.," *New York Times*, May 25, 1990, p. A12; A. Rosenthal, "Bush Called Ready to Renew China Trade Status for a Year," *New York Times*, May 23, 1990, p. A1.

100. R. Pear, "Mideast Tensions: Bush, Meeting Foreign Minister, Lauds Beijing Stand Against Iraq," *New York Times*, December 1, 1990, sec. 1, p. 8; T. L. Friedman, "Mideast Tensions: Chinese Official Is Invited to Washington in Response to Gulf Stance," *New York Times*, November 28, 1990, p. A15; N. D.

Kristof, "China Gains in Mideast Crisis but Loses Cold War Benefits," *New York Times*, November 11, 1990, sec. 1, p. 1; Yangmin Wang, "China, Too, Has a Role to Play in Persian Gulf," *New York Times*, September 26, 1990, p. A24.

101. J. R. Payton, "Our China Initiatives Raising Questions," *St. Petersburg Times*, January 11, 1990, p. 2A.

102. L. R. Brown, *Who Will Feed China? Wake-Up Call for a Small Planet* (New York: W. W. Norton, 1995), p. 104.

103. T. L. Friedman, "U.S. Is to Maintain Trade Privileges for China's Goods; Clinton Votes For Business," *New York Times*, May 27, 1994, p. A1; D. Jehl, "U.S. Is to Maintain Trade Privileges for China's Goods; A Policy Reversal," *New York Times*, May 27, 1994, p. A1.

104. The eventual success of "democracy" in China cannot and should not be measured by U.S. ideals or practices. Political scientist Minxin Pei notes that "In American public discourse, political reform has a narrow meaning: democratization. American politicians and news media measure the progress of political reform in other countries against a single yardstick—the holding of free and open elections. But while democratization may be one element of reform, it is not the only one, especially in countries lacking the most rudimentary institutions of governance." Minxin Pei, "Is China Democratizing?" *Foreign Affairs* (January/February 1998): 69.

105. From State Department collection reported in *Turmoil at Tiananmen*, pp. 184–85.

106. R. L. Stanfield, "Muted Outrage," p. 1719.

107. T. L. Friedman, "Taking the Measure of a 'Measured Response,'" *New York Times*, July 2, 1989, sec. 4, p. 3.

108. Liu Binyan, "How Can We Forget China's Heroes?" *New York Times*, December 1, 1990, sec. 1, p. 25.

Chapter Four

When Icons Collide:
Somalia, 1992–1993

The people who are dragging around bodies of Americans don't look very hungry to the people of Texas.[1]

—Senator Phil Gramm

On May 23, 1994, on the lawn of the White House, President Clinton bestowed the Congressional Medal of Honor, the nation's highest award of military distinction, on two soldiers. Master Sergeant Gary Gordon and Sergeant First Class Randall Shughart were in attendance only in spirit, represented by their families and friends. Both men, members of the elite Delta Force, had been killed on October 3, 1993, in the "Battle of Mogadishu," a helicopter-borne raid by American special forces to capture the top aides of Somali clan leader General Mohammed Farah Aidid. At the award ceremony some eight months later, two months after the last American combat troops had somewhat ignominiously withdrawn from Somalia, the president spoke briefly, reciting the details of the soldiers' heroism: "Sergeants Gordon and Shughart died . . . for a noble and important cause, to give Durant [the helicopter pilot captured by the Somalis] and others a chance to live." Continuing, the president assured those in attendance and, through the press, the nation, that the slain heroes "were part of a larger mission, a difficult one, that saved hundreds of thousands of innocent Somalis from starvation and gave that nation a chance to build its own future."[2]

In reciting these words, the president enacted an age-old ritual of political leadership and military culture.[3] The commander, whose ultimate responsibility it is to assign young men to face death in battle, bestows upon them a ceremony of memorial, a symbolic marker of recognition, and recites an incantation reassuring their survivors that the warriors did not fall in vain. Also as ancient as war itself were the president's troika of rationalizations for honoring the dead servicemen and their mission, conflated for the purposes of justifying the previous actions of the leader. The first "reason" cited by the president was the most personal and immediate: a soldier died to save a comrade. The camaraderie of the trenches that enables one to die for one's buddy is the oldest and most easily identifiable motivation for valor.4 Second, Clinton asserted that the soldiers' death was in service to the nation. This too would have been a familiar homily to a Roman legionary, a Sung Dynasty archer, or a horseman of Custer's Seventh Cavalry. Finally, and perhaps most important, in light of the controversy and recriminations surrounding the Somalia intervention, the president framed the deaths of the two American soldiers as instrumental in a greater humanitarian cause in which the lives of "hundreds of thousands," unrelated by kinship, cohort, or citizenship, were saved through the agency of American benevolence. These soldiers were martyrs of mercy who died serving humankind.

Despite all these honors, Gordon and Shughart are not household names of their generation, as were Ira Hayes and Audie Murphy after World War II. Their deaths, however, and the post-mortem disposition of their bodies, are notorious. My students, who were in their early and middle teens in 1993, strongly identified three icons, one generic and two specific, attached to the cue "American intervention in Somalia." These were, by no coincidence, the icons that Clinton wished to frame the day of the ceremony. The first image was of starvation. It is non-specific, but the details are familiar: an emaciated black child, head grossly out of proportion to a frail body, with flies thickly covering its eyes. This image was employed as the framing icon to define, rationalize, illustrate and support America's decision to send troops to Somalia as a "mission of mercy." The icon also served, however, as a baseline with which many, including my students, compared the seemingly contradictory icons to come.

The other icons were much more specific and were created under unusual circumstances in the aftermath of the Battle of Mogadishu. The first is a fuzzy video image of the face of an American army copilot, Michael Durant. His cheeks, forehead, and nose are covered with congealed cuts and bruises; his expression is dazed, as if he is both angry and alarmed at his predicament. Simply a facial close-up, it is hardly a great moment of action or confrontation captured by a skilled photojournalist. The image was produced by Aidid's men, the Somali captors of the pilot, who filmed him being interrogated and then peddled the tape to the Western media.

The final icon was the one that provoked the greatest evocative response from my students. Most of the icons we discussed did not seem, for these young people, to conjure up any of the emotions that discourse elites claim are inevitable. As suggested earlier, this has two probable causes. The first is that pictures have much less innate power to elicit outrage than discourse elites assign to them. The second is what might be called the proprietary effect: pictures of Vietnam, of World War II, even of Tiananmen Square are neither of their generation nor part of their generational cognitive property.5 Somalia was—hence their enhanced recognition. However, another decisive factor was at work here, absent from the previous icons we have discussed, which made this third image the one that my students reacted to most strongly. Unprompted, they added extra-descriptive elements about the horror of what they saw, the evil of the perpetrators in the picture of the naked body of an American soldier dragged through the streets of Mogadishu by jeering Somalis. My students remembered the ropes used to drag the body, and the bruises and contusions on the corpse. Many even recalled the smiles on the faces of, as one student put it in the eloquence of youth, "those fuckers." The class consensus was clear: how could "those people" (the least vitriolic term employed) have been so ungrateful?

That image, and that of the face of Michael Durant, became the icons associated with America's mission in Somalia. The president's attempted framing was a belated rhetorical buttress against a wave of counter-framing by other political elites, press commentators, many in the military itself, and overwhelmingly in the American public. There was wide consensus on the meaning of the first icon. In late 1992, the generic image of the starving child was offered as an illustration for intervention and as evidence that our actions were not grounded in any motive but human decency. The second two icons, those resulting from the battle of October 1993, seemed to create dissonance with the first. Here, the people we were benevolently trying to save were killing our young men. Although the president framed the mission as altruistic, the consensus of all other elites was that, no matter how many Somalis were "saved," the cause was not worth American deaths. The major effort in American politics became how fast we could pull out and leave the Somalis to suffer without our assistance.

This chapter investigates the process of icon formation and definition during the Somalia intervention, which has been held up as one of the best examples of visual determinism. Indeed, the evidence seems compelling that pictures of one kind "got us in," while pictures of another kind "drove us out." Second, in previous cases a single major icon was seen as summing up events, but here we have a collision of icons. The starving child image was not simply displaced by those of suffering American soldiers; the first icon remained as a paradoxical counterpoint to the second set of icons, hence the anger of the public, many elites, and my students. Finally, the decision to engage in a "humanitarian intervention" is said to be the major foreign policy challenge of the post-Cold War era. Of particular interest are entities such as Somalia, which Secretary of State Madeleine Albright and others have labeled "failed states . . . where effective government has collapsed, or anarchy reigns, or the economy is hopeless, or a humanitarian calamity overwhelms the country and the people [who] are sliding into an abyss cry out for help from the international community."[6] How we answer such cries may be tempered by our reactions to the icons that discourse elites present to and interpret for us.

GETTING IN: FRAMING INTERVENTION

When President George Bush on December 4, 1992, announced that American troops would be sent to Somalia to assist the United Nations' relief efforts, he framed his decision as wholly humanitarian by alluding to the first icons of outrage: "Every American has seen the shocking images from Somalia."7 Bush was ostensibly acting in concert with Resolution 794, which determined that "the magnitude of the human tragedy" in Somalia "constitutes a threat to international peace and security."8 "The people of Somalia," said Bush, "especially the children of Somalia, need our help. . . . Only the United States has the global reach to place a large security force on the ground in such a distant place quickly and efficiently and, thus, save thousands of innocents from death."9 The link between imagery and policy seemed clear. Presidential historian Michael Beschloss argued that Bush "responded to the outrage of the American public over television pictures of the Somalian famine by sending U.S. troops to ensure that domestic turmoil would not prevent food and other supplies from going where they were needed."10 Another writer stated, succinctly, that "In Somalia, television pictures of starving kids" forced us to intervene.11 Similar sentiment was expressed by others. Bush's press secretary Marlin Fitzwater later asserted that "TV tipped us over the top."12

It is instructive to examine the visual coverage of the intervention and the framing of it for the two key periods, early December 1992, when America "got in" to Somalia, and early October, 1993, after the Mogadishu raid, when we decided to "get out." Although the full coverage is beyond the scope of this study, the selective appearance of the icons of Somalia is revealed. When inspected in such a fashion, it becomes clear that the press essentially replicated the president's frames of the icons of outrage. What also emerges is that it is more likely that the images were employed to illustrate the policy, not that the pictures drove the policy-maker. Whatever "outrage" the American public felt was in response to being told by elites that Somalia was a problem. Moreover, that the pictures existed and were presented to the public and the politicians was not, like the famine itself, an act of God, but an act of framing by those same discourse elites. The icons of starvation were framed as evidence for the need for a mission of mercy, and, in the rhetoric of compassion and outragespeak, used as counter-iterations to anyone opposed to the intervention.

Newsmagazines

It was not until late November, 1992, in response to policy balloons of the Bush administration, that *Newsweek* began to focus on the Horn of Africa. This is significant: policy formulation spurred visual focus. *Newsweek*'s December 7 issue offers a two-page spread of a painfully thin child. The headline reads, "Troops To Somalia" with the subheading "Bush Offers Ground Units To Help End The Suffering—And Leaves Clinton With A Foreign Policy Problem." Bill Clinton, in leather jacket, looking jaunty and calm, is pictured on an opposite page. The caption reads, "High Time: The president elect supported U.S action to put an end to the horror." The two remaining pictures in the story feature the chaos, the "death of a nation" and the major problems in Somalia:

starvation and gunmen.

Newsweek's December 14, 1992, cover picture is of a baby-faced American soldier in green uniform, duffel-bag over shoulder. The title reads, "Going In: Should America Be The World's Policeman? Specialist 4, Karl Hanninen, 20, Ships Out For Somalia."[13] The cover story commences with a vertical two-page spread of young, wide-eyed Americans with the caption, "Troops waiting for orders at Fort Drum, N.Y." The headline above them reads, "Mission Of Mercy," clearly framing the military intervention as a sympathetic humanitarian expedition. The next two pages display a single contrasting image, obviously meant to create a sequential link from the soldiers preparing to "go in" for the "mission of mercy" to what we now see: an emaciated human being, collapsed on red, dusty ground, her mouth half-open, her eyes partly rolled back. In the background a similar figure lies under a blanket. The caption informs us that, "At a feeding center in Baidoa, this woman, too weak to eat, lies waiting for help—or death." The montage continues as the next page reveals a crowd of young Somali men, most in light clothing or bare-chested, many holding up sticks and guns. They are representative of "A land of restless young men—and AK-47s." The final picture of the story: "Bodies of dead children are as light as bundled sticks. Here, one waits for its grave."

In the next story, on "Battle Fields of the Food War," the reinforcement of the starvation theme continues. One image shows "gunmen" and the unloading of cargo, but four show the "Kingdom of the dying"—wretched children and old men. The very last image of the Somalia section, however, is of a starving "boy at a feeding center." Within the body-text of the story, the editorial view of the magazine is clear. An "African-American serviceman, mobilized for the Somalia force, has seen the television footage of emaciated babies and starving women, and he has been moved by the realization that 'this could be my family.' Those seeking the *raison d'être* for America's intervention in Somalia can find it here."

In *Time* magazine's November 23 and November 30 issues, no mention or pictorial coverage is made of Somalia. Once more, pictures follow policy declarations, in contradiction to claims otherwise. In the December 7 issue, a small item notes that U.S. forces are likely to be sent. Again, although there is no picture, the item is written as if the sole reason for intervention is the starvation of Somalis. It is in *Time* magazine of December 14, 1992, the first issue after the president's announcement—due to the lead period for printing—that the icon of starvation is employed to frame the policy. The cover is a tight, facial close-up of an emaciated child. His (or her?) face is haggard and drawn. His eye sockets are wells in which we see huge dark, moist eyes.[14] The headline reads, "Somalia: The U.S. To The Rescue." Almost ten pages of surface area are devoted to the story, including several pages of a photo essay on the "Landscape Of Horrors: The Images That Moved The World."

Including the cover, there are thirteen photographs related to the story in the issue. Of these, seven show suffering Somalis. The cover story, mainly credited to Bruce W. Nelan, notes that, "At this time of year, with wrenching pictures of starving Somalis on view, anyone who raises questions about succoring them risks being labeled heartless." In the story we are told that clan chiefs may "delay, obstruct, or simply dodge the Americans while they are there." No mention is made of ambushing and defeating American armies in battle. "In strictly military terms, the venture is not especially daring or dangerous," we are assured. To bolster this line, experts are quoted to instruct the reader that Somalia is "weak" and to "pacify" it is "doable" compared to Bosnia. The worst prognosis is that Americans might get "stuck." Neither is the eventual expansion of the mission predicted or cautioned against. Finally, the icons are prominently featured in generic detail in the photo-essay of the "Landscape Of Death" which is described as "the images that have finally brought the world to Somalia's rescue." The pictures that follow are horrific; they include an infant, his eyes covered in flies, sucking his mother's shriveled breast.

Time's December 21, 1992, cover shows a photo of a young, clean-cut white American servicemen facing a group of smiling Somali children. The American flag on his shoulder faces the camera. The main title reads, "Restoring Hope." The subtitle reads, "Clinton's first foreign policy challenge: If Somalia, why not Bosnia?" The issue contains, including the cover, ten pictures on the Somalia story. Six include images of Somalis and U.S. servicemen interacting. In five we see positive interaction—smiles and handshakes between burly Americans and thin Somalis. In one image, a G.I. holds off two Somalis at gun point after a confrontation at the Mogadishu airport. There is another picture of starvation victims, a graphic of the operations deployment, and one image of the media greeting the soldiers at the beach. The cover story itself makes a case visually and verbally that the Americans are welcome. An introduction informs the reader of "Great Expectations: As Operation Restore Hope begins, Somalis want the U.S. to stay long enough to fix not just their diet but also their society." Indeed, the great danger posed to the mission, the story explains, is that the Somalis want the Americans to solve their problems for them; they are not Anti-American, but rather demand too much from the Americans. Small pockets of fighting are mentioned, but the danger is posed to "foreign troops" who will push inland. Relief workers are quoted complaining that the Marines are not providing them armed protection and are not disarming the militias. In short, the tone of the article is that the United States is expected to do much more, to be more activist. The article concludes, verbally reinforcing the cover image, that "there is a breathless reverence for all things American."

Newspapers

Newspaper coverage maintained the same themes in early December. On December 6, Somalia was a front page story in the *New York Times*. A picture of workmen lugging sacks of grain from a beached boat illustrated a story on how "Efforts to get food out to Somalis fall prey to

Arms and Frustration." Somalia was also the feature of a photo essay by James Nachtwey in the specials section of the *Sunday Times*, showing seven color images of starving children and adults. The introduction to the photographs explains that more than 100,000 people have died in Somalia since January 1991, and that, "This fall, with agriculture in ruins, hungry people streamed into towns like Baidoa, where these photographs were taken. With relief efforts disrupted by warring gangs, Somalis were dying by the hundreds every day, prompting U.N. moves to assemble a military force to get food to the starving." The pictures include a stick-like figure in a threadbare blanket sitting in a wheelbarrow, captioned: "A woman is transported in a wheelbarrow from a hospital to a feeding center." Next, in medium shot, we see "a boy in rags [who] screams with pain as his mother squats alongside." Other variations on the icon of African hunger include: "Bodies awaiting collection outside a destroyed water-pumping station where children gather to pass the time"; "A woman who was found lying near the pumping station is helped to a feeding center"; "In a hovel near the feeding center a boy places a tatter of cloth on his starving father"; and "A body is washed before burial."

Likewise, in the *Washington Post* of December 4, the top section of the front page is dedicated to Somalia and America's intervention plans. White House Press Spokesman Marlin Fitzwater is quoted as saying he hoped that the force of 27,000 U.S. troops would be withdrawn by inauguration day of January 20, 1993. He adds, "We want to make it clear that this U.N. force would be designed to get humanitarian supplies in, not to establish a new government or resolve the decades-old conflict there or set up a protectorate or anything like that." A single photograph illustrates a side story on hunger and chaos in Mogadishu: it shows a group of Somali men sitting placidly by a radio. One elderly man thumbs a string of beads. The captions reads, "Somalis, awaiting word of U.N. decision on sending troops, listen to British newscast on short-wave radio in Mogadishu." The stories are continued inside the newspaper, where once again we see a picture of an emaciated Somali child. On December 6, Somalia is again the front page of the *Post*. A starving child in one photograph is counterposed to another photo of a surly Somali militiaman. Two stories cover the top front section of the paper. One describes "The path to Intervention." The subheadline and story explain how it was the "massive tragedy" that led to U.S. decisions to "do something about that." The last picture is a skeleton-like child, individually named—a sure indication of an attempt to instill human interest into the story.[15]

Television

Television coverage of the major moments before, during, and after the decision to intervene reveals the same themes and images: hyperbole, evidence that the United States has the power to enforce its plans, approval by elites of the mission, and the icons of starvation.[16] For example, on November 21, 1992, when American involvement in a

Somalia intervention and increased United Nations deployment were still in the discussion phase, CBS devoted a 2-minute and 20-second segment to the Somalia story. The story notes that food was not getting through to the hungry because of the interference of warlords, but the main emphasis is on the return of a Congressional delegation, chaired by Rep. John Lewis (D-Georgia), with "an eyewitness account of the tragedy. The delegation visited three sites in Somalia, and what they witnessed spurred them to request an immediate audience with President Bush and President-elect Bill Clinton." Lewis, speaking on a tarmac in front of his colleagues, reads from a statement: "What is happening in Somalia cannot be compared to anything else in modern history. The country is in chaos. Warlords and young kids roam the country with guns." Another delegation member claims that the problem is not food, but the interference of the warlords and the gangs. The reporter, Jim Stewart, goes on to narrate over footage of young Somali men that the gangs and warlords are stealing food, "sometimes taking supplies straight off aircraft as they arrive." The story leaves open whether the Bush administration will choose to intervene, but the reporter closes by instructing us that in the 60 days left in George Bush's tenure, 60,000 Somalis may die.

On NBC's November 21 broadcast, Garrick Utley introduces Somalia as "a land of fighting, refugees and hunger." The main topic of the story is three ships full of food that were not being unloaded because of interference by feuding factions. The situation in Somalia is described as chaotic, with gangs and warlords preventing the hungry from getting food. An underweight baby clings to her thin mother's body, while Utley tells us that "1.5 million people [face] starvation." Then we see a montage of flyblown, crying, emaciated children. The United Nations, however, has been "ineffective." This is followed by the same tarmac clip of the Congressional delegation returning, then an interview with Rep. Lewis from Washington. Utley's first question is, "You come back with all these terrible images, but what stands out in your mind? What struck you as being the worst?" Lewis replies: "I saw little children, a very small child literally dying in her mother's arms. I saw too many children that are suffering without food, starving, dying, and too many people with guns. Somehow, some way, the people of Somalia must get help from the world community."

On ABC *Evening News* of November 26, Forrest Sawyer begins the newscast by noting that intervention was prompted by a "million people hanging on the edge of starvation." In other words, the decision to intervene is framed as having been forced upon a reluctant American government, and, if undertaken, would be a mission born out of purely humanitarian motives. In the story, the United Nations is portrayed as asking for America's help. President-elect Bill Clinton is quoted as supporting the intervention, saying "it is a very, very good thing . . . trying to find a way to make the relief effort work and trying to save people's lives." Opposition to the intervention is cited, but undercut by the language of Bob Zelnick in the report: "Ironically, the prospect of U.S. troops in Somalia is opposed by some of those people it's intended to help. Representatives of some relief agencies fear the use of force against Somalia's gangs could lead to retaliation against them."

To underline this apprehension, there is a report from Don Kladstrup in the town of Bardera "where the gangs forced relief workers to flee." Then he intones—accurately—"Some of the pictures you're about to see are hard to watch but they will help you understand why there is so much pressure to intervene." We see another montage of "looted hospitals and food warehouses" and shot after shot of starving women and children. A Somali is pictured and translated as saying, "We just buried 24 people. Can't anybody help us?" A relief worker states, "We just can't cope." We are told that the death rate in Bardera, because of clan interference in food distribution, has risen to 300 people a day. We view scenes of Somalis fighting over food, and are told there are only seven aid workers for 11,000 people; we see several shots of starving children. A relief worker tells us that there's "no hope at all" for this one. A mother mourns over her dying child, crying to the camera, "It's my only child, but she can't swallow, can't eat."

On NBC's November 26 broadcast, an almost identical framing occurs. Over the shoulder of the anchorwoman, Deborah Roberts, is a graphic of starving children undertitled by the word SOMALIA. She announces: "Somalia seems so far away this Thanksgiving day, but the starvation and factional fighting know no holiday." The mission is described as "getting food already being sent to Somalia into the hands of starving people." Jim Miklaszewski reports on the story, again over a montage of emaciated women and children and sinister gunmen. The troops, we are told, are being sent to ward off a potential human disaster. "In Somalia there is no government, and rival Somali warlords fight for control of the country. Two million people face starvation; one thousand die each day. In Mogadishu, 12 thousand tons of United Nations relief food sits undelivered in warehouses." Again there are several scenes of U.N. troops sitting around, trapped in their bunkers. Again, the opposition of "some relief agencies" is voiced only in contrast to pictures of starving, crying women and children. Over the image of a crowd of children grabbing for a few morsels of food, the reporter assures us that U.S. officials say "their first priority is to feed Somalians, not fight a war." The CBS *Evening News* of November 26 is almost a carbon copy of its sister networks. Connie Chung immediately frames the story of the nation on the Horn of Africa as being one of tragedy and compassion. She opens with: "Happy Thanksgiving. On a day when Americans are filling up on a holiday feast, one million people are in danger of starving to death half a world away."

On December 4, leading off the NBC news, Jane Pauley instructs viewers that: "For most of us, Somalia has been a single image: the desperate face of starvation, a far-away country divided and devastated, almost a footnote to nearer global problems." She continues as the shot expands to encompass her and Garrick Utley sitting in a studio. Between them is the large graphic of the faces of starving Somali children. Thus the icon of outrage is defined by the repetitive graphic design element. "Tonight," Pauley announces, "Somalia has moved to the top of the global agenda." What follows is a standard montage: gaunt refugees fighting for a few grains of food at a relief center; white-bleached bones on a savanna; ragged gunmen firing on a ravaged street; the burial of a child. Then, over another montage, Pauley describes the situation in Somalia as a struggle for dominance in a land where there is "no government, no law, no order, only the power of the guns in the hands of undisciplined soldiers."

On ABC news of December 4, the Somalia story continues. Bob Zelnick instructs us that: "If the Pentagon sticks to plans laid down today, relief could flow to some of Somalia's neediest people within 10 days." These words are spoken over footage presumably taken at a Somali relief camp, where again we see skeleton-like women and children. In contrast, we see an American aircraft carrier and troops hustling onto a huge helicopter. We are told that the Marines will "clear Mogadishu's port and roads of armed gangs." American forces will also move to control "the so-called triangle of death" south of Mogadishu. Zelnick expresses the optimism of the Army that it can work with what he describes as Somalia's "private armies," perhaps even "paying bounty" for their weapons. He assures us, however, that "[Chairman of the Joint Chiefs of Staff Colin] Powell and [Secretary of Defense Richard] Cheney said that 'if threatened, U.S. forces will shoot first.'" The mission, we are reassured, may last as long as two to three months.

Another report from Camp Pendleton, California, follows the preparation of troops for deployment to Somalia. We are told that the Marines "like the idea of going this time not to fight [in contrast to the Gulf War] but to help people who are starving." One Marine is quoted: "Personally, I like to help people, and this gets me a chance to go out and help people that need it the most." Another Marine explains their mission "to help people out, to keep people from dying every day, sure, sure, I feel good about it."

On CBS's news of December 4, the Somalia story is stamped with the imprint of importance by Dan Rather reporting live from Mogadishu. Rather tells us how the airport will be "transformed" once the Marines arrive. The story switches to Marines in America readying for the trip to Somalia. These anecdotes are very revealing of the frame employed to present the intervention. A young Marine expresses "pride for the mission." He states: "There's people there that need our help, they're starvin'." The Marine's young wife—it turns out they are newlyweds— wants her husband to stay home, but Zelnick undercuts this bit of pathos by commenting, "That's what all the wives say, half-jokingly, whenever Camp Pendleton empties out for a crisis." In other interviews, we learn that the camp community is reacting "with joy and sadness"; a "here we go again" spirit seems to prevail among the families.

It is somewhat subtle framing. The images of Americans making sacrifices serve the ideology of intervention: we are giving up husbands and sons at Christmas time; a little girl's father will not be home for her birthday; a wife who has just discovered she is pregnant will be deprived of her husband; a woman will worry about and miss her brother. These elements do not undermine support for the mission. Rather they enhance our self-perception of altruism, and all the "sadness" is reinforced by commentary and quotations that this is a "good thing to do," something noble. Indeed, the newlywed wife, wishing her husband to stay home, is given the last word of the story, and it neatly completes the framing of self-sacrifice. The young wife says: "Poor me, poor me. But I gotta stop and think about the poor people in Somalia, really." In short, the framing of the decision to send American troops may be summed up as a collective visual and verbal pat on our own back. Any other agenda except altruism and any dangers beyond a lengthy mission are essentially ignored or dismissed. It is a clear case of rally 'round the mission.

On the ABC news of December 6, Forrest Sawyer leads off by asserting, "The anarchy in the country continues to make it nearly impossible for relief workers to do their jobs, which means everyone is waiting for the U.S. to arrive." Ted Koppel, reporting live from Mogadishu, comments: "This is a country where the four horsemen of the Apocalypse are on familiar territory. That makes the Marines, expected here any day now, a very desirable alternative." The evidence for this opinion seems to be the interviews with Somali leaders that follow. One clan chief, and the self-appointed president of Somalia, Mohammed Ali Mahdi, chirps: "I'm so happy if the United States has responded and sent in a force to Somalia to settle the peace and deliver the food to the needy people." Then Koppel interviews General Farah Aidid—the clan leader who would later become the nemesis of U.S. and U.N. forces—in a pleasant garden. Aidid states: "Only Americans, I believe, can give this possibility [of hope]. It's a great country." Later in the story, after many disaster scenes of Somalia, we are told that some American diplomats have reservations about the mission, specifically Smith Hempstone, the American ambassador to Kenya, who compares the situation in Mogadishu to that of Beirut; but as is always true in television journalism, it is possible to discern which theme, story, or point is least important by the fact that no extensive interview is made, no footage shown—this question is not explored in any depth. Again, although there are caveats attached to the mission, the possibility that U.S. forces will become mired in a hot war and humiliated is never raised, nor are we reminded that similarly tragic situations exist in many other places in the world in which we have no plans to "do good."

On CBS news of December 7, Dan Rather again reports from Mogadishu. He describes the city as a "killing zone," and then engages in a walking interview with Farah Aidid along a tree-lined path. The Somali leader asserts, "We will protect American troops doing their activities, their military activities . . . in the country. This is our interest, and that is why we welcome them, and we will do our best to help during their stay in Somalia." Rather goes on to interview Aidid's rival, Interim President Mahdi, who sits in the foyer of a hotel in an elegantly carved armchair. Rather narrates, "Now he too welcomes the Americans and says they'll be in no danger." Rather ends the segment by walking through a row of Mahdi's heavy weapons, which could be the stuff of an ominous frame for the intervention. But they are not introduced or described as guns that may one day be turned against the Americans.

Rather, instead, assures us that this is a sign that Mahdi is gathering his weapons to surrender them.

NBC's extensive Somalia coverage on December 7 continues the theme of the "mission of mercy," and supports the idea that the military situation is "under control." The opening graphic is a convoy of American ships including an aircraft carrier. Jane Pauley reports to us from the studio, Tom Brokaw from Somalia. Brokaw reminds us that "this is a humanitarian, not a military mission." He tells us that he will be soon interviewing the warlords and then pauses and comments, "Operation Restore Hope just can't start soon enough." Then begins a montage of the doomed and the dying, emaciated women, old men, a starving child. They are described as refugees who were "caught in a shoot-out between rival gangs." We then see the dim, crowded interior of a hospital where the wounded lie unattended. Then, an American from the "International medical corps" is shown conducting an operation in a cramped, dirty room. Brokaw reports: "Baidoa is barely hanging on, but in Mogadishu there are high hopes for the Marine landing."

Another scene shows U.S. jets flying over the city, and Brokaw assures us that "the local warlords have gotten the message." Then we see a bustling street in Mogadishu and Brokaw proclaims that a "holiday" atmosphere has broken out in anticipation of the American entry. We see small children at a feeding center run by Save the Children. Brokaw sits on a floor curled up among mothers and children in a "special feeding room" for those who are underweight, but then we see a large room filled with children being led in a happy song, and Brokaw tells us that "the 90 percent of children who do survive have a chance at life." Notably, the last story on Somalia is of death at the refugee center. The final image is an icon: as a child collapses in front of the camera, he is carried away by a Somali relief worker in a "Madonna and child" scene.

THE CONTEXT OF INTERVENTION

Such are the major points in the coverage of the prehistory of America's intervention in Somalia. Unquestionably, print and electronic media replicated several consistent themes. The fundamentally unchallenged assertion is that this was a mission of mercy. Every phrase and insight by news reporters, anchors, and commentators, every citation by experts, iterates this premise. Second, the danger is minimized. Our motivations are framed as altruistic, and a supreme self-confidence is expressed and visually emphasized by imagery of American military might. The warlords, while not portrayed as amiable, friendly natives, still are shown to be unlikely as fearsome opponents. Above all, there is the generic icon: the walking skeleton, the rail-thin child, the flyblown infant, the icon of starvation, repeatedly shown and referred to in the coverage. They may be summed up by Tom Brokaw's phrase that the U.S. intervention "just can't start soon enough."

What is left out of this equation is that these pictures were not new, nor, hyperbole aside, was the famine in the horn of Africa unlike "anything else in modern history." As will be discussed below, the same pictures could have been taken in Somalia—or in dozens of other spots around the world—for years previously. The tragedy in the Horn of Africa had been building throughout the late 1980s and through 1992. Similar images had appeared in mid-1992 to accompany President Bush's decision to send economic aid as part of Operation Provide Comfort. In short, no political elite in Washington could have been unaware of the problems faced by Somalia. I would argue, though, that the image of the starving child was not cited by Bush and others until it was clear that it would also be a focus of American policy. It was a generic icon of African disaster; however, thousands of such pictures have been produced and will be produced without prompting a military response by the U.S. government. The cameras went to Somalia *en masse* only after the president of the United States, the number one icon setter and framer, told them to, and only after he connected Somalia to American interest by announcing that thousands of U.S. troops would be dispatched there.

More significantly absent from the framing of the icon of starvation were other possible interpretations for Bush's decision to intervene. Conservative Fred Barnes argued that not pictures on TV, but rather an urgent message by U.N. Secretary General Boutros Boutros-Ghali on November 24, was what suggested the idea.[17] Boutros-Ghali warned the president that all order had broken down in Somalia and the U.N. force at the time—500 Pakistanis—was inadequate. After consulting advisers, and after being reassured by Colin Powell that a small-scale mission could be accomplished quickly and with little cost, Bush then decided on the force option. This line of interpretation, favored by those who saw the United Nations as leading America into disaster, projected that Bush was follower rather than leader.

Another school of thought saw the mission as a sort of self-conscious publicity corrective to the legacy of the Gulf War, where, in contrast to Somalia, the United States mobilized a coalition to punish a Third World, Muslim nation. One commentator suggested that the Bush team "welcomed the opportunity to cast the much-maligned U.S. military in the role of hero to Africans and Muslims abroad, and to blacks and liberals at home."[18] In an earlier meeting with Boutros-Ghali, Bush was told that many Muslim nations had the impression that America was more willing to bomb Muslims than to feed them. Similarly, Representative Donald Payne (D-New Jersey), chairman of the Congressional Black Caucus, wrote in late 1993 that President Bush, by intervening in the nation of Somalia, "proved that the new world order was also for helping Black people as well as the rest of the world, which has strong meaning in my district of greater Newark."[19]

Alternately, Bush's team may have seen Somalia as fitting a mold for a humanitarian mission to close the curtain on a presidency whose most famous event was the Persian Gulf War. Colin Powell, who supported the mission, seemed to feel that it was also a suitable public relations exercise for an American military that was being somewhat chastised for the devastation wrought on Iraq. His comments suggest that he and other

Pentagon chiefs foresaw a "clean mission—it's sort of like the cavalry coming to the rescue, straightening out things for a while and then letting the marshalls come back to keep things under control."[20] Again, this prophecy of an uncomplicated rescue effort was disastrously in error, but was habitually replicated in the media.

Journalists James Petras and Steve Vieux, writing in the alternative press publication *Lies of Our Times*, offer a more sinister set of motives which were recently elaborated by communications scholar Rune Ottosen.[21] They posit a "hidden agenda" for Bush's decision to "invade" Somalia at the top of which was that the mission assisted in the justification of military expenditures because it highlighted a visible and clearly understandable role for the American military in the post–Cold War era. As Ottosen notes, the American military is "in excess of what is needed for defense" of America's territories and possessions. Increased emphasis on special missions in the Third World, such as Operation Restore Hope, thus may be seen as a budget-enhancing tool. It would also be, Petras and Vieux argue, "a vehicle for setting the political priorities and framework for the incoming Clinton administration." Of equal interest may have been the traditional importance accorded to the Horn of Africa as a strategic location, and a site past which much of the world's oil traffic flows. In addition, American companies have explored for oil in Somalia and have listed it as a top "prospective commercial oil producer." In contradiction to ideas that the move may have been seen as a public relations gesture to Muslims, these writers also suggest that the intervention was an act of containment against perceived Muslim radicalism.

Finally, Somalia may have been a testing of the waters (or deserts) for a new doctrine of "philanthropic imperialism."[22] All the evidence from the thinking of the Bush administration was that, while few believed, as Marlin Fitzwater said, the troops might be out before Clinton's inauguration in late January 1993, no one anticipated that it would be a long and bloody mission. This may have been the ideal adventure for both the president and the Pentagon, "an irresistible sip of painless Third World heroism, with no backwash."[23] This crusading spirit, this Kiplingesque conscientiousness, is also suggested as a justification of the Somali mission by anthropologist Anna Simons. She argues that when relief agencies framed the Somalia famine as "the worst in the world" and journalists "herald[ed] their cause. . . . The U.S. government then responded much as France and Britain had to missionaries in the past."[24] The parallel between the self-justifications of the colonialist expansion in the nineteenth century and the "humanitarian intervention mentality" of the late twentieth century is almost inescapable.

Reviewing much of what was said about the mission, it is easy to read it as a variation on a 100-year-old-poem, written by Rudyard Kipling to exhort the nascent United States to take up, as had the empires of the Old World, the "burden" of the race to conquer and control the "Half devil and half child" dark peoples so as to: "Fill full the mouth of Famine,/And bid the sickness cease." Of course Kipling's language is much more direct than the compassionspeak of today's leaders, but the ideal remains the same: we seek only to help, and that is why our soldiers tromp boldly into the lands of the less fortunate. As Dan Rather in his memoirs noted, "The American people don't make the call to arms lightly; they need more than a picture to send their sons and daughters to fight and die."[25] Indeed, it takes a president, but his rallying task is assisted by the evidence of stirring icons of outrage. Bush may or may not have been influenced to intervene by pictures he saw from Somalia, but he probably understood that an intervention would look good on TV.

GETTING OUT: FRAMING THE "BATTLE OF MOGADISHU"

At 3:30 p.m. on October 3, 1993, the United States military unit Task Force Ranger, consisting of 100 combat troops, including members of the elite Delta Force and 16 helicopters from the "Night Stalkers" Special Aviation Unit, deployed on its mission of the day.[26] The Night Stalkers, known as "the best of the best in military aviation," was typically employed to escort American commando missions.[27] Their target was a house in a neighborhood of south Mogadishu often called "Bosnia" because of its reputation as the scene of much fighting. In this house, American and U.N. intelligence had learned, leading supporters and advisers of General Mohamed Farah Aidid—designated by the United Nations as Public Enemy Number One—planned to meet.[28] Despite several attempts to capture him, the thin, limping elderly adversary had thus far escaped.

As the signal was given, the fleet of American helicopters, loaded with elite commandos, heavily laden with modern guns and missiles, rose from its staging point and flew toward the target in full light of the African sun. The only things visible upon their arrival were the "Klingon cruisers," the Toyota light trucks favored by Somali militiamen. Within minutes the "customers" of the Task Force, including Delta Force green berets and U.S. Army rangers, fast-roped to the ground. Another chopper landed on the roof of the building to discharge the soldiers.

Although the occupants of the house, almost thirty associates of Aidid and his clan, were captured and the perimeters secured, a Somali response was not long in coming. Aidid's forces, scattered through the neighborhood and beyond, sped to the site, as did hundreds of fighters who lived in the area. Nor were the Somalis unaware of the Americans' plans and dispositions. During five previous Task Force Ranger operations in September, Aidid's men, under his direct orders, had offered little resistance, rather they "reconnoiter[ed] . . . [and] learned that the Americans always used the same tactical 'template.'"[29] One of the Somali commanders, amused at the arrogance of his opponents, noted sardonically, "If you use one tactic once, you should not use it a third time. And the Americans had already done basically the same thing six times."[30]

The battle began. A Blackhawk helicopter was hit by a rocket-propelled grenade. The chopper crashed to the ground below. Other heli-

copters swooped to cover the downed bird. Task Force Ranger headquarters was alerted. By this time, the area was full of Somalis, some
firing, others watching. Another American helicopter was hit. Soon, so
many Somalis were in the area that "for the 90 or so U.S. soldiers
consolidating near the downed helicopter [this was] a killing zone."[31]
One helicopter crash-landed in a neighborhood of small homes and tin
shacks.[32] Two Delta Force snipers, Sergeants Shughart and Gordon,
jumped to the ground from another helicopter and pulled out the only
man they found alive: Michael Durant. Durant recalled hearing Shughart
crying out, "I'm hit!" A moment later, Gordon appeared from the blind
side of the helicopter and gave Durant a rifle. Then Gordon returned to
his comrade out of Durant's line of sight. Durant never saw either of his
two would-be rescuers again. He found he had no ammunition, and so
lay down the rifle and waited. Captured by Somalis a moment later, he
was stripped and beaten. In the next days his captors made the infamous
video of their prize.[33] The tape, passed to the news media, became an
icon on every major news broadcast, and on the covers of most
newspapers and magazines in North America. Within 12 days, Durant
was released under Aidid's orders.

   After Durant's capture, the battle continued. Paradoxically, the U.S.
Somalia expedition had been denied heavier armor by Secretary of
Defense Les Aspin, who had not wanted to raise the military profile of
the mission.[34] The survivors of Task Force Ranger and their hostages
were not rescued until later that night by a hastily scraped-together
group of Americans, Pakistanis and Malaysians; the latter had the only
tanks. Eighteen Americans died as a result of the October 3 battle;
almost 80 were wounded. In the long tradition of trying to obscure a
disaster with a display of medals, "more Bronze Stars, Silver Stars, and
Distinguished Services Crosses were given for actions during this
evening than in any other single action of this size in U.S. military
history."[35] Shughart and Gordon were the first Congressional Medal of
Honor winners in more than two decades. The Somali dead and
wounded were in the thousands, but they were largely unheralded and
uncounted, and most significantly, unphotographed by the American
mass media. President Clinton, despite some early bluster, promised to
withdraw American troops by March of the next year. Soldiers sent to
reinforce the mission to Somalia attempted no new offensives and
simply hunkered down in their compounds.[36] Aidid eventually struck a
deal with his pursuers and lived long enough to watch the Americans
leave his country. He was later killed by other Somalis, and his son, a
former U.S. Marine, took his place as clan leader.[37] Ironically, as
Michael Maren, a long-time relief worker and one of the more consis-
tently realistic observers of the events, noted, "Most of the [Somali] men
who were captured in that bloody battle probably would have shown up
at the U.N. gates with flowers in their hands if they'd been invited for
dinner."[38]

   A survey of news coverage of the Battle of Mogadishu and its
aftermath uncovers several basic themes. Through frequent repetition,
prominent display, and discourse, two new icons of outrage emerged:

Michael Durant's face and the mob desecrating the bodies of fallen American soldiers. The framing of these events by discourse elites across the ideological spectrum was that these represented outrages by an ungrateful Somali people and were exemplars of why the mission wasn't worth the sacrifice of young American lives. Notably, almost no attention was paid to American actions which may have set off the tragedy, nor to the losses suffered by the Somalis. In addition, no challenge was made to the original premise that these Americans were engaged in a mission of mercy—hence, the augmentation of the sense of aggrieved victimhood. Finally, President Clinton showed indecision and offered no strong plan of action to rally the country.

Newsmagazines

The October 18 issues of *Time* and *Newsweek* are those worthy of analysis here because they were the first to cover in depth the debacle of October 3. *Time* features the still image from the video of Michael Durant's face on its cover. The headline reads, "What In The World Are We Doing?" The issue features some 15 images, of which about 11 display either rampaging Somalis, blamed for the deaths of Americans, or portraits of or funeral services for the Americans. One image is of a Somali man, amid the wreckage of what appears to be a military vehicle or helicopter, holding up clothing from, we infer, a dead American soldier. The caption reads, "A Peace Mission in Somalia Turns Vicious and Ugly." Then, there is a picture of a Somali boy standing among the rubble, backed by a crowd, holding up torn clothing of an American soldier like a trophy. The caption reads, "Images Like This One are Mainlined Directly into the Democracy's Emotional Bloodstream."

In the main feature story, "Anatomy Of A Disaster," we are told, "It seemed simple at first. There were people in need. America would help. But the mission to Somalia, which began with visions of charity, now puts forth images of horror." (No mention is made, of course, that it was the press that framed the mission's simplicity to the public). To visually illustrate this introductory frame, two pictures are shown across two pages. One, we assume, is of the early days of Operation Restore Hope. An American soldier, his flag prominently shown on the sleeve of his desert khakis, leans over, smiling at a Somali child in a crowd of pathetic-looking women and children. Contrasting on the following page is a jeering mob of Somalis, grinning and brandishing sticks, many with fists clenched, standing over the naked, roped body of what we assume to be an American soldier. On the following pages, we see Somali gunmen surrounding the wreckage of a helicopter, the now-rescued Michael Durant in a hospital bed looking bruised and haggard, accompanied in huge type with this quote: "They beat me violently with their fists and sticks." Then there is an Army portrait of a young Ranger, "killed in action last week." Attached is a side-bar of excerpts he had written to a "hometown friend." The first begins, "I love my country and everything it stands for. I am in a position that I may have to give my life for my country."

The articles are most scathing of Clinton and Defense Secretary Aspin. Huge letters read "'How Did This Happen?' Clinton Demanded Of Les Aspin." A side-bar interview with Secretary of State Warren Christopher is titled "Defending His Boss." The last word, a commentary by columnist Michael Cramer, makes the case that President Clinton has a "second-rate" defense policy team, and "lacks his own clear bearings." The title of the piece is "It's All Foreign to Clinton." Cramer's main complaint is a lack of leadership: "Clinton is responding like Everyman rather than as the Commander in Chief and leader of the free world."

Michael Durant's battered face, staring in fear and seeming bemusement at the camera, overlaid by the title "Trapped In Somalia," is also the cover of *Newsweek* on October 18, 1993. Inside, opening the section dealing with the cover story, two pages show the color version of the desecrated body icon. The caption informs us that this is "Humiliation In Somalia: The Body Of A U.S. Servicemen Is Dragged Through The Streets Of Mogadishu." The headline of the story is, "Bloodbath: What Went Wrong?" The story itself is divided into several sections. First there is a piece on "The making of fiasco: Somalia, An inside look at how Washington blundered into misguided 'two track' policy." The story is illustrated by four images. The lead is the image of grinning Somalis flaunting a piece of "battle-torn camouflage pants from a dead United States soldier." The second image is of armor loaded on a transport plane headed for Somalia. The next picture is a podium shot of President Clinton. This is captioned by quotes from Clinton on Somalia: "If we . . . leave today, we know what would happen"; George Bush on Iraq: "It would be a signal to tyrants and potential despots around the world"; and Richard Nixon on Vietnam: "[It] would result in a collapse of confidence in American leadership." The quotes are intended as ironic commentary on the rhetoric of presidents calling upon America to "stay in the fight."

The final picture of the story is a medium shot of Aspin, looking chastened. The caption, reinforcing the story line, tells us that it was Aspin who, trying not to raise the profile of the mission, decided against sending heavier armor earlier. Inside the story is a side-bar on Aidid: "When The Bad Guy Has No Phone To Tap." He is shown in sinister pose and described in the caption as a "low-tech escape artist." One of the other side-bars, without illustration, includes excerpts from the "horrifying tale" of Michael Durant as told to a British news correspondent allowed to speak with him during his incarceration. Among Durant's comments: "Americans mean well. We did try to help. Things have gone wrong."

The Somalia section continues on to the story of the "Bloody Sunday" raid itself and its aftermath, "Fire Fight From Hell: What went wrong during the rout that stunned America." The lead picture is set in Arlington National Cemetery where we see an Army honor guard carrying a coffin draped with the Stars and Stripes. In the foreground are the white stone crosses of America's past war dead. In the back of the small procession, a military escort holds the arm of a young woman, dressed in black, her head bowed in grief. The caption tells us this is the funeral of "U.S. Army Sgt. James Joyce, killed in action in Mogadishu." As the story continues we see graphics that show the overview of what happened during the botched raid—the "anatomy of disaster." Then, reminiscent of the issues of *Life* magazine that showed numerous Vietnam War dead, there are 13 portraits detailing the "Rising American Death Toll."

Newspapers

In the *Washington Post* of October 4, 1993, the defeat of the American task force is a page-one story, but is unaccompanied by pictures on the front page. A picture with the continuing story on page A13 shows the "burning wreckage of a U.S. humvee destroyed by a mine in Mogadishu." Within the story, various political elites from both parties express grave doubts about the mission. Senator Sam Nunn (D-Georgia), a supporter of the administration, is quoted as wanting a "narrower mission." Senator Bill Bradley (D-New Jersey) states: "We ought to leave now." President Clinton and Secretary of Defense Les Aspin defend the mission, but offer no support for extending it. In the *New York Times*, no Somalia picture is shown on October 4. However, on October 5, Somalia is on the front page. The photograph shows one of the main sets of "exit" icons: "The body of a U.S. soldier being dragged yesterday through Mogadishu. The soldier was one of at least 12 Americans killed on Sunday." We view another often-repeated picture that became almost a sub-genre icon of the failure of the American mission: smiling Somalis holding up shreds of a U.S. soldier's uniform. At the bottom of the page is a tight close-up of the video still of airman Michael Durant. The caption reads, "An American soldier held captive and identified as U.S. Army Chief Warrant Officer Michael Durant, shown yesterday on a videotape from Somalia television."

Similarly, in the October 5 *Washington Post*, the image of the U.S. soldier being dragged by the crowd is repeated as part of the front of the World News section. The caption reads, "The body of an American soldier is dragged by ropes along a Mogadishu street by celebrating Somalis." A U.N. military spokesman expressed shock at the incident, saying, "We don't treat Somali casualties that way." In the story more description is given of the soldier's body "trundled through the streets on a wheel barrow by about 200 cheering Somalis."

On October 6, the *Washington Post* front page headline reads, "Somalia Options Reviewed as Discontent in Congress Grows." The front page image is the huge mouth of a C-5B transport vehicle being loaded with American troops and a tank which are "Somali-bound." On page A12, another bold counterposition is made. In the top front picture we see General Aidid, in glasses, fist raised in the power salute. A caption, reinforced by a similar headline, reads, "Public relations gains by Mohamed Farah Aidid, shown in June, have historical parallels in the Vietnam War." Below this is the video still of Durant. The caption reads, "The image of captive U.S. pilot Michael J. Durant prompted friends in his hometown of Berlin, N.H., to display yellow ribbons to signal their support." The picture accompanies a story on "Grim skepticism on the home front: Military towns await word on casualties, sadness mixes with doubts about U.S mission." In the story, several soldiers and dependents, and residents of towns near military bases, are quoted showing concern and pride. Most want the mission to end. Several react to the Durant picture. Durant's father is quoted: "He looked scared. He has a black eye and some cuts. We could see dirt on his face." The story informs us that the "videotape and the picture of a dead U.S. soldier in a Mogadishu street sparked a visceral reaction."

The concluding quote of the article is by a female base clerk and "retired Air Force Staff Sergeant" (and thus, in the code of journalism, qualified to speak for the American people): "They went over there on a humanitarian mission to feed them. We've done our part. We've fed them. It's time to come home." Finally, on page A16, we see a photograph of "Somali children play[ing] around the wreckage of a U.S. Blackhawk helicopter shot down during the battle in Mogadishu." This accompanies a continuing story on how "Discontent in Congress Grows."

In the *Times'* October 6 issue, the focus is on reinforcements sent to Somalia; the airlift picture shown on the same day for the *Washington Post* is presented here as well. Stories profile Michael Durant and the division among political elites about Somalia policy. At the bottom of the page is the military portrait, complete with American flag, of Sgt. Eugene Williams, an African-American soldier killed in Mogadishu. The story describes funeral services for him, and the sorrow felt for others lost in Somalia. Opinions of the relatives are divided: one says her son "died in vain." Counterposed to Sgt. Williams is a photograph of "President Clinton returning to the White House . . . for a meeting on Somalia." Clinton carries a briefcase, and his head is bent, suggesting weariness and discouragement.

The headlines on the front page add to the air of indecisiveness among political elites. "Clinton Reviews Policy In Somalia As Unease Grows"; "Reinforcements For U.S. Troops Delayed 9 Hours"; "Bid To Clarify Aims"; and "Congress Turning Hostile After Hostage-Taking And Heavy Losses." Within the latter story, we are told that "the deaths on Sunday" had "thrown the administration off balance, adding a layer of complications and crystallizing Congressional opposition." Bob Dole is quoted: "If we had a vote today, we'd be out today." Later in the story, "angry legislators" are described as besieging Secretary of Defense Aspin and Secretary of State Warren Christopher "with demands for a clear road map for an exit from Somalia, coupled with bitter complaints that the policy goals were unclear or unrealistic." In short, the events outpaced the administration's slow reaction and muddled response. Viewers and readers would have absorbed a message of divided government and uncertain policy making.

On October 7 in the *New York Times*, Somalia was again on the front page, with the somewhat contradictory headlines of "Clinton sending more troops to Somalia" and "A firm deadline for a pull-out will be set."

The only front-page picture is one dated June 1993, of General Aidid. His fist is extended toward the camera; he wears an angry expression, seemingly in the middle of speech making. The headline of the side-bar story tells us, "An elusive clan father is peacekeepers' nemesis." Inside there is a picture of crew-cut young Americans in a hospital bed. They are identified as "two of the American wounded" from the Battle of Mogadishu. Finally, two images illustrate a story of how "Relatives recount dreams of two killed in Somalia." One picture is a military portrait of Cpl. Jamie Smith: "one of two Rangers from New Jersey killed on Sunday in Mogadishu." Relatives and friends of Smith are interviewed, recounting his honor, virtue and skills as a soldier. The final picture crowns the theme of pathos and loss: the dead Ranger's father, a middle-aged man, his eyes slightly lowered, his fingers clutching "the letter he received in the mail yesterday in Long Valley, NJ, from his son."

The pattern of indecisiveness continued the next day, an eternity in the modern televisual world. On October 8, 1993, the *Washington Post* front-page headline reads, "Clinton to Double Force in Somalia." An official quoted in the story, however, states: "We still have to clarify the mission." The accompanying picture is of Clinton speaking before Congressmen in a White House meeting. (The same picture is on the first page of the October 8 *New York Times*.) Again the headlines are contradictory and hint of division among political elites. Forces are to be added, but withdrawal within six months is promised, and "critics question Clinton policy." The *Washington Post*'s front page of October 9 offers two pictures of Michael Durant, one from the Somali video, the second from the house in Mogadishu where he was held. The headline reads, "U.S. Captive Says He's Well Treated." In parallel, the *New York Times'* front cover of October 9 shows a picture from the funeral of Sgt. Joyce at Arlington. The picture is of the genre that is the most heart-rending and familiar in the iconography of war. The escort soldier and others in the background wear grim expressions. Joyce's mother and wife hold under their arms triangulated American flags. The headlines of the three Somali stories that border the picture read: "The U.N.'s Glow is Gone: After Months of Frustration and Setbacks, U.S. Turns Away from Joint Peacekeeping"; "A Common Cry Across the U.S.: It's Time to Exit"; "U.S. Mixes Signals to Somali General on its Next Steps."

In the weeks to come, the outrage icons are repeated and commented upon, but other scenes and iterations frame our understanding of them. These include the funerals of the dead soldiers, criticism of the president's policies, and the reinforcement of the unpopularity of the mission among the public, political leaders, and commentators, editorialists, and pundits.

Television

TV coverage of the events of October 3 reveals similar patterns. News of the details of the raid did not clearly arrive until October 4. On the CBS *Evening News* with Dan Rather and Connie Chung, the opening

graphic that signals the main news item is an American flag overlaid by
the title: "Americans Killed." Rather reports: "One American is captive,
12 are dead and 78 others are wounded in fighting in Mogadishu . . . in
the hellhole that is Somalia." We see video footage of the bruised face of
Michael Durant, speaking to the camera, identifying himself. David
Martin reports from Mogadishu over a series of shots of burning
vehicles, milling Somalis, and then the image of the naked body of an
American held by ropes and surrounded by Somalis who grin at the
camera. We hear the voice of Paul Watson of the *Toronto Star* (Watson
won the Pulitzer Prize for his photographs of the incident): "You could
see quite clearly that his face had been mutilated and that he had a large
gash wound along one of his thighs. This crowd followed it down the
street, and around a corner, pausing every once in a while for people to
kick at the corpse, to spit on it, and to stomp on it." Then we are shown
more footage of burning vehicles, and American troops loaded on a
transport plane to be sent as reinforcements. We view file footage of
American helicopters, tanks, and troops. David Martin narrates, saying
that U.S. officials are "fed up" with the United Nations. When Aidid's
name is mentioned, we see him speaking but we don't hear what he is
saying. Senators "from both parties" make statements on camera. Robert
Byrd (D-West Virginia): "The end game of U.S. participation in Somalia
should be measured in days and weeks"; Bob Dole (R-Kansas): "It
seems to me that enough Americans have died in Somalia." Then, in
summing up this initial segment, David Martin, standing in front of the
Pentagon, undermines any positive spin put on the story by the military
establishment with his own Pyrrhic framing: "Despite all the casualties,
Pentagon officials say they've succeeded in capturing 19 of Aidid's
followers, including two of his key lieutenants. But if this operation was
a success, then the U.S. can't stand much more success in Somalia."

In the next segment, we learn that Bill Clinton's health agenda has
been ambushed by foreign policy questions. We see him jogging by the
bay in San Francisco, and then giving a speech. He "spent much of the
day defending his policies in [Somalia]." Clinton is then quoted
speaking in tortuous diplomatic rhetoric: "The United States, not the
United Nations, the United States will view this matter very gravely and
take appropriate action." No journalist needed to explain to American
viewers that this was hardly bold leadership.

NBC's *Nightly News* of October 4 begins with Tom Brokaw
announcing: "Stunning news from Somalia: the deadliest battle yet
involving U.S. forces." Then we see the desecration footage. Reporter
Ed Rable: "Images of Somalis dragging through the streets of Mogadishu the body of one of the dead Americans. The scenes described for
us today by eyewitness Paul Watson, a reporter for *Toronto Star*."
Watson then gives an almost identical description to that which he
narrated to CBS of Somalis dragging, stomping, and spitting on the
bodies of the American dead. The Durant video follows. Once again, Les
Aspin is filmed at the Pentagon reading a limp statement. We are told
(and shown) that the United States will be sending tanks, troops and
aircraft to Somalia, but only for protection, not an offensive against

Aidid. The president is shown giving a speech in which he intones, "We have issued the sternest possible warning" not to harm the captured American, hardly a thundering rallying cry in response to the icons of outrage. In contrast, George Bush is shown "criticizing the operation." Dissatisfaction is cited also from Capitol Hill where senators such as Patrick Leahy (D-Vermont) state: "It is time to get out." On the Senate floor, John McCain (R-Arizona) implores: "Mr. President, it is time to come home."

In the ABC news broadcast of October 4, Peter Jennings announces: "Over the weekend the U.S. military suffered one of the worst battlefield tragedies in several years. Twelve Americans have been killed, 75 wounded, and half a dozen are missing. It was another frustrating operation against the Somali warlord Mohamed Aidid." Reporter John McWethy speaks over the desecration video, essentially the same footage shown on the other networks, in the news magazines, and in the newspaper. Again, Canadian journalist Paul Watson describes the scene, but this time with an extra gruesome detail: "I saw one being pulled by ropes. I watched it for probably 10 minutes. I saw a second burnt body, which was burnt beyond recognition, which was being pulled by a small crowd of children." Then we see the Durant video. Also, as in the other broadcast, Aspin, like Clinton, provides a rather tepid reaction to the video: "We will respond forcefully if any harm comes to those who are being detained." Once more as well, we see the American troops and tanks being sent to reinforce the mission, but no hint is given that they plan to engage in offensive action. John McWethy then adds: "The failure to capture Mohamed Aidid and the mounting American casualties drew more criticism from Capitol Hill." On the Senate floor, Robert Byrd speaks, "Why in the world should we drag these fatal cops-and-robber operations on any longer? Let's vote and let's get out."

Finally, as in the other broadcasts, the administration's attempt to put a positive light on the mission is undercut by the reporter's concluding: "As bad as the situation looks in Somalia, the Clinton administration argues that it is making crucial progress in trying to put Aidid out of business by capturing his top lieutenants. But that argument is getting harder to sell as American casualties go up and Aidid remains free." From the studio, Peter Jennings adds his own commentary that equally undermines the official story. "Indeed, it is harder to sell and there are indications tonight that the Clinton administration is ready to undertake a serious review of the U.S. commitment to Somalia and the role of American troops in the United Nations contingent." From California, correspondent Brit Hume adds to the unfavorable frame of the Somalia story. "Mr. Clinton was overtaken by the bad news from Somalia about the deaths of some U.S. soldiers and the possible capture of others." Clinton is then shown making the same warnings against Aidid. Hume finalizes the overturning of the governmental rhetoric by noting that Clinton had, earlier in the year, tried very hard to associate himself visibly with the success of Operation Restore Hope—"hugging" it—and now would have difficulty disassociating himself.

FRAMING OUTRAGE

It is beyond the scope of this study to discuss all the news coverage of October 1993, but across all media, the same themes and images recur. Overwhelmingly such themes—outrage at the scenes; pictures "getting us in" and "driving us out" from the "hellhole that is Somalia"; lack of inspiring leadership from the president; the contrast between our good intentions and the perfidy of the Somalis—were replicated in further commentary from many sources.[39] [See Appendix C.] Although the administration sent new troops to Somalia, they quite clearly were intended not to escalate the conflict, but to protect the troops already in place. The chief executive, Bill Clinton, is framed as indecisive; his secretary of defense is immediately indirectly blamed for the disaster. In terms of public opinion (and icon) management, the president of the United States did not attempt to lead press, public, or lawmakers toward any bold new policy. If Lyndon Johnson was largely silent during Tet, and George Bush was too "muted" for his critics as the Tiananmen events occurred, Clinton's diplospeak was inappropriate in the extreme. When I played tapes of the Clinton administration's broadcasts for my classes, the reaction to Aspin's "warning," contrasted with the gruesome images, was shaken heads and snorts. It is with this frame of indecisiveness that the effects of the images should be taken into context. Clinton defaulted the frames of policy to others. Into this vacuum, spurred by strong public reaction and sniping by politicians of both parties, the press was allowed to interject its own cynicism about government optimism. Little mention is made, however, that most major media faithfully replicated both the previous administration's and the Pentagon's optimistic predictions about the mission. Also, the changing of the mission by the United Nations and the Clinton administration from food distribution to anti-insurgency and government building was seldom noted by the U.S. press while it was occurring. Boosterism was followed by silence; the inevitable result was shock and surprise.

Polls reinforced this view: strong support was shown for President Bush's decision to send troops in December 1992; post-October 3, 1993, polls showed overwhelming opposition to the mission in Somalia.[40] Polls taken by the television networks, Gallup, and the *Washington Post* in October 1993 showed approval of the president's handling of the crisis below 40 percent; in contrast, 73 percent had approved of Bush's decisions in December of 1992. In reporting such findings, the *New York Times* undercut the framing of the president in the most effective rhetorical strategy journalism has at its option: quoting "ordinary" Americans who reject continued American presence in Somalia. An emergency health care administrator stated: "Bring the boys home. . . . If I have to choose between pictures of starving Somalian babies or dead American soldiers being dragged through the streets of Mogadishu, well, I don't want to see any more dead Americans. . . . What the President proposed doesn't change a thing for me."[41] As the report argued, "The pictures of a dead American soldier being dragged through the streets of Mogadishu seem to have made it all but impossible for Mr. Clinton to change many minds."[42] Press frames, thus, made it appear that the pictures could drive policy in only one direction: out of the Horn of Africa, with the only debate being on how fast.

It is not clear, however, whether both sets of images (the starvation and desecration icons) actually drove policy, or were employed as examples for and against policy. The public was, by one measurement, surprised by the events in Mogadishu. According to a series of Times Mirror polls, public attention paid to Somalia was slight until the events of October 1993; no more than a few percent were following the story. Notably, however, the pictures may have confirmed more than reversed a policy trend. In a Times Mirror poll taken on September 15, 1993, approval was already at the low figure of 41 percent. In the case of the icons of starvation, such images had appeared before without initiating a military mission.

It is self-evident that the second set of images were more likely to touch the American psyche because they involved Americans. A Time/CNN/Gallup survey a day after the pictures of Durant and the desecrated soldiers ran found that 50 percent of respondents who had seen the images favored withdrawal from Somalia as opposed to only 33 percent who had not. People reacted to the events; the icons focused their reaction. This is a crucial distinction in assessing the power of an image. Pictures are not just forms and shapes; they show things and people. How much we care about those things and people affects the power of the image over us.

As in the case of Vietnam, increasing casualties led to decreasing support for the conflict, or rather lessened support for how it was being "handled." Americans can withstand the sight of dead "others," especially if our leaders and media classify such people as enemies (Iraqis during the Gulf War) or unimportant (Rwandan Tutsis), but the empathy for dead Americans is intense and real. That empathy is an effective tool for rallying action, but it is a reasonable question to pose (the same query we could raise in reaction to Tet '68): what if the American president at the time was a strong, aggressive, popular leader? Interestingly, a series of ABC polls in the wake of the events of October 3–4, 1993, found the country divided on what exactly to do, but over 50 percent of the respondents did not approve of Clinton's "handling of the situation." What if Clinton had "handled" the battle of Mogadishu differently, that is responded with a cry for vengeance, a massive commitment of troops, and the requisite demonizing of the enemy? President Clinton, however, like Lyndon Johnson at Tet, decided that the battle was not worth escalating, and signaled not a rally but a retrenchment. The rhetorical arena was thus left open to critics of the policies. Again, though, the pictures were not all-powerful and monodirectional in their influence. Bush could have reacted in 1992 with simply more food aid; in October, 1993, Clinton could have declared war or at least called for punishment and vengeance on a smaller scale; the visuals could have been driven by them toward other policies. Like history itself, icons do not move inexorably in one direction with one predetermined outcome.

UNASKED QUESTIONS: THE FRAMES NOT PRESENTED

Part of the "shock" expressed by discourse elites was disingenuous: politicians, military leaders, and journalists who were paying attention knew very well that Operation Restore Hope had quickly adopted a heavy-handed martial profile. Media coverage, however, as is always the case, dropped to almost nothing for the bulk of 1993—until the battle. The signs of escalation continued, however. In January, U.S. Marines began raiding arms depots and arsenals of Somali clans, including that of General Aidid. The first American soldier was killed on January 12. Later that month, U.S. helicopter gunships, in coordination with Belgian paratroops, fought with other militiamen. In February, the United Nations delivered an ultimatum to all 14 major clan leaders to submit an itemized list of their heavy armaments. Anyone who did not comply would face censure and the confiscation of weapons. None of the warlords met the deadline. In late February, U.S. and U.N. troops were stoned in Mogadishu by a crowd of Aidid supporters. Leaving Somalia on March 2, Special U.S. Envoy Robert B. Oakley announced that the mission "to restore hope and to stop the killing from war, famine and disease has largely been accomplished." A few weeks later, U.S. forces engaged in a battle between two rival warlords in the city of Msmayu.

At the end of March, the U.N. Security Council passed Resolution 814, creating UNOSOM II, the multinational peace-keeping force command structure. Among its mandates was to disarm the Somali clans. Throughout these months, withdrawals of American troops coincided with increasingly frequent confrontations with Somalis. On June 5, three Americans were wounded and 24 Pakistani soldiers killed in a battle with the forces of General Aidid. Less than a week later, U.S. forces raided suspected Aidid strongholds, arsenals, or communication centers. On June 17, a battle between Aidid and U.N. and U.S. forces left 60 Somalis dead and 44 U.N. soldiers wounded. On July 12, fifteen Somalis died in another raid by the United States on an Aidid headquarters building. On August 8, four American soldiers died under mysterious circumstances, killed either by a land mine or a remote-control bomb. Later that month, the United States sent a unit of Army Rangers to Somalia. On August 30, the Rangers began commando missions searching for Aidid. At the beginning of September, seven Nigerian U.N. troops were shot. Throughout the month, more clashes and Ranger raids continued. At least 60 Somalis were killed in one encounter. On September 25, Somalis shot down an American helicopter, killing three soldiers aboard and wounding three others in the ensuing firefight. In short, the "mission of mercy" had evolved into an anti-insurgent war. This evolution was never adequately expressed to the American people; even many in the political hierarchy seemed unaware, or rather unwilling to pay attention.

Accordingly, to most viewers, the perception of discordance between icons was understandable. The middle story between pictures of starvation and those of betrayal was not told. To continue the Kipling analogy, the "devils" that the white man must face had utterly displaced the suffering children. There is no evidence that this framing was imposed on the news media by political elites and every evidence that reporters reacted in the same way to the images that politicians and many ordinary Americans (including my students) did: with revulsion and blame. Dan Rather commented later that, "These were soldiers who'd been sent to help—to save children—on a humanitarian mission. Yet, they had died, evidently at the hands of the neighbors of the people they'd been sent to save. It made me sick to think about it."[43] If, however, the pictures of the dead servicemen had an "effect," once again the effect must be assessed relative to the framing of the icons of outrage and what they actually showed. However natural Americans' reaction to the pictures of atrocities visited upon our soldiers, it is important to consider the images we were not shown, and the questions not asked about the context of the events.

Were Lives Saved?

President Clinton's assertion that "hundreds of thousands" of lives were saved by the intervention was unchallenged even by his critics. In light of new research, however, we may legitimately ask: were lives saved because of the introduction of American combat troops? Most sober observers agree that this question is not fully answerable; the media, however, demand numbers and these were provided by aid agencies desperate for publicity. Short-term success was suggested, especially by many nongovernmental aid and relief organizations involved in the feeding of the country's hungry. Former aid worker Michael Maren argues that claims of lives saved from the U.N. and U.S. mission were vastly exaggerated, and that wiser members of the press admitted after the Americans had left that "we were wrong."[44] Rakiya Omaar, former head of Africa Watch, concluded:

Ironically, Somalia's overall food supply problem was in fact solved more than one month *before* the intervention began: the intervention was designed to address a problem that had already been largely solved. .... [It] had no discernible impact on fine-targeting of food to the most vulnerable, public health or rehabilitation—and indeed, has damaged the prospects for the economic recovery of farming communities by oversuppling [*sic*] imported food.[45]

More important was an assessment by the respected Refugee Policy Group (RPG) in 1994. They candidly admit that it is extremely difficult to determine how many people died in Somalia during the years 1990–1993.[46] Nevertheless, the RPG estimated that the highest rates of excess mortality were in the early months of 1992 and around September 1992. At the time that extra food aid was sent, supposedly in response to pictures of starvation from Somalia, the excess mortality rate had in fact been decreasing for most of the year. Moreover, as the RPG report suggests, many of those at the edge of death die anyway, regardless of intervention. Most of the people in the starvation icons of Somalia perished; only earlier assistance could have helped them. The report, for example, notes that in the period 1991–1992, "many of those who received aid at therapeutic feeding centers went on to die. In effect, the food aid postponed these deaths but did not avert them."

That frame, of course, was not allowed to occlude America's self-congratulation on engaging in a mission of mercy. In short, there is some evidence that the intervention did not directly save the hundreds of thousands claimed as its beneficiaries. In absence of verifiable figures, journalists (and aid agencies, and eventually politicians) brandished large numbers or ritually repeated figures without verification.[47] Moreover, in parading the starvation icons in front of viewers, Western media never captioned the scenes with the uncomfortable truth: these people will die whatever we do. The icon of starvation, then, masked the real horror that was beyond being erased by our guns and grain.[48]

How Many Lives Were Lost Because of the Mission?

It is revealing that we are unsure of the precise number of Somalis killed by the U.N.-U.S. mission. In reciting the losses of the October 3 battle, *Newsweek* (October 18) claims that 300 to 400 Somalis were killed and 700 to 800 wounded. These losses are mentioned in passing. "Americans did not see pictures of the Somali casualties," reported *Time* magazine, which proceeded *not* to show us those casualties. Indeed, in every major channel of American mass media the enemy dead were unpictured.[49] What about "losses" before October 3? As related above, these were not prominently cited as being an influence on the events that day. According to the United Nation's own figures, more than 200 Somalis had been killed by U.N. or U.S. forces in the first 100 days of the intervention.[50] By no means were all these people killed in self-defense or shoot-outs with warlords. Many incidents small and large continued throughout the year leading up to October 3: Marines shot to death a twelve-year-old Somali who they thought was holding a gun on them;[51] Canadian troops tortured Somalis to death;[52] and Pakistani troops fired on a crowd and killed at least 20 people. Even more important, earlier in 1993, in a "real destroy mission" as described by an American officer, gunships fired missiles into a house where tribal elders, including Aidid supporters, were reportedly meeting. As many as seventy were killed. As Michael Maren notes, it was a questionable objective: "most of [those killed were] respected members of the community. . . . Some were even there to urge Aydiid to step down."[53]

General Aidid's line was that 10,000 Somalis were killed by intervention forces between June 5 and October 3.[54] While no one, probably including Aidid himself, believed this was an accurate figure, it is interesting to note that Western intelligence officials only thought it "high," not preposterous.[55] Finally, in the October 3 raid, it is estimated that a third of the Somali dead were women and children.[56] This context, however, was absent from the framing of events in American media. As shown, the framing of icons made it appear that *all* Somalis were unified in opposition to us. That this was General Aidid's propaganda line as well only piles yet another irony on top of the miscues and misdirections of Operation Restore Hope. Moreover, those who would think that identifying the costs of the mission in Somali lives somehow gives support to the "enemy" and dishonors our dead should consider the following: ignoring earlier Somali casualties increased anger, resentment, and resistance. The price of blindness and ignorance was borne not only by the Somalis, but by the young American servicemen sent in harm's way with inadequate support for an overambitious mission.

Could Anything Have Been Done Earlier?

Former President Jimmy Carter concluded that, "We've gotten started only after the crisis became so acute that U.S. television stations primarily began to show the starving Somali children."[57] This assumes that the story itself drove the media agenda, not the reverse. The icons of Mogadishu obscure a deeper issue: could anything have been done earlier? Could those icons have been avoided? Deciding whether or not the intervention in Somalia was "successful" begs the question, compared to what? By simply judging Operation Restore Hope on its own balance sheet we are creating a false dilemma; by making alternatives, we ignore other choices.[58] Yet we should ask if the United States could have avoided the pitfalls of a military intervention. If lives were indeed saved by actions in 1993, could more have been done previously at a lower cost of people, material, and money?

One of the unambiguous findings of the 1994 Refugee Policy Group Report was that the crisis in Somalia was essentially preventable because "simple health care interventions could have saved most of the lives lost during the crisis."[59] "[A] negligible amount of money was invested in diplomatic efforts to solve the root political cause of the problem," argued John Sommer, director of the Somalia Humanitarian Aid Society. "This was tantamount to treating the symptom while downplaying the disease," because "intensive diplomacy" might have prevented the crisis as it developed later.[60] His report concludes that as many as 240,000 Somalis died before any real attention was paid by the international community. Jan Westcott, the former special relief coordinator for Somalia at the Office of U.S. Foreign Disaster Assistance, points out that there were opportunities for assisting the Somalis to bring internal order to the country but these efforts were insufficiently supported by the United Nations and the international community.[61] Among the scrapped plans that may have been successful was a Somali police force, but American funding for such a unit was delayed three years until a few weeks before the Mogadishu raid.[62] In a similar vein, a report by Africa Watch and Physicians for Human Rights of March 26, 1992, argued that "[T]he U.S. did not make any serious efforts to head off the current disaster. . . . It failed to provide the much-needed leadership internationally that would have encouraged the U.N. to act on Somalia much earlier."[63] It seems evident that earlier intervention of reduced proportions through diplomacy and aid targeted toward economic and agricultural rejuvenation would have circumvented the tragedies to come, both Somali and American.[64]

THE ICONS OF ARROGANCE?

Days before the fateful raid on Mogadishu, Bill Clinton spoke to reporters and asserted that the Americans were in the Horn of Africa "to stop the killing, to stop the disease, to stop the famine. And that has been done with broad support among the Somali people, with the exception of that small portion in Mogadishu where General Aideed and his supporters are."[65] Before, during, and after the mission, the administration's frame, passed on by the Bush presidency, was that Somalia was solely a mission of mercy and that any opposition was feeble and limited. The former frame, that of the humanitarian mission, remains to this day, despite critiques and expositions of it in sources ranging from the left alternative press to military publications. The contention that the mission was a military "success" convinced no one in Somalia—"spinning Dunkirk," Michael Maren so perceptively called it, with the big difference being, of course, that one day the British army returned to Dunkirk in triumph and was welcomed by its citizens.[66]

Suffering Americans, an evil warlord, jubilant taunting Somalis: these icons were put in collision with others, those of the starving child. America, and especially the sympathetic, well-meaning American soldiers, were portrayed as victims, either of incompetence by politicians, or of an ungrateful, sinister, and callous people. We went, we told ourselves, to save a nation, but were blinded by the vainglory that Kipling accurately forecast as the sin of all empires. This arrogance of self-congratulation, unanimously expressed by discourse elites, led to the deaths of many American soldiers who probably honestly did want to help a suffering people they had seen on TV. The U.S. forces, which were engaging in so many attack missions in October of 1993, were at the lowest ebb of their equipment and manpower. The intervention force had been drawn down from 28,000 to 4,000, and was allowed no medium tanks. The original mission of safe-guarding feeding centers had been expanded by the U.N. command and the Clinton administration with little notice by the press or complaint by other political elites.

In an intervention full of ironies, however, the Somalia story did not turn out to be as touristic a form of journalism as no doubt many in the media expected. The best journalists, like the best soldiers, are the ones most likely to be in the front line, and to fall in the service of their profession. Somalia was the graveyard of many young American soldiers, but it was the same for more than a dozen journalists. Did they, too, die in vain? Certainly Somalia produced several icons of outrage; some will live forever as examples of "great" photojournalism, more for their content than for their composition, but the pictures undoubtedly were symptoms of international politics and prejudices, not their cause. Ronald Reagan, in response to the pictures of the famine in Ethiopia in 1984–1985, commented that "a hungry child knows no politics." He was correct in the sense that the victims of famine as well as the victims of the other three Horsemen of the Apocalypse are often those least aware of the causes of their suffering. Unfortunately, those who allow, encourage, or create the conditions for famine are equally ignorant or, rather, willfully blind.

The lesson of the icons of Somalia seems to be that even when a picture demonstrably has some power to influence, that influence is largely due to contextual factors. The content of the pictures is what counts: in this case, dead Americans. Also of importance are the decisions of elites to make a policy or, in contrast, to show indecision and weakness. Clinton's response to the "outrages," warning that Aidid "ought to stop the violence because that's a good thing" was hardly comparable to the battle cries of Churchill ("We shall fight them on the beaches"); Stalin ("Fight to the last drop of blood"); or Roosevelt ("Day of Infamy").[67] The icons of outrage of Somalia were framed in a distinct way, and all other possible framings, all contexts that may have suggested different ways to understand the relevance, representativeness, and indeed the causes of these images, were either ignored or shunted to obscurity. The icons of Somalia masked much more than they revealed.

NOTES

1. "In or Out, or What?" *Economist*, October 9, 1993, p. 60.

2. "Remarks at the Presentation Ceremony for the Congressional Medal of Honor," *Weekly Compilation of Presidential Documents: Administration of William J. Clinton*, May 23, 1994, pp. 1150–1151.

3. E. Goffman, *The Presentation of Self in Everyday Life* (New York: Anchor, 1959).

4. A. Mendelsohn-Bartholdy, *The War and German Society: The Testament of a Liberal* (New Haven: Yale University Press, 1937).

5. H. Schuman, R. F. Belli, and K. Bischoping, "The Generational Basis of Historical Knowledge," in *Collective Memory of Political Events: Social Psychological Perspectives*, ed. by J. W. Pennebaker, D. Paez, and B. Rimé (Mahway, NJ: Lawrence Erlbaum, 1997), pp. 47–77.

6. M. K. Albright, *U.S. Department of State Dispatch*, June 28, 1993, pp. 463–67. See also M. Mandelbaum, "The Reluctance to Intervene," *Foreign Policy* 95 (1994): 3–18.

7. "Address to the Nation on the Situation in Somalia," *Weekly Compilation of Presidential Documents: Administration of George Bush*, December, 1992, p. 2329.

8. R. Watson, "Mission of Mercy; It's Our Fight Now," *Newsweek*, December 14, 1992, p. 26.

9. C. P. Freund, "Images from Somalia," *Washington Post*, December 6, 1992, p. C3.

10. M. R. Beschloss, "The Video Vise," *Washington Post*, May 2, 1993, p. C1. See also R. Ciolli, "Eyes on the Battlefront," *Newsday*, May 9, 1993, p. 53.

11. B. Harden, "Who Killed Liberia?" *Washington Post*, May 26, 1996, p. C1.

12. N. Gowing, *Real-Time Time Television Coverage of Armed Conflicts and Diplomatic Crises: Does it Pressure or Distort Foreign Policy Decisions?* Working Paper 94–1, Joan Shorenstein Barone Center on the Press, Politics and Public Policy, Harvard University, John F. Kennedy School of Government, p. 68.

13. The soldier's rank as reported is in error. Specialist 4 (along with Specialist 5 and Specialist 6) were removed from U.S. Army ranks in the 1980s. Hanninen was probably simply a "Specialist."

14. Interestingly, within a reflection in the eyes we also see the shadowed face of the photographer.

15. This is unlike the "Viet Cong suspect" in Eddie Adams's Tet offensive photo and the "man who stood against the tanks" at Tiananmen.

16. The CNN telecasts were not available for this analysis.

17. F. Barnes, "Last Call," *New Republic*, December 28, 1993, pp. 11–13.

18. J. Muravchik, "Beyond Self-Defense," *Commentary* (December 1993): 19.

19. D. M. Payne, "Somalia is a Test of U.S. Commitment for Africa," *The Washington Report on Middle East Affairs* (November/December 1993): 39.

20. Quoted in S. Blumenthal, "Why Are We in Somalia?" *The New Yorker*, October 25, 1993, pp. 57–58.

21. J. Petras and S. Vieux, "The Somali Invasion," *Lies of Our Times* (January-February 1993): 14–16. See also R. Ottosen, "'Rambo' in Somalia? A Critical Look at Media Coverage of Operation Restore Hope," in *International News Monitoring*, ed. by M. Griffin and K. Nordenstreng (Boston: Hampton Press, 1998, forthcoming).

22. R. Omaar and A. DeWaal, "Somalia: Adding 'Humanitarian' Intervention to the U.S. Arsenal," *Covert Action* 44 (1993): 4–11.

23. J. Stevenson, *Losing Mogadishu: Testing U.S. Policy in Somalia* (Annapolis, MD: Naval Institute, 1995), p. 53.

24. A. Simons, *Networks of Dissolution: Somalia Undone* (Boulder: Westview, 1995), p. 202.

25. D. Rather, *The Camera Never Blinks Twice: The Further Adventures of a Television Journalist* (New York: William Morrow, 1994), p. 253.

26. See R. Atkinson, "Night of a Thousand Casualties," *Washington Post*, January 31, 1994, pp. A1, A26–A27; J. Stevenson, *Losing Mogadishu*, pp. 94–95; K. DeLong and S. Tuckey, *Mogadishu: Heroism and Tragedy* (Westport, CT: Praeger, 1994), pp. 9–10, 39–59, 100; M. Maren, *The Road to Hell: The Ravaging Effects of Foreign Aid and International Charity* (New York: Free Press, 1997), pp. 216, 230.

27. Little is popularly known about the unit because of its "super-secret" status. Until recently, the government did not even acknowledge its existence. See K. DeLong and S. Tuckey, *Mogadishu*, p. 2.

28. As Jo Ellen Fair notes, "Writing about representations of individuals in non-Western contexts is sometimes difficult because of the language the researcher finds herself needing to use." In this case, Aidid (the spelling of whose name varies depending on the source) was ritually referred to in the American press as a "warlord." Among Somalis not of his faction or clan, even more negative monikers were employed. Obviously, a host of labels could be used to frame Aidid. I have striven in this essay neither to replicate standard media frames nor to retreat to semantic banalities. When I am speaking in my own voice, Aidid is a general, a Somali leader, or a clan leader. "Gunmen" and "thugs," or, as could be posed, Somali Freedom Fighters, are described here as militiamen. Obviously, no label is entirely satisfactory, and attention should always be paid to the context and implications of any description applied to groups and persons. See J. E. Fair, "The Body Politic, the Bodies of Women, and the Politics of Famine in U.S. Television Coverage of Famine in the Horn of Africa," *Journalism & Mass Communication Monographs* 158 (August 1996): 29 [f2].

29. J. Stevenson, *Losing Mogadishu*, p. 94.

30. "The Raid That Went Wrong," *Washington Post*, January 30, 1994, pp. A1, A26–27; R. Atkinson, "Night of a Thousand Casualties."

31. R. Atkinson, "Night of a Thousand Casualties."

32. K. DeLong and S. Tuckey, *Mogadishu*, p. 40.

33. Durant in an interview recalls that he could not "play John Wayne" and live, so while not giving his captors all the answers they wanted, he did give them some intelligence, though none that would "endanger his comrades." In K. DeLong and S. Tuckey, *Mogadishu*, p. 57.

34. The 1st Armored Division stationed in Germany had on call a Division Ready Force that consisted of heavy tanks and other armor and support vehicles. This unit was designed for missions in heavy-fire zones like the site of the Battle of Mogadishu. It could have been deployed to Somalia within 18 hours. Inexplicably, it was not called in, even after the fighting began and the American ground commander asked for assistance.

35. K. DeLong and S. Tuckey, *Mogadishu*, p. 100.

36. J. Stevenson, *Losing Mogadishu*, p. 106; K. B. Richburg, "Weapons of War, Words of Peace Blur Somalia's Future," *Washington Post*, January 27, 1994, p. A3; "President Resists Somalia Pull-Out Now," *New York Times*, October 14, 1993, p. A6.

37. The troubles of Somalia continue: factional fighting, kidnapping of aid workers, and sabotaging of relief efforts. Familar stories and pictures trickle into the news stream, but no rush to intervene and no herd of cameras. See J. C. McKinley, Jr., "Somali Gunmen Kidnap 9 Foreign Red Cross Workers," *New York Times*, April 16, 1998, p. A3; J. C. McKinley, Jr., "How a U.S. Marine Became Leader of Somalia," *New York Times*, August 12, 1998, p. A3.

38. M. Maren, *The Road to Hell*, p. 230. See also M. Maren, "Somalia: Whose Failure?", *Current History* (May 1996): 201–5.

39. Nicholas Gowing notes that, "[The images produced an] intense and effective pressure . . . [through] thousands of phone calls made to lawmakers on Capitol Hill." N. Gowing, "Behind the CNN Factor; Lights! Camera! Atrocities! But Policy Makers Swear They're Not Swayed by TV Images," *Washington Post*, July 31, 1994, p. C1.

40. See reports of polls in J. Keen, "Public Feels 'Confusion' about Goals," *USA Today*, October 5, 1993, p. 1; T. Quitieri, "U.S.: Return our Men," *USA Today*, October 6, 1993, p. 1A; "*Time* Poll Oct. 7," *Time*, October 18, 1993, p. 42; J. Byrd, "Picture from Somalia," *Washington Post*, October 17, 1993, p. C6; R. Benedetto, "Poll: Most Now Say U.S. Troops Should Get Out," *USA Today*, October 6, 1993, p. 2A; ABC *News*, "Americans React to Fate of U.S. Soldiers in Somalia," October 5, 1993.

41. B. Drummond Ayres, Jr., "A Common Cry Across the U.S.: It's Time to Exit," *New York Times*, October 9, 1993, sec. 1, p. 1.

42. Ibid.

43. D. Rather, *The Camera Never Blinks Twice*, p. 252.

44. M. Maren, *The Road to Hell*, p. 213.

45. R. Omaar and A. de Waal, *Somalia—Operation Restore Hope: A Preliminary Assessment* (London: African Rights, 1993), p. 1.

46. S. Hansch, *Lives Lost, Lives Saved: Excess Mortality and the Impact of Health Interventions in the Somalia Emergency*, Refugee Policy Group Report (Washington, DC: Refugee Policy Group, 1994).

47. Ibid.

48. The role that drought played in the famine is highlighted in D. Keen, *The Benefits of Famine and Relief in Southwestern Sudan, 1983–1989* (Princeton: Princeton University Press, 1994).

49. It is unlikely that a montage of the Somali dead would have modified American public and political elite reaction. What is significant for this analysis, however, is that the American media felt no need to picture the enemy at all.

50. R. Omaar and A. de Waal, *Somalia—Operation Restore Hope*, p. 36. See also J. Stevenson, *Losing Mogadishu*, p. 68.

51. J. Stevenson, *Losing Mogadishu*, p. 66.

52. C. Truehart, "Canadian Guilty of Killing Somali," *Washington Post*, March 18, 1994, p. A26; C. H. Farnsworth, "Torture by Army Peace Keepers in Somalia Shocks Canada," *New York Times*, November 27, 1994, p. 14.

53. M. Maren, *The Road to Hell*, p. 229.

54. G. Anderson, "UNOSOM II: Not Failure, Not Success," in *Beyond Traditional Peacekeeping*, ed. by D.C.F. Daniel and B. C. Hayes (New York: St. Martin's Press, 1995), pp. 267–81.

55. Ibid.

56. J. Stevenson, *Losing Mogadishu*, p. 95; P. J. Sloyan, "How the Warlord Outwitted Clinton's Spooks," *Washington Post*, April 3, 1994, p. C3. This does not mean that American forces were targeting civilians. It is a universal strategy of insurgents to fight from within populated areas to confound their more powerful, technologically-advanced attackers, as well as maximizing the propaganda potential when civilian deaths occur. In the case of General Aidid, his power base was inside heavily populated areas of a major city.

57. D. Oberdorfer, "Bush Sends Forces to Help Somalia," *Washington Post*, December 5, 1992, p. 1A.

58. See discussion of the problems of exploring "historical alternatives" in K. Monsma, "Beyond Dependency: Historical Sociology and Social Change in the Southern Cone of South America. A Review Article," *Comparative Studies in Society and History* 33 (October 1991): 791–99.

59. S. Hansch, *Lives Lost, Lives Saved*, p. 35.

60. J. G. Sommer, *Hope Restored? Humanitarian Aid in Somalia, 1990–1994*, Refugee Policy Group Report, 1994, p. 113.

61. J. Westcott, *The Somalia Saga: A Personal Account, 1990–1993* (Washington, DC: Refugee Policy Group, 1994), p. 37.

62. "Presidential Memorandum for the Secretary of State, the Secretary of Defense. Presidential Determination, No. 93–43," *Weekly Compilation of Presidential Documents: Administration of William J. Clinton*, October 1, 1993, pp. 1947–48.

63. Africa Watch and Physicians for Human Rights, *Somalia, No Mercy in Mogadishu: The Human Cost of the Conflict and the Struggle for Relief* (Washington, DC: Africa Watch and Physicians for Human Rights, 1992), p. 26.

64. J. G. Sommer and C. C. Collins, *Humanitarian Aid in Somalia: The Role of the Office of U.S. Foreign Disaster Assistance (OFDA) 1990–1994*, Refugee Policy Group Report, November, 1994, p. 2.

65. "Exchange with Reporters Prior to a Meeting with Congressional Leaders," *Weekly Compilation of Presidential Documents: Administration of William J. Clinton*, September, 28, 1993, p. 1913.

66. M. Maren, "Spinning Dunkirk," *The New Republic*, December 9, 1993, pp. 18–20.

67. "Exchange with Reporters at Yale University in New Haven," *Weekly Compilation of Presidential Documents: Administration of William J. Clinton*, October 9, 1993, p. 2054.

Chapter Five

Managing Icons of Outrage

The subject of this book has been the icon of outrage, the photograph, video, or film onto which people attempt to impose fame, importance, greater meanings and ideological certainties. Icons, of course, come in many types, from the "hard news" photo of an immolated monk to the boudoir shot of a Hollywood ingénue. As the border between news and entertainment becomes indistinct, the values of the latter merge with the significance of the former—so too with their icons. Indeed, as a recent example of the issues surrounding icons, we need look no further than Princess Diana. Hers is often referred to as the most photographed face in the world, and even posthumously that face, in its many expressions, constituted a generic icon. As *Newsweek*'s Jonathan Alter reported after her death, "Diana [magazine] covers of the past two weeks were the best sellers not only of the year but of the entire decade."[1]

Moreover, issues concerning wolf-pack coverage of celebrities are similar to the question of the style and scope of coverage of international crises. Paparazzi who hounded Diana, perhaps to her death, were interested in procuring her picture, which they would then sell. The public bought those pictures. Even in the early days after her death, when there was considerable anti-tabloid sentiment in Great Britain and America, the tabloids, which sensationally covered Diana's life and death, sold out. For one brief moment, public attention was called upon the process of procuring an icon, but that did not disturb the hunger for obtaining those very icons. Diana was, then, a brand name product, a unique item, and those who wished to sell her likeness had to travel to photograph the original. In this sense, her body and her face had the aura of what Walter Benjamin called the original work of art that has been subsumed in an era of mechanical reproduction of images. With Diana's death, the original has been destroyed, perhaps the equivalent of the burning of a painting or the smashing of a sculpture; but the copies live forever. Likewise, the horrors that photojournalists shoot continue, change, or reappear, but the photographs, if they are chosen to enter the pantheon of icons, outlive their subjects and creators.

Princess Diana's death also raised the issue of to what extent an icon can be managed. There is no question that the young Englishwoman was pursued, photographed, and videotaped in compromising situations against her will, sometimes reducing her to anger and tears. What later emerged, however, is the ambiguous relationship Diana had with the paparazzi. Clearly, she attempted to use their lenses in service of personal p.r. as much as they were exploiting her face and body for cash. To cull sympathy during her battles with the House of Windsor, she would leak her own itinerary, especially if her exposure would reveal pictures of herself in positive situations, such as a trip to the amusement park with her sons. She played the game and, it could be said, the game resulted in her death. On the other hand, in historical terms, the same cruel insight made about another living icon, Elvis Presley, could be made about the princess; for Diana, death may truly have been a "smart career move." The foundation of her icon status was not just her position and her actions but her (photogenic) beauty. As she aged, with all the accompanying prejudice society holds against a woman with sagging skin and wrinkles, she could only look forward to an increasingly harsh stigmatization of that image.[2] But at no point did any picture, favorable or unfavorable, posed or caught, really provide much in the way of understanding the person behind the mask.

Likewise, news photographs are remarkably selective windows on the world. The myriad other vistas of reality and events that occur beyond the range of the lens, the eye of the photographer, or the scope of the newscast or newspaper, are ignored. The icon takes precedence over the event. That certain realities are chosen for presentation and certain of these are taken as metonyms of the news that day or of a particular set of events is the most powerful way that an icon acts to limit our knowledge about the world. This circumscription occurs concurrently with a limiting of explanations for the icon and interpretations of its greater and lesser meanings. The icon and the discourse about it thus constitute a frame of understanding. Frames are devices of limitation and focus. A relevant body of psychological research has shown that people's reasoning to produce an explanation for a phenomenon is significantly constrained by the set of explanations that are offered at the same time as the phenomenon is presented.[3] In such situations, we rarely reach beyond those offered explanations for any others that are unspoken or for which, as in the case of the news picture, examples are not given. Nor do we accept that we don't know enough to make a decision. What is out of sight is also out of mind, and the icon of outrage of news photography blinds us as well as presents us with visions of crises in foreign lands.

How does this affect the study of the relationship between media and society? In his recent work on *Capitalism and Communication*, Nicholas Garnham argues that concentration on the "privileged" texts (the view assumed by much literary-oriented media studies) is "perfectly designed as an ideology of intellectuals or cultural workers for it privileges their special field of activity, the symbolic, and provides for cheap research opportunities, since the only evidence required is the unsubstantiated views of the individual analyst."4 The icon of photojournalism is interesting because such a privileged status has been imposed upon it, not only by academic analysts, but by important and influential members of society. The problem of substantiation is the crucial one nonetheless, and it is clear that icons elicit many unsubstantiated claims of significance and effects. What we see is that there is a strong degree of separation between those who comment on "privileged" images in journalism, in books, and in other media, and the non-specialist public. In a way, those of us who study images for a living, who are steeped in visual culture, who explore nuances of the pictures in the press, are the least qualified to talk about them. Our attachment to these texts mirrors that of the other elites whom we attempt to critique. Neither do we view or "receive" the pictures with the same frames of interpretation as the mass audience.

While a special text, the icon is a measurable economic product of value, and can be studied as such. Once famous, it is a cash cow, selling copies for generations to come. Commodified, yet it is not fully a commodity because in the case of the specific icon, there is an original; treated as a work of art, yet not quite because the originality is assumed to be more in the (assumedly non-recreateable) scene that was captured. The generic type, of course, can be shot to match the expectation. To answer Garnham's challenge, then, what is studied here, the news photograph of tragedy, is not just a symbolic entity but a revealing component of an international system of creation, production, and distribution. All those involved in the process—though least of all its subjects—stand to profit in prestige and money by its celebrity and maximum dispersal.

Illustrative is the genre of hunger and horror images from Africa. First, Africa is an "easy" target. Despite the difficulty of traveling to many locations within the continent, generally somewhere in Africa on any given day a photojournalist can produce a "money" shot of any of the apocalypse's four horsemen.5 Africa also has no single powerful lobby in the United States pressing for greater, more complex, more sensitive, or more pro-active coverage. Third, stories about Africa can be easily packaged; good and bad guys are unambiguously denoted without fear of domestic controversy. Reporters may or may not feel any moral obligation to cover Africa, but they rarely experience domestic political backlash because of their coverage, unless, of course, Americans are involved. Finally, Africa, however cruel the scenery, provides a pleasant looking-glass for the American audience; asserting that there is a "Third World" always implies that we are first. This feeling can be useful for the programs of charities; most "save the X" advertising has the connotation that we, the Western observers, are superior to the huddled masses. A product, we should recall, must be sold as a tool to make the purchaser feel better. As shown previously, however, in the analyses of various icons of outrage, from the girl in Kevin Carter's picture, to the man who faced the tanks at Tiananmen, or the dying children at Somali feeding stations, the icon dwellers are not necessarily the better for our contributions.

How, then, can we more thoroughly engage the picture? Talking to photojournalists is a start. Of most interest is to what extent they think images show what they want them to. Susan Moeller, who interviewed famous modern war photographers, noted that "the photographer's intent in taking a photograph could bear little relation to the later impact of that image."[6] People besides those of us who read histories of photojournalism should have access to such contexts. Certainly it is possible, as Howard Gardner has suggested, that some people are blessed with a superior visual intelligence while their lexical-verbal skills may not be commensurate.[7] This is the stereotype of the photojournalist, but since only in specialty books and dinner conversations are these women and men allowed a voice, it is unfair to characterize them as mute. As I hope the dense contexts of the few photographs discussed in this book demonstrate, there is a great deal of insight and context available for investigation around any photograph. For an image that achieves star status, and is claimed to have an effect on foreign policy, such hidden contexts are all the more important to illuminate. Letting the photojournalist speak up—not just in retrospect to historians—may be one step along one path in that revelation.

This is crucial because of the two-dimensional nature of most photojournalism and, unfortunately, even of the icon of outrage. Because we think pictures show us the truth, because we think the meanings in an image are self-evident, because we think modern news imagery truly gives us an expansive window on the world, we do not consider the third dimension of the pictures that we see in our newspapers and magazines and on television, that of depth. It is important to reach into the image and to step back from the image, to understand the how and the why of a picture, to question its metonymic status, even to engage in dispute over its meaning.

Why do we have innumerable discussion programs that conduct an autopsy on every utterance of the president but so little combative, or even thoughtful, visual analysis in the public sphere? There is a fundamental laziness about the way we look at images, especially considering their purported importance. It is so easy to proclaim that a picture "scarred the nation"; so tedious to admit we have no idea what the picture did. By reaching into the third dimension, we can and should ask questions about what pictures were not taken and why, about whether photojournalism has any right or duty to show more than one visual side of a story. Such questions, such engagement would undermine the sacred doctrine of modern visual journalism, that photographs are capturing reality and transferring it to us without any interpretation. The death of a myth, however, is often the liberation of a people. In this case, it would allow the beginning of a new model of enlightened, engaged, and open photojournalism.

Another line of research would be either experimental or field studies on the impact, influence, or effects of *particular* news images. To what extent are the importance and interpretations of prominent news images shared throughout society? Does the first-person effect work both ways?

Do people assume that others react in the same way as they do to certain kinds of media stimuli, such as icons of outrage? Conversely, do people tend to concur with the first-person definitions of the meaning of a prominent image made by discourse elites? It would be interesting, for example, if news organizations conducted polls about people's reactions to pictures of prominent events as they occurred. Ethnographers might observe the reaction to icons in the home and perhaps track how ordinary people do or do not employ them in their discussion of news events. All such studies obviously have shortcomings of validity and reliability, but they would allow us to learn more about the influence of icons than is provided by first-person assumptions. The audience's share, then, is as fruitful an area of research as that of the creators or disseminators of prominent pictures in the news.

Another reason why researchers, journalists, and even ordinary people should try to engage icons in the dimension of depth is to address the enormous distance between the publicity of international journalism and the reality. Almost every article in mass communication research that assesses Western coverage of other nations, peoples, and events, including this book, comes to the same conclusion: American news media oversimplifies, decontextualizes, and fails to meaningfully translate foreign affairs to the American people. In a sense, this criticism is unfair, asking journalists to pretend they have the time and the space accorded to academics who address narrow subjects. This book is an example: limited to 75,000 words, I have only cursorily contextualized and explored the cases presented here. Other researchers could take the same cases and provide different contexts. Perhaps political scientists, sociologists, historians, and anthropologists of the Sudan, Vietnam, China, and Somalia would find my excursions naive and narrow.

The irony, often unrecognized by academics, is that news editors and journalists feel that in many cases they are doing good by publishing the stories that appear in the paper because the kind of news stories which attract discourse elites are widely, and I think correctly, perceived as being uninteresting to the general reader. Considerable marketing evidence supports this prejudice. As said, it is a commonplace that cover pictures that show foreign news unrelated by topic or by content to America are poor sellers even when elites may consider the events—wars in Bosnia or Ethiopia, or the fall of the Berlin Wall—to be of great importance. Foreign news "sells" when it involves Americans: the Gulf War, or pictures of dead G.I.s in Somalia. International celebrities like Diana are also an obvious exception. This is true as well in television. CNN's highest ratings ever were during its coverage of the Gulf War. Tiananmen Square and the fall of the Berlin Wall did not register significant public attention.

Moreover, attention may not, although most academics write as if they assume it will, heighten knowledge. For example, in a December 6, 1992, CBS News poll only 65 percent of those surveyed knew that Somalia was an African country. News coverage had little positive effect on this figure; when polled shortly after the events of the Battle of Mogadishu, only 57 percent of those surveyed in a *Time*/CNN Poll

(October 7, 1993) placed Somalia in Africa.

Journalists may also feel that the simplification, or oversimplification, in the view of academics, of foreign news, is a legitimate public service of their profession. The viewers who know nothing of the foreign land and care less need to have their news world translated into symbols, ideas, and slogans that make sense to them.[8] In short, journalists often feel that reporting foreign news at all—in the face of public disinterest—is itself an act of good citizenship that should be respected if not praised. Hence their resentment at academic carping.

Another defense for journalists is that academic and think-tank critics and pundits so often get things wrong themselves. It is well known in the news business that one of the guises that journalists don when reporting a story or commenting upon it is that of pseudo-expert. Reading a few articles or a book, or talking to a few professors, the journalist then makes on-air comments that sound as if they are the product of intense study; the same journalist offering us insight into the political situation in Indonesia is, a week later, a pseudo-expert on Kazakhstan. Or, journalists deploy selective quotes, often highly edited, from "experts" to support their own theories on an issue or an event. Such ruses are part of the game, and obviously disingenuous to an extent, but however simplistically the journalists translate the information and opinions of experts, the fact is that expertise, in politics and society, is no guarantee of accuracy. Social scientists are astute retrodictors; they can often articulately explain why something must have happened the way it did. Prediction, on the other hand, largely eludes them as much as the tabloid psychics. Few experts counseling reporters about the Tiananmen events predicted the outcome. The same was true in Vietnam, in Somalia, and a host of other major events of this century, from the rise of Adolf Hitler to the fall of communism in eastern Europe. Is it really fair to chastise journalists for being simplistic when we, in our understanding of complexity, so often fail to sense what will happen next?

On the other hand, criticism of mainstream news by scholars and the alternative press is fully justified in light of the inflated self-congratulation of the news industry. As viewers of news, we are assured that we are being brought "the world," that we are receiving "all the news," that the globe is being covered for us, and a hundred other clichés of journalistic vanity. To say that this is an exaggeration is an understatement. So much occurs in the world that is ignored by Western media and so much of what does happen is not covered in any way commensurate to its actual impact on human populations that at times it seems almost a cruel joke to watch the promotional spots of the news industry and their grandiose claims of total coverage. It is of course too much to ask that a nightly news broadcast begin with a product label warning, *NOTE: You are about to see only a few things that happened in the world today; many other important things occurred but we couldn't, or wouldn't, cover them.* A more open engagement with icons and other images might at least provide some sort of corrective—a limited one.

In pretending that what they are showing us is all that is going on in the world or all that is important, news media do a disservice to national public and political decision making, even when they are simply following the agenda and presenting the frames already set by political elites. This may be a sort of visual echo chamber. In Somalia, for example, perhaps there would have been less pressure to intervene if we had both seen and understood that the misery in the Horn of Africa was being reenacted in a dozen other places in the world.

The cult of simplicity in foreign affairs reporting may be critiqued on similar grounds. It is undoubtedly difficult, time-consuming, and expensive to provide a complex, sensitive, nuanced, multi-vocal understanding of an international event or issue to the American people through mass media. There is no doubt, as well, that such an endeavor would have trouble finding viewers outside those traditionally concerned with foreign affairs. This said, the dangers of simplicity are manifold, for the public, the press, and the nation. A simple point may be simply wrong. It was certainly unambiguous to show and describe the initial American intervention in Somalia as an altruistic mission of mercy with no chance of failure. Somalia, however, turned out to be a complex entity, as did Vietnam and Tiananmen. In addition, the simplest idea is often the one with which we are most comfortable, that most plays into our prejudices, and that best fits the pre-existing pictures in our heads. Simplicity in a complex world is a siren song that supports unwarranted optimism, encourages overambitious missions, and blinds the viewer—including political elites—to the messy facts of life.

Thus, icons are also worthy of study as social thermometer; the analogy is not strained because even the hottest images may eventually blow cold. It is a paradox of the icon that one of the ways we identify it is through repetition, and yet repeated identical stimuli lose their effectiveness over time; excitatory habituation and desensitization may occur in the reception of icons of outrage.[9] Musician Bob Geldof, who was prompted by TV pictures of starvation in Ethiopia to form the relief organization LiveAid in the mid-1980s, later observed what he called "compassion fatigue." People were simply tired of seeing the same images showing the same problems over and over. We can equally wonder if we are entering an era of icon fatigue. Have the great shots of photojournalism all been done—is there anything new under the sun? Is a starving child or a man blocking a tank or a street execution still shocking? Probably outrage will always be felt against visualizations of attacks on Americans, but repetition may induce weariness and numbness to the world's pain. This is another reason for the more meaningful engagement with the icon, for only by exploring it in depth may we rejuvenate its power to touch us.

In addition, we might also ask: do we really need a picture? Is a visual image required as a component of outrage, or is it enough to express outrage and cite an event itself? A recent case was the persuasion campaign to support an American military response to Saddam Hussein's invasion of Kuwait. This campaign was funded by some $12 million of the sheikdom's money and organized by the public relations firm Hill & Knowlton, whose president had been chief of staff to George Bush when he was Ronald Reagan's vice president. One of the major atrocity claims made against the Iraqis was the "baby incubator story."

On October 10, 1990, a Congressional Committee heard testimony from a 15-year-old Kuwaiti girl who gave her name as "Nayirah."[10] She claimed to have been a volunteer at a hospital where babies had been flung from incubators by Iraqi soldiers, who left "them on the floor to die," and then stole the incubators. President Bush took up the story, repeating it six times over the next five weeks as an example of the horrors of the Iraqi occupation.[11] Hill & Knowlton also arranged more "eyewitnesses" to be presented to the United Nations and organized a campus mailing campaign. In argumentation in the Senate, pro-war lawmakers cited the baby incubator massacre as one of the main reasons for action against Saddam. Yet, as early as December, an independent eyewitness denied that incubators had been stolen from civilian hospitals in Kuwait, but said that some babies had died because of lack of staff for the pre-natal units.[12] Nayirah turned out to be the daughter of the Kuwaiti ambassador to the United States. To this day, it still has not been resolved how many incubators were stolen, under what circumstances and if any babies died as a result.

The outrage that President Bush, the Kuwaiti government in exile, Bush administration officials, and allies in Congress tried to stir with this story was neither incited by a visual nor had a visual around which to coalesce. This is not completely a negation of the utility of an iconic image as a tool of outrage, because even though there was no picture to accompany the story, it was visualizable in the minds of all who heard it. We do not need a picture of a child molester's deeds to feel anger toward the perpetrator and empathy for the child. Perhaps, even if we do not need a visual, outrage is enhanced if the event can be visualized in language and the imagination—and, of course, if it plays into omnipresent prejudices. But prejudices are fueled by familiarity. It assisted greatly that the press replicated the verbal and visual discourse of the administration that was designed by Hill & Knowlton, in the pay, ironically, of a foreign government.[13]

That George Bush went on to lose re-election in a contest dominated by domestic issues does not diminish his accomplishments in managing foreign policy icons. In Somalia, Bush seemed to appreciate that his policies would be justified by the icons of outrage replicated in the press. At Tiananmen, Bush reacted with some expressions of outrage; though his restrained actions did not satisfy everyone, he sensed, correctly, that the outrage against the Chinese government was fleeting and could be assuaged by rhetorical flourishes and token measures. He did so because he understood that though icons may endure, outrage fades. Indeed, opinion surveys confirmed that the majority of Americans did not favor a complete break in relations with mainland China. But it was during the Gulf War that the most intriguing management of the icon of outrage was made. When pictures appeared that might have cast an unfavorable light on Bush's policies, such as the bombing of an air raid shelter in Baghdad, the administration responded rapidly and energetically with a plausible counter-story that overturned the negative implications of the images: it was really an Iraqi command post; Saddam placed women and children there on purpose to act as human shields; and so on. Revealingly, public support for the war did not decrease because of infants incinerated by our precision-guided munitions. Again, prejudice and spin may count more than the picture itself.

Most brilliantly, the Bush administration did what governments have done for thousands of years, although with greater subtlety. Rather than try to manipulate the interpretation of pictures already in the press, the administration flooded news media with vivid, kinetic videos of "smart" bombs going down chimneys and cruise missiles precisely splitting bridges. Only later did we learn many of those images were misrepresented and non representative. Icons, then, are not only reflections or refractions of wars, civil conflicts, and natural disasters, they can also be tools for fighting, managing, and shaping them. American foreign policy can only be overturned by an icon if policy makers mismanage their reaction to the images or abstain from engaging them at all. Accordingly, icons of outrage are less a danger to the traditional system of foreign policy-making than an opportunity and a challenge. We are also—as perhaps we have always been—living in the era of the managed icon.

Words shape that management; so do our prejudices. Physical images are often the manifestations of our mental images. The numerous quotations that I have deployed in this book from journalists, pundits, generals, academics, and politicians often express a tendency for lyrical description to frame an icon of outrage: "America was shocked," "the whole world was watching," "the world weeps," "scarred the psyche of the nation," "the public was repulsed," and so on. Such language acts to thrust greatness upon a picture and install it in the pantheon of photojournalism. Yet plainly the icon is not a hypodermic stimulus that haphazardly overturns sound public policy. Even among the elites, time and circumstance can expose the ephemeral nature of rhetoric attached to icons of outrage. If I have accomplished anything in this book, I hope it is to suggest greater caution when asserting the wider impact of a news image. Proclamations about power and effects, and feverish effusions about "changing the world," must be spoken and written based upon careful surveying of evidence, not inspiration and imagination. Effects, from outrage to action, must be proven, not extended automatically from the first person to the entire world. When talking about pictures in the press, prudence should restrain the use of language better suited to describing chemical reactions or 19th century Russian novels.[14]

In addition, as has been implied in all the discussions here on the long-term reaction to an icon of outrage, we should never underestimate the ability of the human mind to forget. If the complex organ known as the brain can have its data processing and recalling strategies summed up in a few words, it is that we seek out things of relevance to ourselves.[15] It has long been recognized by philosophers and lived by the common man that we cannot pay attention to everything. Dante, one of the premier discourse elites of the 12th century, understood "the domestic and civic cares by which the greater number of people are quite properly absorbed, so that they have no leisure for speculation."[16] Likewise, today, a daughter's flu, a missed deadline at work, or Hoosier basketball occlude the attention and undermine retention of visual or verbal information about such relatively unimportant matters as genocide in the Sudan, rough justice on a Saigon street, or one man who stood for democracy. Non discourse elites are not necessarily ignorant or stupid when they neglect and remember less about events and images in the news of foreign lands that objectively and properly have little relation to the "cares" of their daily lives. The shadow memory of an icon, then, may linger, but the knowledge of the issue will probably evaporate.

Leaders may take note (and courage) from these probabilities. Certainly, feeling pressured to respond to instant images of outrage may be a new development in the age of the cable news network and the satellite feed. But no polling data have ever shown that the people of the United States are eager to seek out yet more foreign commitments for aid and troops. This is not isolationism, but rational prudence. Political leaders can assert that foreign wars, peace-keeping missions and interventions are not the correct response to a problem summed up by an icon of outrage. There is no need for anyone, especially a president, to fear the visual bogey man.

This is basically because the icon is a symptom of the modern age, not a cause of it. Pictures can be powerful tools of political argumentation, but what they show and what they connote are largely imposed upon them. The greater public is, in most cases, much less uniform or emotive in their reactions, or rather we don't know as much about their reaction and the sources of it as we assume. Pictures can change the world, but only if the fire they fan is already burning—only if those effects follow preexisting channels of prejudice. The context of the image often reveals much more than its visual elements, assuming, of course, that people are exposed to that context and that they care. And above all content matters—not all victims are, in the eyes of all observers, equally worthy of sympathy.

Yet, this does not mean that the icon of outrage is a peripheral phenomenon. Its importance arises from the fact that it is believed to be important, that the public affairs machineries of governments feel they must respond to such icons and either deflect, circumvent, or utilize their power. The first person effect is an assumption about other people's feelings (and likely behaviors); it can also be an incentive to one's own utterances and actions. Mediation, event, and comment upon mediation thus interweave, making complex the ascription of cause and effect. So it has been in the past with stirring, powerful texts. The classical scholar L. R. Farnell once commented of 6th and 7th century BCE Greece: "Much Hero-cult was directly engendered by the powerful influence of Homeric and other epics. . . . We so often hear how saga reflects cult that we are in danger of ignoring the reverse truth that cult may reflect saga; for cult was often the mimetic of past events, and the memory of these was preserved mainly by saga-poetry."[17] Today as well, if we believe in the power of media, that will further fix its power.

The perception of the icon's power, then, is a very real force in foreign policy—more so as its reality, projected or not, becomes a commonplace assumption. Icons of outrage have been, are, and will continue to be at the center stage in the foreign policy arena. Foreign policy actors, including the mass media, struggle to select, censor, distort, define, or deny them. To understand such battles we must begin to appreciate what an icon of outrage is and can be. The power of the content of the icon, and the power of its aesthetic properties may contribute to its political power and the reverse; yet each quality may also wax or wane independently. As Arthur Koestler wrote, "Myths grow like crystals . . . as soon as a suitable core is found, they group themselves around it and the crystal is formed. . . . The question, of course, is who makes a suitable core."[18] However manufactured and imposed their qualities, icons of outrage are the best candidates for the cores of myths in the mass mediated age. Any insight into their nature must begin by shedding vain first-person delusions about pictorial naturalness and transcendent truth. The best preliminary caption we can apply to icons of outrage is to assert that no picture can truly say it all.

NOTES

1. J. Alter, "Genuflect Journalism," *Newsweek,* September 22, 1997, p. 37.

2. The "stigma" of beauty and the eventual failure to uphold the idealized criterion is discussed in E. Tseelon, "What is Beautiful is Bad: Physical Attractiveness as Stigma," *Journal for the Theory of Social Behaviour* 22 (September 1992): 295–309.

3. S. A. Sloman, "When Explanations Compete: The Role of Explanatory Coherence on Judgments of Likelihood," *Cognition* 52 (1994): 1–21.

4. N. Garnham, *Capitalism and Communication: Global Culture and the Economics of Information* (London: Sage, 1990), pp. 1–2.

5. R. D. Kaplan, *Surrender or Starve: The Wars Behind the Famine* (Boulder: Westview Press, 1988), pp. 39–40.

6. S. D. Moeller, *Shooting War: Photography and the American Experience of Combat* (New York: Basic Books, 1989), pp. 354–55; M. W. Browne, "Viet Nam Reporting," *Columbia Journalism Review* 3 (Fall 1964): 7.

7. H. Gardner, *Frames of Mind: The Theory of Multiple Intelligences* (New York: Basic Books, 1983).

8. Alvin Goldman calls this phenomenon "'epistemic paternalism'—the deliberate attempt to simplify, to make the news understandable and digestible to a large audience." A. I. Goldman, "Epistemic Paternalism: Communication Control in Law and Society," *Journal of Philosophy* 85 (1991): 123.

9. D. Zillmann, "Television Viewing and Arousal," in *Television and Behavior: Ten Years of Scientific Progress and Implications for the 80s, Vol. 2. Technical Reviews,* ed. by D. Pearl, L. Bouthilet, and J. Lazar (Washington, DC: U.S. Government Printing Office, 1980), pp. 53–67; V. B. Cline, R. G. Croft, and S. Courrier, "Desensitization of Children to Television Violence," *Journal of Personality and Social Psychology* 27 (1973): 260–365.

10. The complications of the story are discussed in many sources. R. Williams, "300 Babies Killed in Kuwait," *Press Association Newsfile* [wire], December 19, 1990; J. Chancellor, "War Stories," *New York Times,* April 1, 1991, p. A17; J. R. MacArthur, "Remembering Nayirah, Witness for Kuwait?" *New York Times,* January 6, 1992, p. A17; M. Abley, "Persian Gulf War,"

Toronto Star, February 26, 1994, p. C5; S. A. Roschwalb, "The Hill & Knowlton Cases," *Public Relations Review*, September 22, 1994, p. 267; M. O'Kane, "Bloodless Words, Bloody War," [London] *Guardian*, December 16, 1995, p. T12; B. Livesey, "Rough Handling," [Toronto] *Financial Post*, May 10, 1997, p. 26.

11. See, for example, George Bush, "Why We Are in the Gulf," *Newsweek*, November 26, 1990, pp. 28–29; "The President's News Conference," *Public Papers of the Presidents, Weekly Compilation of Presidential Documents*, October 9, 1990, pp. 1553–54.

12. J. Arraf, "Doctor Says Babies Dying In Kuwait Hospitals," *Reuter Library Report*, December 9, 1990.

13. Cf. M. Miller, *Spectacle: Operation Desert Storm and the Triumph of Illusion* (New York: Poseidon Press, 1994).

14. I am not saying that the American public or "the world" is indifferent to icons of outrage or the human suffering and horror they contain. But before we automatically impose on an entire nation or planet a strong emotional or political reaction, some attempt must be made to gauge its existence, its depth and its meaning. Also, we can never pretend that the frames erected around such images by discourse elites play no role in the selection and the elevation of one of the millions of pictures in the news stream to an icon of outrage; but the effects of pictures in the press must always be judged in relation to what is said about them as well as the prejudices of the audience.

15. D. Sperber and D. Wilson, *Relevance: Communication and Cognition* (Cambridge, MA: Harvard University Press, 1988).

16. Quoted in Dante, *The Comedy of Dante Alighieri, The Florentine. Cantica II: Purgatory*, trans. D. Sayers (London: Penguin, 1955), p. 122.

17. L. R. Farnell, *Greek Hero Cults and Ideas of Immortality* (Oxford: Oxford University Press, 1921), pp. 340, 342.

18. R. Hewison, *Under Siege: Literary Life in London 1939–1945* (London: Oxford University Press, 1977), p. 48.

Appendix A

Comments on
the Saigon Execution Incident and Image

The [Saigon execution] photograph and the film shocked the world, an isolated incident of cruelty in a broadly cruel war, but a psychological blow against the South Vietnamese nonetheless.

—William C. Westmoreland
A Soldier Reports
(Garden City, NY: Double Day, 1976).

[The Saigon execution footage's] impact was arguably the turning point of the war, for it coincided with a dramatic shift in American public opinion, and may well have helped to cause it.

—Godfrey Hodgson
America in Our Time
(Garden City, NY: Doubleday, 1976).

But no portrayal of the South Vietnamese military and security forces had the impact of Eddie Adams' photographs—and ABC's and NBC's film—of Brig. Gen. Nguyen Ngoc Loan executing a captured, mufti-clad Vietcong officer near the An Quang Pagoda.

—Peter Braestrup
Big Story: How the American Press Reported and Interpreted the Crisis of Tet 1968 in Vietnam and Washington, 2 Volumes
(Boulder: Westview, 1977).

[The Saigon execution] was an act of cruelty which did not help the world image of the South Vietnamese at a critically important time for them.

—Douglas Kinnard
The War Managers
(Hanover, N.H.: University Press of New England, 1977).

A world-wide furor was created by the publication of photographs taken by Eddie Adams of Associated Press, showing a civilian-clothed Viet Cong prisoner being executed—with a pistol, at point-blank range—by Brigadier Nguyen Ngoc Loan, Chief of the Saigon Police Force....

[Eddie Adams' picture was] Summary justice that shocked world opinion.
—Charles B. MacDonald
"Communist Thrust—The Tet Offensive of 1968," in *The Vietnam War, An Illustrated History of Conflict in Southeast Asia*, pp. 148–155. (New York: Crown, 1979).

The public killing of a Vietcong terrorist by General Loan, Chief of South Vietnam's National Police, had a particularly shocking effect.
—Carlos D'Costa
Media Coverage of the Tet Offensive 1968, Ph.D. dissertation. (Florida Atlantic University, Boca Raton, Florida, 1981).

The brutality of the South Vietnamese against captured Vietcong shocked the American consciousness as nothing in the war had done before.
—Joseph A. Amter
Vietnam Verdict: A Citizen's History
(New York: Continuum, 1982).

[T]he Loan shooting seemed to many people to confirm the suspicion that this was a "wrong war" on the "wrong side." . . . The NBC-Television film footage . . . originally in color, brought the cruelty of the war into the nation's living rooms.
—Don Oberdorfer,
TET! The Turning Point in the Vietnam War
(New York: Da Capo, 1983 ed.).

The impact of the Tet Offensive on the American people, however, results primarily from one episode shown on TV: Saigon Police Chief General Loan executing a captured enemy soldier.
—John Clark Pratt
Vietnam Voices: Perspectives on the War Years, 1941–1982
(New York: Viking, 1984).

Pictures like *Life* photographer Eddie Adams's shot of General Loan shooting a captured Vietcong in the head were extraordinarily powerful. They crystallized the war's brutality without providing a context within which to understand the events they depicted. [T]he immediate reaction to such scenes was a gut revulsion to the barbarity of the war which tended to supersede more rational, long-term considerations.
—Bui Diem (with David Chanoff)
In the Jaws of History
(Boston: Houghton Mifflin, 1987).

No film footage did as much damage as AP photographer Eddie Adams's 35-mm shot taken on a Saigon street on February 1. [It was] a sickening image of the brutality of our esteemed ally. Here was another horrifying image of the Vietnam War to add to the others. . . . [It] . . . possibly did more to damage to the Saigon government than Tet itself.
—Irwin Unger and Debbi Unger
Turning Point, 1968
(New York: Charles Scribner's Sons, 1988).

But the most memorable image [the Adams picture] of the upheaval in

Saigon—and one of the most searing spectacles of the whole war—was imprinted the next day on a street corner in the city.

—Stanley Karnow
Vietnam: A History
(New York: Viking Press, 1989).

This graphic illustration [Adams' photo] of the ugliness of guerrilla war shocked and troubled millions of Americans.

—Anthony James Joes,
The War for South Viet Nam, 1954–1975
(New York: Praeger, 1989).

This [Adams'] photograph became the grimmest visual souvenir of those times. The shooting has been called the most significant gunshot of the war—not because (like the rifle shot that heralded the beginning of the American Revolutionary War) it was "heard around the world," but because it was seen around the world. . . . The American public was repulsed by what was perceived as the blatant barbarity of its South Vietnamese ally. [T]he photograph would remain in memory as one of the most sinister and ugly images of the Vietnam War.

—Lorraine Monk
Photographs that Changed the World: The Camera as Witness, The Photograph as Evidence
(New York: Doubleday, 1989).

[I]mages, such as . . . Adams's Tet execution . . . overwhelmed the photographer's intent and willy-nilly defined as well as described the conflict. In the media and in the memory, photography, intentionally or not, selectively paraphrased the war.

—Susan D. Moeller
Shooting War: Photography and the American Experience of Combat
(New York: Basic Books, 1989).

Loan shooting the Vietcong—became [one of the] symbols of the Tet offensive.

—James Stuart Olson and Randy Roberts
Where the Domino Fell: America in Vietnam, 1945–1990
(New York: St. Martin's Press, 1991).

[I]t was profoundly disturbing to wake up to a photograph of a man putting a bullet into another man's brain. [The picture became] a key memory and a potent symbol of a war that harshly divided Americans and left a bitter legacy.

—Vicki Goldberg
The Power of Photography: Photographs That Changed Our Lives
(New York: Abbeville Press, 1991).

[The Saigon execution] was an act of such naked brutality, so at odds with civilized notions of justice and decency, that it served graphically to confirm the charges that America's allies in Vietnam were brutal men, morally indistinguishable from the brutal men on the other side.

—David W. Levy
The Debate over Vietnam
(Baltimore: John Hopkins University Press, 1991).

[T]he [execution] pictures captured what was most disturbing about the war to many Americans: the disparity between the barefooted bound prisoner and the general, with his flak jacket, his heavy American pistol, the callous indifference to constituted rules of war; the terror of death meted out in America's name, with American means, by men like Loan.

—Marilyn B. Young
The Vietnam Wars, 1945–1990
(New York: Harper Collins, 1991).

The photograph of the execution was on front pages all around the world—leading our best and oldest friends to ask, more in sorrow than in anger, what has happened to America?

—Robert F. Kennedy
quoted in George Katsiaficas, ed.
Vietnam Documents: American and Vietnamese Views of the War
(Armonk, NY: M. E. Sharpe, 1992).

Everyone who saw them [the images of the execution] knew immediately that both pieces of film [Adams' and NBC] were special.

—Clarence R. Wyatt
Paper Soldiers: The American Press and the Vietnam War
(New York: W. W. Norton, 1993).

Images [of Tet] proved indelible. They scarred the American psyche.

—John Hanchette
"25 Years Ago, America Fell into Throes of a Revolution,"
Gannett News Service, January 28, 1993.

[The image] seemed to many people to confirm the suspicion that this was a "wrong war" on the "wrong side."

—Justin J. Gustainis
American Rhetoric and the Vietnam War
(Westport, CT: Praeger, 1993).

[T]he [Adams] photo became the most famous and talked about picture of the Vietnam War.

—Ronald H. Spector
After Tet: The Bloodiest Year in Vietnam
(New York: Free Press, 1993).

Every day, NBC aired the [Saigon execution] film and shocked the world. The war was considered the most barbaric in the US history and Americans resented their children's participation.

—Lac Hoang and Viet Mai Ha
Why America Lost the Vietnam War
(Sugarland, TX: self-published, 1996).

[News reports] encapsulated the corruption of the South Vietnamese government and military with the stomach-wrenching scene of General Loan, the national police chief, putting a bullet through the head of a captive, apparently in cold blood and without reason.

—David Harris
Our War: What We Did in Vietnam, What Vietnam Did to Us
(New York: Times Books, 1996).

Americans viewing Eddie Adams picture said to themselves "that's enough, we've had it, we're not going to support a dictatorship, that's no democracy as we know it."

—Wallace Terry
Time Deputy Bureau Chief, Saigon, 1967–69.
Vietnam, The Camera at War (History Channel, 1997).

Of all the images of terror, none was more brutal than the day viewers watched an execution of a suspected Vietcong on the streets of Saigon by General Loan, an ally of the Americans.

—Narrator
Newsreels to Nightly News: Episode IV
Vietnam, The Camera at War (History Channel, 1997).

The [Saigon] execution was added to people's feeling that this is just horrible. This is just terrible. Why are we involved in a thing like this? People were just sickened by this, and I think this added to the feeling that the war was the wrong war at the wrong place.

—John Chancellor
NBC *News*, 1950–1993,
Newsreels to Nightly News: Episode IV
Vietnam, The Camera at War (History Channel, 1997).

[Eddie Adams'] picture captured the brutality that was common to General Loan and the war.

—Peter Arnett
Live from the Battlefield: From Vietnam to Baghdad,
35 Years in the World's War Zones
(New York: Simon & Schuster, 1994).

Appendix B

Descriptions of the Man Killed in the "Saigon Execution"

DATE	SOURCE	DESCRIPTION OF MAN KILLED
Feb. 2, 1968	*NBC*	Chancellor (in studio): "Captured Viet Cong officer" Tuckner (on scene): Commander of the Viet Cong commando unit; enemy officer
Feb. 2, 1968	*CBS*	(No description of shooting) Walter Cronkite: "Heaviest fighting in Saigon at militant Buddhist pagoda that government claims was VC command post"
Feb. 2, 1968	*Atlanta Constitution*	Viet Cong Officer; Captured guerrilla was carrying pistol and wearing civilian clothes
Feb. 2, 1968	*Chicago Tribune*	Viet Cong officer; captive
Feb. 2, 1968	*Los Angeles Times*	A Viet Cong officer; guerrilla
Feb. 2, 1968	*New York Times*	Guerrilla; identified as a Vietcong terrorist; Man wore civilian dress and had a pistol; Identified as a Vietcong officer; He was carrying a pistol when captured; prisoner

DATE	SOURCE	DESCRIPTION OF MAN KILLED
Feb. 2, 1968	*Washington Post*	Vietcong officer; The officer, in civilian garb and carrying a pistol
Feb. 3, 1968	*New York Daily News*	Vietcong (communist) officer caught disguised and armed. . . . The executed Vietcong was out to kill as many people on our side of this war as he could; (b) so are all his surviving pals.
Feb. 3, 1968	*AP log*	Vietcong officer; a tousle-haired Vietnamese in civilian garb; Vietcong officer; the prisoner
Feb. 4, 1968	*AP log*	Captured Vietcong
Feb. 9, 1968	*Time*	Viet Cong officer
Feb. 12, 1968	*Newsweek*	(In story): manacled Viet Cong suspect. . . . Dressed in civilian clothes, the prisoner was wearing an arm band stamped with the letter "X 2 B 27"—possibly a coded identification for "Cell Two, Platoon 27"; suspect; prisoner. (caption): Viet Cong terrorist
Feb. 23, 1968	*Time*	guerrilla suspect—a thin, frightened, but stubborn-looking man in plaid shirt and pants; the suspect's; But in Viet Nam, what is a uniform? The Viet Cong dress in the black pajamas of the country peasantry or in ordinary street clothing, like Loan's victim, and wear red armbands or other identifying badges only in combat. And what, in Viet Nam, are the laws and customs of war?
March 1, 1968	*Life*	Shana Alexander: His face is square to the camera, squinched in its instant of death, distorted by the bullet's impact like a pilot's in a power dive.

Appendix C

Comments on Somalia Icons

JOURNALISTS AND COMMENTATORS

These pictures of dead American soldiers and the captive helicopter pilot were driving an increasingly emotional debate that could result in the cutoff of money to run the Somalia operation within weeks.

—John McWethy
ABC News, October 5, 1993.

It was pictures like these that provoked the U.S. to send over 25,000 American troops to Somalia. . . . It may be pictures like these which finally make the U.S. leave. . . . We're seeing them again, pictures from another land so shocking that we're moved to call Congress, call the President, tell them what the United States should do. This time they're gruesome, horrible scenes of the brutalized bodies of American soldiers dragged through the streets of Mogadishu, pictures of a young American GI held hostage, painfully reciting the words his captors dictate.

—Cokie Roberts
ABC *Nightline*, October 5, 1993.

For Mr. Clinton, the stakes in Somalia were raised exponentially with the broadcast of those chilling pictures, the shaky images of the young helicopter pilot held captive and grotesque scenes of dead American soldiers have triggered a new wave of worry, outrage and confusion.

—Chris Bury
ABC *Nightline*, October 5, 1993.

[T]he ghastly images of American dead being desecrated by followers of Mohammed Farrah Aidid, touched off a rush of reconsideration about the cloudy U.S. role in the stricken East African country.

—Tom Baxter
"Analysis: Are Television Images of Crises Driving U.S. Foreign Policy?" *Atlanta Journal and Constitution*, October 10, 1993, p. A7.

The pictures from Somalia have always been wrenching. . . . At first the images were of children starving to death, photos awful enough to rouse

the world's humanitarian instincts. And on Oct. 5, the image that
sickened and gripped us showed a crowd of Somalis celebrating around
the body of an American soldier being dragged down a street in
Mogadishu. It is impossible to avoid reacting to these pictures. They stir
our emotions, focus our attention, compel us to act.

—Joanna Byrd
"Picture from Somalia,"
Washington Post, October 17, 1993, p. C6.

[The images of Durant and the desecrated body were] threatening to
drown reasoned judgment with emotion.

—Arthur Spiegelman
"Somali War Images Haunts U. S.,"
The Reuter Library Report [wire], October 5, 1993.

Wherever TV cameras go, foreign policy seems to come lapping
obediently behind. . . . Images of hunger got us into a mess in Somalia we
never understood.

—Ronald Steel
"Bosnia Lessons: Why U.S. Policy has Failed,"
Dallas Morning News, April 26, 1994, p. 15A.

[It was] a foreign policy that's driven by image.

—David Halberstam
"The Somalian Conflict and the Power of TV Images,"
CNN, *Larry King Live*, October 5, 1993.

We went into Somalia because of pictures. . . . Nonetheless, we have
been driven out of there too. We leave with Somalia again on the brink of
chaos and with 30 American dead.

—Charles Krauthammer
"Intervention Lite: Foreign Policy by CNN,"
Washington Post, February 18, 1994, p. A25.

The American public was right to want to scuttle the Somalia expedition
as soon as American corpses appeared on the television screen.

—David Fromkin
"Don't Send in the Marines,"
New York Times Magazine, February 27, 1994, pp. 36–37.

[Durant's] terrified face . . . turned many Americans against the whole
involvement.

—George. J. Church
"In and Out,"
Time, Oct. 25, 1993, pp. 26–32.

[Starving child] pictures prompted President Bush's military adventure—
now they will justify it.

—Rakiya Omaar
"Disaster Pornography from Somalia,"
Los Angeles Times, December 10, 1992, p. B7.

[Somalia was an example that] all too often these days emotional reactions to television pictures contribute to both injudicious involvement in a foreign conflict, then later premature withdrawal.

—Robert Akerman
"A Note of Doubt Creeps into Somalia Coverage,"
Atlanta Journal and Constitution, June 16, 1993, p. A16.

POLITICAL LEADERS

Americans have no desire to see their men and women degraded, killed and defiled by lawless infidels who drag the bodies of Americans through the streets to be kicked and spat upon.

—Sen. Trent Lott (R-Mississippi)
ABC *News*, October 5, 1993.

When an American gets killed, suddenly the opinion changes. . . . In Somalia, we were there to help feed Somalis, but if somebody kills an American, then "To hell with it, we're going home. If they starve, they starve."

—Les Aspin
quoted in Jennifer Talhelm, "Aspin: U. S. Faces Post-Cold War Puzzle,"
[Durham, NC] *Herald-Sun*, March 28, 1995, p. C7.

Pictures of starving children would rightly encourage Americans to press their government to intervene, then equally dramatic pictures of American casualties would force a premature withdrawal before the job was done.

—Ambassador Rozanne Ridgway
quoted in Harlan Cleveland, "A Too-National Intervention; Rescue Force Should Have Carried Flag of UN, Not U.S."
[Minneapolis] *Star Tribune*, December 13, 1992, p. 29A.

There's no doubt that, especially in the Congress in this case, the pictures of that soldier raised the absolute demand for us to get out and do something, change and so on, and that had a clear impact on our Somalian policy.

—"President Bush Won't Spill Beans on Somalia Mission,"
CNN, December 2, 1992.

[It] would be fair to say that the foreign policy of the United States was influenced by the gruesome TV pictures from Mogadishu.

—Boutros Boutros-Ghali
"U.N. chief urges patient diplomacy, not soundbites,"
Reuters North American Wire, May 23, 1996.

[It was a] tale of two pictures. When the Americans went into Somalia in the first place, the pictures were of big, strong Marines feeding poor, starving Somalis. And Americans thought this was wonderful. It played to all of our best sense of ourselves. Now in the pictures are Somalis dancing around a downed American helicopter. That brings back all the echoes of Vietnam, all the echoes of big-footed Americans going places where they're not wanted. And that has helped cause this tremendous decline in support.

—Anthony Lake [Bill Clinton's National Security Adviser]
PBS, *Washington Week in Review*, October 1, 1993.

This past weekend we all reacted with anger and horror as an armed Somalia gang desecrated the bodies of our American soldiers and displayed a captured American pilot, all of them soldiers who were taking part in an international effort to end the starvation of the Somali people themselves.

—President William J. Clinton
"Address to the Nation on Somalia,"
Weekly Compilation of Presidential Documents: Administration of William J. Clinton, October 7, 1993, p. 2022.

Selected Bibliography

Allison, Graham T. *Essence of Decision: Explaining the Cuban Missile Crisis.* Boston: Little, Brown, 1971.

Almond, Gabriel A. *The American People and Foreign Policy.* Westport, CT: Greenwood, 1977.

Antaki, C., and A. Lewis, eds. *Mental Mirrors: Metacognition in Social Knowledge and Communication.* London: Sage, 1986.

Arlen, Michael J. *Living-Room War.* New York: Viking, 1969.

Arnett, Peter. *Live From the Battlefield: From Vietnam to Baghdad, 35 Years in the World's War Zones.* New York: Simon and Schuster, 1994.

Barilleaux, Ryan J., and Mary E. Stuckey, eds. *Leadership and the Bush Presidency: Prudence or Drift in an Era of Change?* Westport, CT: Praeger, 1992.

Barthes, Roland. *Image-Music-Text.* Steven Heath, trans. New York: Noonday Press, 1988[1977].

Bennett, W. L. *News: The Politics of Illusion.* New York: Longman, 1983.

Bernstein, Irving. *Guns or Butter: The Presidency of Lyndon Johnson.* New York: Oxford University Press, 1996.

Biocca, Frank, ed. *Television and Political Advertising: Signs, Codes, Meaning.* Vol. 2. Hillsdale, NJ: Lawrence Erlbaum, 1991.

Black, George, and Robin Munro. *Black Hands of Beijing: Lives of Defiance in China's Democracy Movement.* New York: John Wiley and Sons, 1993.

Bonior, David E., Steven M. Champlin, and Timothy S. Kolly. *The Vietnam Veteran: A History of Neglect.* New York: Praeger, 1984.

Braestrup, Peter. *Big Story: How the American Press Reported and Interpreted the Crisis of Tet 1968 in Vietnam and Washington,* Vols. I and II. Boulder: Westview, 1977.

Brody, Richard A. *Assessing the President: The Media, Elite Opinion, and Public Support.* Stanford, CA: Stanford University Press, 1991.

Brook, Timothy. *Quelling the People: The Military Suppression of the Beijing Democracy Movement.* New York: Oxford University Press, 1992.

Brown, Lester R. *Who Will Feed China? Wake-Up Call for a Small Planet.* New York: W. W. Norton, 1995.

Bryan, C.D.B. *The National Geographic Society: 100 Years of Adventure and*

Discovery. New York: Harry N. Abrams, 1987.

Bryson, L., ed. *The Communication of Ideas*. New York: Institute for Religious and Social Studies, 1948.

Calhoun, Craig. *Neither Gods nor Emperors: Students and the Struggle for Democracy in China*. Berkeley: University of California Press, 1994.

Carey, J., ed. *Media, Myths, and Narratives*. Beverly Hills: Sage, 1985.

Chang, Tsan-Kuo. *The Press and China Policy: The Illusion of Sino-American Relations, 1950–1984*. Norwood, NJ: Ablex, 1993.

Chomsky, Noam, and Edward S. Herman. *Manufacturing Consent: The Political Economy of the Mass Media*. New York: Pantheon, 1988.

Cioffi-Revilla, C., R. L. Merritt, and D. A. Zinnes, eds. *Communication and Interaction in Global Politics*. Beverly Hills: Sage, 1987.

Cohen, Bernard C. *The Press and Foreign Policy*. Princeton: Princeton University Press, 1963.

———. *Foreign Policy in American Government*. Boston: Little, Brown, 1965.

———. *The Public's Impact on Foreign Policy*. Boston: Little, Brown, 1973.

Crabb, Cecil V., Jr., and Pat M. Holt. *Invitation to Struggle: Congress, The President and Foreign Policy*. 3rd ed. Washington, DC: Congressional Quarterly, 1989.

Cronkite, Walter. *A Reporter's Life*. New York: Alfred A. Knopf, 1996.

Daniel, Donald C. F., and Bradd C. Hayes, eds. *Beyond Traditional Peacekeeping*. New York: St. Martin's Press, 1995.

DeLong, Kent, and Steven Tuckey. *Mogadishu: Heroism and Tragedy*. Westport, CT: Praeger, 1994.

Denton, Robert E. Jr., and Rachel L. Holloway, eds. *The Clinton Presidency: Images, Issues and Communication Strategies*. Westport, CT: Praeger, 1996.

Des Forges, Roger V., Luo Ning, and Wu Yen-Bo, eds. *Chinese Democracy and the Crisis of 1989: Chinese and American Reflections*. Albany: State University of New York Press, 1993.

Dreze, J., and A. Sen. *Hunger and Public Action*. New York: Oxford University Press, 1991.

Duke, Michael S. *The Iron House: A Memoir of the Chinese Democracy Movement and the Tiananmen Massacre*. Layton, UT: Peregrine Smith, 1990.

Ebert, James R. *A Life in a Year: The American Infantryman in Vietnam, 1965–1972*. Novato, CA: Presidio Press, 1993.

Elder, R. E. *The Policy Machine: The Department of State and American Foreign Policy*. New York: Syracuse University Press, 1960.

Epstein, E. J. *News from Nowhere: Television and the News*. New York: Random House, 1973.

Errington, Elizabeth Jane, and B.J.C. McKercher, eds. *The Vietnam War as History*. Westport, CT: Praeger, 1990.

Farnell, L. R. *Greek Hero Cults and Ideas of Immortality*. Oxford: Oxford University Press, 1921.

FitzGerald, Frances. *Fire in the Lake*. Boston: Little, Brown, 1972.

Flexner, Abraham. *Universities: American, English, German*. New York: Oxford University Press, 1930.

Frey-Wouters, Ellen, and Robert Laufer. *Legacy of a War: The American Soldier in Vietnam*. Armonk, NY: M. E. Sharpe, 1986.

Friedland, Lewis A. *Covering the World: International Television News Services*. New York: Twentieth Century Fund, 1992.

Gans, Herbert J. *Deciding What's News: A Study of CBS Evening News, NBC Nightly News, Newsweek and Time*. New York: Vintage, 1979.

Gardner, Howard. *Frames of Mind: The Theory of Multiple Intelligences*. New

York: Basic Books, 1983.

Gargan, Edward A. *China's Fate: A People's Turbulent Struggle with Reform and Repression, 1980–1990.* New York: Doubleday, 1990.

Garnham, Nicholas. *Capitalism and Communication: Global Culture and the Economics of Information.* London: Sage, 1990.

Geyelin, Philip. *Lyndon B. Johnson and the World.* New York: F. A. Praeger, 1966.

Gibson, James William. *The Perfect War: Technowar in Vietnam.* Boston: Atlantic Monthly Press, 1986.

Gilbert, Marc Jason, and William Head, eds. *The Tet Offensive.* Westport, CT: Praeger, 1996.

Goffman, Erving. *The Presentation of Self in Everyday Life.* New York: Anchor, 1959.

Goldberg, Vicki. *The Power of Photography: How Photographs Changed Our Lives.* New York: Abbeville, 1993.

Griffin, Michael, and Kaarle Nordenstreng, eds. *International News Monitoring.* Boston: Hampton Press, 1998, forthcoming.

Halberstam, David. *The Powers That Be.* New York: Alfred A. Knopf, 1979.

Hallin, Daniel C. *The "Uncensored War": The Media and Vietnam.* Berkeley: University of California Press, 1986.

Hammond, William M. *Public Affairs: The Military and the Media, 1962–1968.* Washington, DC: Center of Military History, United States Army, 1988.

Han, Minzhu, and Hua Sheng, eds. *Cries for Democracy: Writings and Speeches from the 1989 Chinese Democracy Movement.* Princeton: Princeton University Press, 1990.

Harris, David. *Our War: What We Did in Vietnam and What It Did to Us.* New York: Times Books, 1996.

Harris, Louis, and Associates. *Myths and Realities: A Study of Attitudes toward Vietnam Era Veterans.* Washington, DC: U.S. Government Printing Office, 1980.

Hewison, Robert. *Under Siege: Literary Life in London 1939–1945.* London: Oxford University Press, 1977.

Hicks, George, ed. *The Broken Mirror: China after Tiananmen.* Chicago: St. James Press, 1990.

Hilsman, Roger. *The Politics of Policy Making in Defense and Foreign Affairs: Conceptual Models and Bureaucratic Politics.* Englewood Cliffs, NJ: Prentice-Hall, 1987.

Hoang, Lac, and Viet Mai Ha. *Why America Lost the Vietnam War.* Self-published, 1996.

Human Rights in China. *Children of the Dragon: The Story of Tiananmen Square.* New York: Collier Books, 1990.

Iyengar, S., and D. R. Kinder. *News that Matters: Television and American Opinion.* Chicago: University of Chicago Press, 1987.

Jamieson, Kathleen Hall. *Dirty Politics: Deception, Distraction, and Democracy.* New York: Oxford University Press, 1992.

———. *Eloquence in an Electronic Age: The Transformation of Political Speech-making.* New York: Oxford University Press, 1988.

Joes, Anthony James. *The War for South Viet Nam, 1954–1975.* New York: Praeger, 1989.

Kaplan, Robert D. *Surrender or Starve: The Wars Behind the Famine.* Boulder: Westview Press, 1988.

Karnow, Stanley. *Vietnam: A History.* New York: Penguin, 1983.

Kearns, Doris. *Lyndon Johnson and the American Dream.* New York: Harper and Row, 1976.

Keegan, John. *The Face of Battle*. New York: Penguin, 1988[1976].

Keen, D. *The Benefits of Famine and Relief in Southwestern Sudan, 1983–1989*. Princeton: Princeton University Press, 1994.

Keen, Sam. *Faces of the Enemy: Reflections of the Hostile Imagination*. San Francisco: Harper and Row, 1992.

Kegley, C. W., Jr., and E. R. Wittkopf. *American Foreign Policy: Pattern and Process*. New York: St. Martin's Press, 1979.

Kern, M., P. W. Levering, and R. B. Levering. *The Kennedy Crises: The Press, the Presidency, and Foreign Policy*. Chapel Hill: University of North Carolina Press, 1983.

King, Larry, with Mark Stencel. *On the Line: The New Road to the White House*. New York: Harcourt Brace, 1993.

Kolko, Gabriel. *Anatomy of a War: Vietnam, the United States, and the Modern Historical Experience*. New York: New Press, 1994.

Kusnitz, L. A. *Public Opinion and Foreign Policy: America's China Policy, 1949–1979*. Westport, CT: Greenwood Press, 1984.

Ky, Nguyen Cao. *Twenty Years and Twenty Days*. New York: Stein and Day, 1976.

Larson, J. F. *Television's Window on the World: International Affairs Coverage on the U.S. Networks*. Norwood, NJ: Ablex, 1984.

Lederer, William J. *Our Own Worst Enemy*. New York: W. W. Norton, 1968.

Lederman, Jim. *Battle Lines: The American Media and the Intifada*. New York: Henry Holt, 1992.

Lee, Feigon. *China Rising: The Meaning of Tiananmen*. Chicago: Ivan R. Dee, 1990.

Lester, Paul. *Photojournalism: An Ethical Approach*. Hillsdale, NJ: Lawrence Erlbaum, 1991.

Li, Peter, Steven Mark, and Marjorie Li, eds. *Culture and Politics in China: An Anatomy of Tiananmen Square*. New Brunswick, NJ: Transaction Publishers, 1991.

Lin, Nan. *The Struggle for Tiananmen: Anatomy of the 1989 Mass Movement*. Westport, CT: Praeger, 1992.

Lippmann, Walter. *Public Opinion*. New Brunswick, NJ: Transaction, 1991 [1922].

Lorell, Mark A., and Charles Kelley, Jr., with Deborah Hensler. *Casualties, Public Opinion, and Presidential Policy During the Vietnam War: A Project Air Force Report*. Santa Monica, CA: Rand, 1985.

Lung, Hoang Ngoc. *The General Offensives of 1968–1969*. Indochina Monographs. Washington, DC: U.S. Army Center of Military History, 1981.

Maclear, Michael. *The Ten Thousand Day War: Vietnam, 1945–1975*. New York: St. Martin's Press, 1981.

Manheim, Jarol B. *All of the People, All the Time: Strategic Communication and American Politics*. New York: M. E. Sharpe, 1991.

Marchand, Roland. *Advertising the American Dream: Making Way for Modernity, 1920–1940*. Berkeley: University of California Press, 1985.

Maren, Michael. *The Road to Hell: The Ravaging Effects of Foreign Aid and International Charity*. New York: Free Press, 1997.

Margolis, Michael, and Gary A. Mauser, eds. *Manipulating Public Opinion: Essays on Public Opinion as a Dependent Variable*. Pacific Grove, CA: Brooks/Cole, 1989.

McNamara, Robert, with Brian VanDeMark. *In Retrospect: The Tragedy and Lessons of Vietnam*. New York: Times Books, 1995.

Mendelsohn-Bartholdy, Albrecht. *The War and German Society: The Testament of a Liberal*. New Haven: Yale University Press, 1937.

Messaris, Paul. *Visual "Literacy": Image, Mind, & Reality.* Boulder: Westview Press, 1994.

Miller, Mark. *Spectacle: Operation Desert Storm and the Triumph of Illusion.* New York: Poseidon Press, 1994.

Milstein, J. S. *Dynamics of the Vietnam War: A Quantitative Analysis and Predictive Computer Simulation.* Columbus: Ohio State University Press, 1974.

Moeller, Susan D. *Shooting War: Photography and the American Experience of Combat.* New York: Basic Books, 1989.

Monk, Lorraine. *Photographs that Changed the World: The Camera as Witness, the Photograph as Evidence.* New York: Doubleday, 1989.

Morrison, Donald, ed. *Massacre in Beijing: China's Struggle for Democracy.* New York: Warner Books, 1989.

Mosher, S. W. *China Misperceived: American Illusions and Chinese Reality.* New York: Basic Books, 1990.

Moyes, Norman B., ed. *Battle Eye: A History of American Combat Photography.* New York: Metrobooks, 1996.

Mu, Yi, and Mark V. Thompson. *Crisis at Tiananmen: Reform and Reality in Modern China.* San Francisco: China Books and Periodicals, 1989.

Mueller, John E. *War, Presidents and Public Opinion.* New York: John Wiley and Sons, 1973.

Muqi, Che. *Beijing Turmoil: More than Meets the Eye.* Beijing: Foreign Languages Press, 1990.

Neuman, Johanna. *Lights, Camera, War: Is Media Technology Driving International Politics?* New York: St. Martin's Press, 1996.

Oberdorfer, Don. *TET! The Turning Point in the Vietnam War.* New York: Da Capo, 1984.

Ogden, Suzanne, Kathleen Hartford, Lawrence Sullivan, and David Zweig, eds. *China's Search for Democracy: The Student and the Mass Movement of 1989.* Armonk, NY: M. E. Sharpe, 1992.

Omaar, R., and A. de Waal. *Somalia—Operation Restore Hope: A Preliminary Assessment.* London: African Rights, 1993.

Page, Caroline. *U.S. Official Propaganda During the Vietnam War, 1965–1973: The Limits of Persuasion.* New York: Leicester University Press, 1996.

Paletz, D. L., and R. M. Entman. *Media, Power, Politics.* New York: Free Press, 1981.

Paret, Peter, Beth Irwin Lewis, and Paul Paret. *Persuasive Images: Posters of War and Revolution from the Hoover Institution Archives.* Princeton: Princeton University Press, 1992.

Pearl, D., L. Bouthilet, and J. Lazar, eds. *Television and Behavior: Ten Years of Scientific Progress and Implications for the 80s. Vol. 2. Technical Reviews.* Washington, DC: U.S. Government Printing Office, 1980.

Pedelty, Mark. *War Stories: The Culture of Foreign Correspondents.* New York: Routledge, 1995.

The Peking Massacre: A Summary Report of the 1989 Democracy Movement in Mainland China. Taipei: Kwang Hwa, 1989.

Pennebaker, James W., Dario Paez, and Bernard Rimé, eds. *Collective Memory of Political Events: Social Psychological Processes.* Mahway, NJ: Lawrence Erlbaum, 1997.

Peters, F. E. *Greek Philosophical Terms: A Historical Lexicon.* New York: New York University Press, 1967.

Peyrefitte, Alain. *La Tragedie Chinoise.* Paris: Fayard, 1990.

Plato. *Republic*, Part X, 595c. 2nd ed. D. Lee trans. London: Penguin, 1987 [1955].

Prados, John. *The Hidden History of the Vietnam War.* Chicago: Ivan R. Dee, 1995.

Rather, Dan. *The Camera Never Blinks Twice: The Further Adventures of a Television Journalist.* New York: William Morrow, 1994.

Rhodes, Anthony. *Propaganda: The Art of Persuasion in World War II.* Secaucus, NJ: Wellfleet, 1987.

Rieff, David. *Slaughterhouse: Bosnia and the Failure of the West.* New York: Simon and Schuster, 1995.

Rosemont, Henry, Jr. *A Chinese Mirror: Moral Reflections on Political Economy and Society.* La Salle, IL: Open Court, 1991.

Schell, Orville. *Mandate of Heaven: The Legacy of Tiananmen Square and the Next Generation of China's Leaders.* New York: Touchstone, 1995.

Schettler, C. *Public Opinion in American Society.* New York: Harper, 1960.

Schramm, Wilbur, and D. Roberts, eds. *The Process and Effects Of Mass Communication.* Urbana: University of Illinois Press, 1971.

Schudson, Michael. *The Power of News.* Cambridge: Harvard University Press, 1995.

Serfaty, Simon, ed. *The Media and Foreign Policy.* London: Macmillan, 1990.

Simons, Anna. *Networks of Dissolution: Somalia Undone.* Boulder: Westview, 1995.

Sperber, Daniel, and Deidre Wilson. *Relevance: Communication and Cognition.* Cambridge: Harvard University Press, 1988.

Stevenson, Jonathan. *Losing Mogadishu: Testing U.S. Policy in Somalia.* Annapolis, MD: Naval Institute, 1995.

Suls, J., and T. A. Wills, eds. *Social Comparison: Contemporary Theory and Research.* Hillsdale, NJ: Lawrence Erlbaum, 1991.

Thomas, Gordon. *Chaos Under Heaven: The Shocking Story of China's Search for Democracy.* New York: Birch Lane Press, 1991.

Thompson, W. S., and D. D. Frizzell. *The Lessons of Vietnam.* New York: Crane, Russak, 1977.

Tuchman, Gaye. *Making News: A Study in the Construction of Reality.* New York: Free Press, 1978.

Turner, Kathleen J. *Lyndon Johnson's Dual War: Vietnam and the Press.* Chicago: University of Chicago Press, 1985.

Valentine, Douglas. *The Phoenix Program.* New York: William Morrow, 1990.

Wasserstrom, Jeffrey N., and Elizabeth J. Perry, eds. *Popular Protest and Political Culture in Modern China.* 2nd ed. Boulder: Westview Press, 1994.

Weiss, Thomas G., and Larry Minear, eds. *Humanitarianism Across Borders: Sustaining Civilians in Times of War.* Boulder: Lynne Rienner, 1993.

Weissberg, Robert. *Public Opinion and Popular Government.* Englewood Cliffs, NJ: Prentice-Hall, 1976.

Werner, Jayne S., and Luu Doan Huynh, eds. *The Vietnam War: Vietnamese and American Perspectives.* Armonk, NY: M. E. Sharpe, 1993.

Westcott, Jan. *The Somalia Saga: A Personal Account, 1990–1993.* Washington, DC: Refugee Policy Group, 1994.

Westmoreland, William C. *A Soldier Reports.* Garden City, NY: Doubleday, 1976.

Willenson, Kim. *The Bad War: An Oral History of the Vietnam War.* New York: New American Library, 1987.

Wirtz, J. J. *The Tet Offensive: Intelligence Failure in War.* Ithaca, NY: Cornell University Press, 1991.

Wright, Charles. *Mass Communication: A Sociological Perspective.* 3rd ed. New York: McGraw-Hill, 1986.

Wright, Will. *Six Guns and Society: A Structural Study of the Western.* Berkeley: University of California Press, 1975.

Wyatt, Clarence R. *Paper Soldiers: The American Press and the Vietnam War.* New York: W. W. Norton, 1993.

Yim, Kwan Ha, ed. *China Under Deng.* New York: Facts on File, 1991.

Yu, Mok Chiu, and J. Frank Harrison, eds. *Voices from Tiananmen Square: Beijing Spring and the Democracy Movement.* Montreal: Black Rose Books, 1990.

Index

About the Author

DAVID D. PERLMUTTER is an Assistant Professor at Louisiana State University's Manship School of Mass Communication and was recently named to the board of directors of the American Association of Political Consultants. He has previously written for the *Journal of Communication, Visual Communication Quarterly, Visual Anthropology,* and other academic and popular publications.